The mini **Rough Guide** to

New York City

written and researched by

Martin Dunford

with additional contributions by

Shea Dean and Zora O'Neill

ROUGH
GUIDES

NEW YORK • LONDON • DELHI

www.roughguides.com

Contents

3

◄◄ New York City skyline ◄ Lincoln Center

Introduction to

New York City

New York City is like no other place on earth. A teeming metropolis that never sleeps and rarely apologizes, its adrenaline-charged buzz lives up to even the most inflated expectations. As home to some of the world's most conspicuous icons, New York is packed with views of something famous at almost every turn, from the soaring Art Deco facade of the Empire State Building to the defiant but welcoming visage of the Statue of Liberty. But look a little deeper and you'll find still more to

love – lively neighborhoods with homespun boutiques and restaurants, raucous live-music clubs, and cutting-edge theaters and galleries, for starters.

It is a testament to New York's unique strength and resilience that the city rebounded so quickly following the terrorist attacks of **September 11, 2001**. Although there continues to be a heightened awareness of the possibility of terrorism all over the city, the physical (if not emotional) scars of that day continue to heal, as construction on the World Trade Center Memorial is firmly underway.

You could spend weeks in New York and still barely scratch the surface, but there are some key attractions and pleasures you should find time for regardless of the length of your stay. One of the best things about the city is its various **ethnic neighborhoods**, chiefly lower Manhattan's Chinatown and the formerly Jewish enclave of the Lower East Side (still good for its delis and bakeries), as well as the artsier concentrations of SoHo, TriBeCa, Chelsea, and the East and West Villages. No trip to the city would be complete without gaping up at the celebrated **architecture**, especially the skyscrapers that dominate Midtown and the Financial District. And then there are the **museums** – not just the Metropolitan and MoMA, but countless other, smaller collections that reward days of happy wandering. In between sights, you can **eat** just about anything, at any time, cooked in any style; you can **drink** in any kind of company; and sit through any number of

On the menu

Food, and lots of it, is one of the city's biggest pleaures. The Lower East Side is great for Jewish-American deli fare, such as overstuffed pastrami sandwiches and bagels with cream cheese and lox, while all over town (Midtown especially) are traditional steakhouses featuring massive aged porterhouse or tender sirloin. The city is also rife with pizza places serving the classic New York slice: thin, crunchy crust covered with red sauce and cheese, typically eaten folded in half and on the go. And even snack food – from hot dogs to large, salted pretzels – bought from street vendors is an experience.

Take the A train

While it may seem intimidating at first, New York's subway and bus system is quite easy to navigate, as well as efficient, fast, and relatively safe. After securing a good map, if you're still at all unsure, just ask for some help – New Yorkers are accurate direction-givers and take a surprising interest in initiating visitors into the great mysteries of their city.

obscure **films**. The more established arts – **dance**, **theater**, and **music** – are superbly represented, while New York's clubs are as varied and exciting as you might expect. For the avid consumer, the choice of **shops** is vast – almost numbingly so, in this heartland of the great capitalist dream.

What to see

New York City comprises the central island of **Manhattan** along with four outer boroughs – **Brooklyn**, **Queens**, **the Bronx**, and **Staten Island**. But Manhattan, to many, *is* New York, and it's likely that this is where you'll stay and spend most of your time. While the subway is ideal for getting around the city quickly, New York is very much about its neighborhoods and therefore best explored on foot – a fact reflected in the chapters of this guide, which are organized to facilitate the best walking tours.

In New York Harbor, the **Statue of Liberty** and **Ellis Island** constitute up the first part of New York (and America) that most nineteenth-century immigrants would have seen. Moving inland to the southern tip of Manhattan, the **Financial District**, which includes Wall Street, boasts many of the city's skyscrapers and historic buildings, and was hardest hit by the destruction of its most famous landmark, the World Trade Center. Just northeast is the area around **City Hall**, New York's well-appointed municipal center, which adjoins **TriBeCa**, known for its swanky restaurants and galleries. Moving east, **Chinatown** is Manhattan's most populous ethnic neighborhood, full of vibrant markets and restaurants. Largely engulfed by Chinatown, **Little Italy** continues to hang on to a few blocks of Mulberry Street, while the **Lower East Side**, the city's traditional gateway neighborhood for new immigrants, is nowadays a stronghold for inventive restaurants and edgy bars. To the west, **SoHo** is one of the premier districts for shopping and also has a smattering of commercial art galleries. Continuing north, the **West and East Villages** are two of the city's most appealing residential neighborhoods, their tree-lined streets home to bars, restaurants, trendy boutiques, and theaters. Best known for its contemporary art galleries – more than three hun-

▲ The Statue of Liberty

▼ Times Square

dred to date – and active gay scene, **Chelsea** borders the old (and still somewhat seedy) **Garment District**. East of the Garment District, on the western fringe of the residential **Murray Hill** neighborhood you'll find the city's tallest skyscraper, the Empire State Building.

Beyond 42nd Street, the main east–west artery of **Midtown**, the character of the city changes quite radically, with the neon jungle of **Times Square** giving way to some of New York's most awe-inspiring, neck-cricking architecture. You'll find some of the city's best shopping as you work your way north up **Fifth Avenue** past Rockefeller Center to 60th Street, the southern border of **Central Park**, a supreme piece of nineteenth-century landscaping without which life in Manhattan would be unthinkable. Flanking the park, the **Upper East Side** boasts some of the swankiest addresses in Manhattan; topdrawer shopping along Madison Avenue in the seventies; and, most pertinently for visitors, "Museum Mile," a string of magnificent art institutions on Fifth Avenue including the vast Metropolitan Museum of Art. On the other side of the park, the mostly residential and fairly affluent **Upper West Side** holds Lincoln Center – Manhattan's temple to the performing arts – and the American Museum of Natural History. Immediately above Central Park, **Harlem**, the historic African-American neighborhood, appeals for its soul-food restaurants and gospel churches; a jaunt further north is most likely required only to see the unusual Cloisters, a nineteenth-century mock-up of a medieval monastery, packed with great European Romanesque and Gothic art and (transplanted) architecture.

When to go

New York's **climate** ranges from the stickily hot and humid in mid-summer to well below freezing in January and February: mid-winter and high summer (many people find the city unbearable in July and August) are much the worst time you could come. Spring is gentle, if unpredictable, and often wet, while fall is perhaps the best season to visit. Whatever time of year you come, dress in layers: buildings tend to be overheated during winter months and air-conditioned to the point of iciness in summer. Also be sure to bring comfortable and sturdy shoes – you're going to be doing a lot of walking.

Average temperatures and rainfall

	Jan	Feb	Mar	Apr	May	June	July	Aug	Sept	Oct	Nov	Dec
Max. temp. (°F)	38	40	50	61	72	80	85	84	76	65	54	43
Min. temp. (°F)	26	27	35	44	54	63	69	67	60	50	41	31
Max. temp. (°C)	3	4	10	16	22	27	29	29	24	18	12	6
Min. temp. (°C)	-3	-3	2	7	12	17	21	19	16	10	5	-1
Rainfall (inches)	3.5	3.1	4.0	3.8	4.4	3.6	4.4	4.1	4.0	3.4	4.4	3.8
Rainfall (mm)	89	79	102	97	112	91	112	104	102	86	112	97

12

things not to miss

It's not possible to see everything that New York City has to offer in one trip – and we don't suggest you try. What follows is a selective taste of the city's highlights: its liveliest events, standout architecture, and most engaging museums. They're arranged in five color-coded categories, which you can browse through to find the very best things to see and experience. All highlights have a page reference to take you straight into the Guide, where you can find out more.

02 The Metropolitan Museum of Art Page **120** • You could spend weeks inside this, the country's largest – and arguably best – art museum.

01 Ice-skating at Rockefeller Center Page **300** • Taking a turn on the ice surrounded by skyscrapers and holiday decorations is an experience you won't soon forget.

03 **The Museum of Modern Art (MoMA)** Page **98** • Gleaming new quarters show off Picasso's Blue Period paintings, van Gogh's *Starry Night*, and a slew of other modern marvels.

10 **A baseball game at Yankee Stadium** Page **294** • There's no better way to feel like a real New Yorker than to cheer on the Bronx Bombers at home.

05 **Central Park** Page **112** • The "lungs of the city" has something for everyone, whether lounging on Sheep Meadow or taking in a summer concert.

06 **Grand Central Terminal** Page **94** • This Beaux Arts masterpiece is impressive enough, though taking a tour will let you in on some of its many secrets.

07 **The Brooklyn Bridge** Page **46** • A walk across this stately marvel, during the day or at night, is the best way to see Manhattan's downtown skyline.

ACTIVITIES | CONSUME | EVENTS | NATURE | SIGHTS

09 Coney Island Page 166 • Eat hot dogs at *Nathan's Famous*, dip your feet in the ocean, and take a ride on the Cyclone (if you dare).

08 The American Museum of Natural History Page 146 • The dinosaur exhibit and the Rose Space Center are among the must-sees at this beloved New York institution.

10 Katz's Deli Page 213 • Savor the incredible pastrami and corned beef at this Lower East Side mainstay, serving massive sandwiches and pickles since 1888.

11 Empire State Building Page 85 • The view from the top of the city's tallest building has to be seen to be believed.

12 Radio City Music Hall Page 110 • The tour of this Art Deco masterpiece is one of the city's best – and the sunset view from the stage is particularly impressive.

Basics

Basics

Arrival

New York's major airports are all within an hour from the city center by taxi or bus, depending on traffic conditions. The city's train and bus terminals are centrally located and connected to major subway stations.

By air

Three major **airports** serve New York. International and domestic flights are handled at John F. Kennedy (JFK) (℡718/244-4444), in the borough of Queens, and Newark (℡973/961-6000), in northern New Jersey; LaGuardia (℡718/533-3400), also in Queens, handles domestic flights only.

Taxis are the easiest way to head to your destination if you are in a group or are arriving at an antisocial hour. Expect to pay $25–35 from LaGuardia, a flat rate of $45 from JFK, and $40–55 from Newark; you'll be responsible for the turnpike and bridge and tunnel tolls – an extra $5 or so. And don't forget a tip for the driver of fifteen to twenty percent.

Another good way into Manhattan is by **bus**; the two Manhattan terminals, used by all airport buses, are Grand Central and the Port Authority. For further general information (driving directions, etc) on getting to and from the airports, call ℡1-800/AIR-RIDE or check out the airline sites at Ⓦwww.panynj.gov.

JFK

New York Airport Service **buses** leave JFK for Grand Central Terminal, Port Authority Bus Terminal, Penn Station, Bryant Park, and Midtown hotels every fifteen to twenty minutes between 6.15am and 11.10pm. In the other direction, they run from the same locations every fifteen to thirty minutes between 5am and 10pm. Journeys take 45–60 minutes, depending on the time of day; the fare is $15 one way, $27 round trip. For further details, call ℡212/875-8200 or check Ⓦwww.nyairportservice.com.

AirTrain JFK – a train service that connects the airport and various subway lines – runs every few minutes, 24 hours daily, from JFK to Jamaica Station on the #E and #J/#Z subway lines, as well as on the Long Island Rail Road (LIRR); AirTrain also runs to the Howard Beach stop on the #A line. The cost is $5 on a MetroCard (see p.18). From the Jamaica and Howard Beach stations, one subway fare ($2 on a MetroCard) takes you anywhere in the city. This isn't your best option late at night, though, as trains run infrequently and can be rather deserted.

LaGuardia

New York Airport Service **buses** run between LaGuardia and Manhattan (Grand Central Terminal, Port Authority Bus Terminal, and Penn Station) every fifteen to thirty minutes. From LaGuardia, the service operates 7.20am to 11pm. From Grand Central, the service runs from 5am to 8pm; from Port Authority 5.50am to 7.40pm; and from Penn Station 7.40am to 7.10pm. Journey time is 40–60 minutes, depending on traffic, and the fare is $12 one way, $21 round trip. For more details, call ☎212/875-8200 or see ⓦwww.nyairportservice.com.

The best bargain in New York airport transit is the #M60 bus, which for $2 (MetroCard or exact change only) takes you into Manhattan, across 125th Street and down Broadway to 106th Street. You can also hop off the bus at 31st Street in Astoria, Queens, and take the #N or #W subway train into the city. Journey time to Manhattan ranges from twenty minutes late at night to an hour in rush-hour traffic, and from fifteen to twenty-five minutes to the subway in Queens.

Newark

Newark Airport Express **buses** leave for Manhattan every fifteen to thirty minutes (4am to 1am), stopping at Port Authority, Bryant Park, and Grand Central Terminal; going the other way, they run just as frequently (4.45am to 1.45am); the journey takes 30–60 minutes depending on traffic, and the fare is $14 one way, $23 round trip. For details, call ☎1-877/863-9275 or see ⓦwww.coachusa.com.

AirTrain Newark takes you from the airport to the Newark Liberty International Airport train station, where you can connect with **New Jersey Transit** trains, which terminate at New York's Penn Station. The fare is $14 one way including the AirTrain. From the airport train station you can also take an **Amtrak** train to New York, though this is significantly more expensive. For details, call ☎1-888/397-4636 or visit ⓦwww.panynj.gov.

By bus or train

If you come by Greyhound, Trailways, Bonanza, or any other **long-distance bus line**, you'll arrive at the Port Authority Bus Terminal at 42nd Street and Eighth Avenue. If you come by **Amtrak** train, you'll arrive at Penn Station, on 32nd Street between Seventh and Eighth avenues. Both the bus terminal and train station are well positioned for all manner of subway service.

City transportation

Public transit in New York is on the whole quite good, cheap, and comprehensive, covering most conceivable corners of the city, whether by bus or by subway. Don't be afraid to ask someone for help if you're confused – it will likely take you a while to become familiar with the system. You'll no doubt find the need for a taxi from time to time, especially if you feel uncomfortable in an area at night; you shouldn't ever have trouble tracking one down – the ubiquitous yellow cabs are always on the prowl for passengers. Don't eschew walking, either: it's a great way to get around and maybe the best way to get to know the city.

The subway

Initially intimidating, the New York **subway** system is the fastest and most efficient way to get from point A to point B in Man-hattan and the outer boroughs, so put aside your qualms: seven million people ride the subway every day, quite a few for the first time.

Any subway journey costs $2, payable by MetroCard, which allows you to transfer (for free) from subway to bus, bus to subway, or bus to bus within a period of two hours. The card is available from station vending machines or station agent-manned booths in one of two forms: as a simple amount from $2 to $100, or an "unlimited ride" version, which allows for unlimited travel over a certain period of time. A one-day "Fun Pass" costs $7, a seven-day unlimited pass $24, and a monthly unlimited pass $76. Subway **maps** can be obtained from any subway station that has a manned booth, as well as the main concourse of Grand Central and the Convention and Visitors Bureau, at Seventh Avenue and 53rd Street. A subway map can also be found at the back of this book; for general subway and bus information, including service changes, call ☎718/330-1234 (24hr daily) or visit Ⓦwww.mta.nyc.ny.us.

Buses

The **bus system** is simpler than the subway, and you can see where you're going and hop off at the sight of anything interesting. It also features many more crosstown routes. The major disadvantage is that the buses can be extremely slow – in peak hours slower than walking pace – and extremely full to boot. In response to cries of overcrowding along several routes, the MTA introduced "accordion buses" – two buses attached by a flexible rubber accordion, which helps the big vehicle turn corners. However, because these run slightly less frequently than the ones they replaced, they still get crowded.

Anywhere in the city the bus fare is $2, payable by MetroCard (the most convenient way) or with exact change (no pennies and no bills). Bus maps, like subway maps, can be obtained at the main concourse of Grand Central or the Convention and Visitors Bureau; you can also often (though not always) pick up bus maps from subway stations.

Taxis

Taxis are always worth considering, especially if you're in a hurry or in a group, or it's late at night. Always use medallion cabs, immediately recognizable by their yellow paintwork and medallion on the hood; gypsy cabs – unlicensed, uninsured operators who tout for business wherever tourists arrive, should be avoided, especially at the airports, where sketchy characters hustle for business.

Up to four people can travel in an ordinary medallion cab. Fares are $2.50 for the first fifth of a mile and 40¢ for each fifth of a mile thereafter (or for each minute in stopped or slow traffic). Between the hours of 8pm and 6am there is a 50¢ surcharge, and from Monday to Friday between the hours of 4pm and 8pm there's a "peak hour" surcharge of $1. Trips outside Manhattan can incur toll fees; not all of the crossings cost money, however, and the driver should ask you which route you wish to take. Don't forget to tip, either: this should be fifteen to twenty percent of the fare; you'll get a dirty look (or comments) if you offer less. Note that cab drivers don't like splitting anything bigger than a $10 bill, and are in their rights to refuse a bill over $20.

Walking

Few cities equal New York for street-level stimulation. As such, **getting around on foot** is often the most exciting – if tiring – method of exploring. Figure ten to fifteen minutes to walk ten north–south blocks – rather more at rush hour. Twenty north–south blocks equal one mile, while crosstown blocks are much longer: about five or six to a mile. Footwear is important (sneakers are good for spring/summer; winter needs something waterproof). So is safety: a lot more people are injured in New York carelessly crossing the street than are mugged. Pedestrian crossings don't give you automatic right of way unless the WALK sign is on – and, even then, cars may be turning, so be alert.

Information and websites

The best place for information is New York City's Official Visitor Information Center, 810 Seventh Ave, at 53rd St (Mon–Fri 8.30am–6pm, weekends and holidays 8:30am–5pm; ☎212/484-1222, ⊛www.nycvisit.com). Here you can get up-to-date leaflets on what's going on in the arts and elsewhere plus bus and subway maps and information on hotels and accommodation – though staffers can't actually book a room for you. The free quarterly *Official NYC Guide* is a useful resource, giving cursory rundowns on what's what with restaurants, hotels, shopping, sights, and mainstream arts events.

Visitor centers

Chinatown Visitor Information Kiosk At the intersection of Canal, Walker, and Baxter sts; Sun–Fri 10am–6pm, Sat 10am–7pm; ☎212/484-1222, ⊛www.nycvisit.com.

Federal Hall 26 Wall St, btw Nassau and Williams sts; Mon–Fri 9am–5pm; ☎212/825-6888, ⊛www.nps .gov/feha.

NYC Heritage Tourism Center Southern tip of City Hall Park, on Broadway near Park Row; Mon–Fri 9am–6pm, Sat & Sun 10am–6pm; ☎212/484-1222, ⊛www.nycvisit.com.

Times Square Visitor Center 1560 Broadway, btw 46th and 47th sts; daily 8am–8pm; ☎212/768-1560, ⊛www .timessquarenyc.org.

Websites

CitySearch NY ⊛www.newyork .citysearch.com. A solid site with listings, customer reviews, and "best of" picks for every category you can imagine.

New York Magazine ⊛www.nymag .com. Best website for all things cultural in the city, with discriminating and up-to-date reviews of shows, shops, bars, and restaurants, as well as a handy "best of New York" section to help narrow down your choices.

NYC & Company ⊛www.nycvisit .com. Website of the city's tourism marketing group, which also runs several of the visitor centers cited above.

NYC Transit Authority ⊛www.mta .nyc.ny.us. Official subway, bus, and commuter-rail website, with schedules, maps, fare info, service advisories, history, and trivia.

Open Table www.opentable.com. Browse menus and make free online reservations at five hundred Manhattan restaurants.

Time Out New York www .timeoutny.com. What's on this week in music, clubs, book readings,

museums, and movies, plus other features.

The Village Voice www .villagevoice.com. The best thing about this older (some say out-of-touch) alternative weekly is the easy-to-use Movie Clock, with times and locations for all films playing in the city.

City tours

There are many different ways to take in the city: exploring streets and neighborhoods on your own; heading up to the tops of buildings like the Empire State, to get a good perspective on the lay of the land; or going on any number of city tours, which might let you experience New York from angles you'd never considered. If you're nervous about exploring the city, or overwhelmed by the possibilities New York offers, look into Big Apple Greeter, 1 Centre St, 19th floor (☎212/669-8159, ⓦwww .bigapplegreeter.org), a nonprofit organization that matches visitors with its corps of 500 volunteer "greeters" – locals trained to give tips and tours depending on your interests. The service is free.

Bus tours

Apart from equipping yourself with a decent map, perhaps the most obvious way to get oriented with the city is to take a narrated, "hop on, hop off" double-decker bus tour. For around $44 you can get two days' worth of access to buses that run in continuous loops through the best neighborhoods and past the most famous sights of the city.

21

They're most fun in warm weather, when you can gawk at the skyscrapers from the open-air top deck. Buses run seven days a week, from (approximately) 9am to 6pm, with special rates and times for evening tours. The most professional tour company is **Gray Line**, based out of Port Authority at 42nd St and 8th Ave (☎212/397-2600, ⓦwww.coachusa.com/newyorksightseeing).

Helicopter tours

A more exciting option is to look at the city from the air, by **helicopter**. This is expensive, but you won't easily forget the experience. **Liberty Helicopter Tours**, with locations including the Downtown Manhattan Heliport, at Pier 6 on the East River, and the VIP Heliport, 30th St and 12th Ave (☎212/967-6464, reserve online at ⓦwww.liberty-helicopters.com), offers excursions ranging from $30 for two and a half minutes to $186 for about a quarter hour. If you leave from 30th Street, the best seat for photos is on the right in the back; note there's a $15-per-passenger surcharge on all flights leaving from this location. Helicopters take off regularly between 9am and 9pm daily unless winds and

visibility are bad. You don't need a reservation for tours from 30th Street, but you do for other locations. Keep in mind, though, that in high season and nice weather you may have quite a wait if you just show up.

Boat tours

A great way to see the island of Manhattan from the water is to ride the **Circle Line Ferry** (☎212/563-3200, ⓦwww.circleline42.com). Departing from Pier 83 at W 42nd St and 12th Ave, the ferry circumnavigates Manhattan, taking in everything from downtown's skyscrapers to the more subdued stretches of Harlem and the Bronx – complete with a live wisecracking commentary; the three-hour tour is $29 for adults, $16 for children under 12, and $24 for seniors. Circle Line also runs super-fast 30-minute cruises on its "Beast" speedboat (May–Oct; $17, $11 for kids under 12), as well as summertime live-music cruises – check the website for the latest details on who's playing.

One of the city's true bargains is the free **Staten Island Ferry** (see p.30), which leaves regularly from South Ferry on the lower tip of Manhattan. The ferry offers great views of New York Harbor and the Statue of Liberty as it makes its way to the underappreciated borough of Staten Island.

Walking tours

Options for **walking tours** of Manhattan or the outer boroughs are many and varied. Usually led by experts, such fact-filled strolls meander through neighborhoods or focus on particular subjects. Most walking-tour organizations will arrange custom and group tours based on your particular interests. Detailed on below are some of the more interesting tour groups: phone ahead or check their websites for complete schedules, which vary by the week or the season.

Walking-tour organizations

The 92nd Street Y 1395 Lexington Ave, between 91st and 92nd ☎212/415-5500, @www.92y.org. Offers an assortment of walking tours ranging from straight historical explorations of specific New York neighborhoods to art, political, and gourmet tours. Average costs are $20–55 per person; advance reservations highly recommended.
Big Onion Walking Tours ☎212/439-1090, @www.bigonion .com. Big Onion specializes in tours with an ethnic and historical focus: pick one

particular group, or take the "Immigrant New York" tour and learn about everyone. Cost for the two-hour tour is $15, $10 for students, and $12 for seniors; the "Multi-Ethnic Eating Tour," including food (reservations required), costs $20 (students $15, seniors $17).
Downtown Alliance ☎212/606-4064, @www.downtownny.com. This well-funded booster group for the Financial District offers a free ninety-minute historical walking tour of Wall Street and environs every Thursday and Saturday at noon, rain or shine. Meet on the front steps of the US Custom House at One Bowling Green.
Greenwich Village Literary Pub Crawl ☎212/613-5796, @www .bakerloo.org. A two-and-a-half-hour guided tour of the most prominent pubs in New York literary history led by actors from the Bakerloo Theatre Project, who also read from associated works. Tours meet at the *White Horse Tavern*, 567 Hudson St, at 2pm every Saturday. Reservations are highly recommended: $15, students and seniors $12.
Harlem Heritage Tours 104 Malcolm X Blvd ☎212/280-7888, @www.harlemheritage.com. Cultural tours of Harlem, general and specific (such as "When Harlem Was Jewish"), are led midday and in the evening by very helpful tour guides. Walking tours are $20–40 (higher-priced tours usually include food or entertainment); the "Harlem Jazz Nights" tour is $115. Reservations are recommended.

Lower East Side Tenement Museum 108 Orchard St ☎ 212/431-0233, ⓦ www.tenement.org. The museum organizes weekend walking tours of the Lower East Side, focusing on the heritage of the various ethnic groups who live there and the furious pace of development. April–Dec only, Sat & Sun 1pm & 3pm; $15, students and seniors $11; combined tickets for museum admission and a tour are available at a reduced price.

Municipal Art Society 457 Madison Ave, between 50th and 51st ☎ 212/935-3960, ⓦ www.mas.org. Opinionated tours look at neighborhoods in all five boroughs from an architectural, cultural, historical, and, often, political perspective. Wednesday lunchtime tours ($10 donation) of Grand Central Terminal start at 12.30pm from the information booth in the main concourse. Most other tours are held Fri–Sun and cost $12, with discounts for students, seniors, and members.

Media

The days are long gone when New York could support twenty daily newspapers. Today, only three remain: the *New York Times* and the tabloids the *Daily News* and the *New York Post*.

The widely revered *New York Times* is the closest thing America has to a quality national daily newspaper (the much more conservative *Wall Street Journal*, now produced in New Jersey, is a close second). The *Times* has solid, sometimes stolid, international coverage, and places much emphasis on its news analysis. The Sunday edition is a thumping bundle of newsprint divided into a number of supplements that take days to read. The legendary crossword puzzle in Sunday's *New York Times Magazine* should keep you occupied all day.

The *Times'* arch rivals concentrate on local news, usually screamed out in humorous banner headlines. The *Daily News* is renowned as a picture newspaper but has occasional intelligent features and many racy headlines.

The *New York Post*, the city's oldest newspaper, started in 1801 by Alexander Hamilton, is known for its sensationalism and conservative slant.

Of the weekly papers, the free *Village Voice* was once widely read for its arts coverage and investigative features, but most New Yorkers now prefer the better-written, more fashionable, and easier-to-carry (though not free) magazines *New York* and *Time Out New York*, both of which have good listings, are released every Wednesday, and can be purchased at any newsstand or bookstore; of the two, *New York* is more sophisticated. The venerable *New Yorker*, while geared for a national audience, also has a nicely edited selection of local arts listings.

Guide

Guide

The Statue of Liberty and Ellis Island

The southern tip of Manhattan and the enclosing shores of New Jersey, Staten Island, and Brooklyn form the broad expanse of New York Harbor, one of the finest natural harbors in the world and one of the things that persuaded the first Dutch settlers to make their home here several centuries ago. Take to the water via ferry to get the best views of the classic downtown skyline or to get out to the **Statue of Liberty** on Liberty Island and **Ellis Island**, two high-priority targets for a trip to the city.

The best way to reach the ferries is to take the #1 to South Ferry or the #4 or #5 to Bowling Green.

The Statue of Liberty

Daily except Dec 25th 9:30am–5pm (extended hours in summer); free; ☎212/363-3200, ⓦwww.nps.gov/stli.

Getting to the islands

Circle Line **ferries** go to both Liberty and Ellis islands and leave from Battery Park in lower Manhattan year-round daily from 9:30am to 3pm (extended hours in summer) every 20–30min (round-trip $11.50, seniors $9.50, children ages 3–12 $4.50; purchase tickets from Castle Clinton in the park, by phone on ☎1-888/782-8834, or online at ⒲www.statuereservations.com). The ferry goes first to Liberty Island and then continues to Ellis.

It's best to **buy tickets in advance** and to leave as early in the day as possible, both to avoid long lines and to ensure you get to see both islands; if you take the last ferry of the day, you won't be able to visit the Statue of Liberty. Liberty Island needs a good hour at least, especially if the weather's nice or if you take the Observatory Tour, which lasts 90 minutes; Ellis Island demands a minimum of two hours for its Museum of Immigration. If you'd like to go inside the Statue of Liberty, you have to take a tour, which, though free, must be booked online in advance (same details as above).

If you want a good, up-close look at the statue but don't have the time or money to actually visit it, consider taking a (free) ride on the **Staten Island Ferry** (☎212/639-9675, ⒲www.siferry.com; take the #R or #W to Whitehall Street). Ferries depart every half-hour or so from the new Whitehall Terminal in Lower Manhattan, dock at St George Terminal on Staten Island, and then return. The trip takes about 25 minutes each way.

The **Statue of Liberty** has for a century been a monument to the American Dream, a potent reminder that the US is at its heart a land of immigrants. It was New York Harbor where the first big waves of European immigrants arrived, their ships entering through the Verrazano Narrows to round the bend of the bay and catch a first glimpse of "Liberty Enlightening the World."

The statue, which depicts Liberty throwing off her shackles and holding a beacon to light the world, was built by Frédéric Auguste Bartholdi in Paris between 1874 and 1884. Bartholdi started with a terracotta model and enlarged it through four successive versions to its present size – 151 feet tall and about 35 feet across. It's constructed out of thin copper sheets bolted together and supported by an iron framework designed by Gustave Eiffel. The arm carrying the torch was exhibited in Madison Square Park for seven years, but the whole statue wasn't officially accepted on behalf of the American people until 1884, after which it was taken apart, crated up, and shipped to New York. The statue was unveiled by President Grover Cleveland in 1886 in a flag-waving celebration that has never really stopped.

You can take one of two **tours**: the one-hour **Promenade Tour**, which takes in the statue's entrance hall and an upstairs exhibition, and the 90-minute **Observatory Tour**, which also includes the 192 steps to the top of the pedestal (the crown has been closed since 9/11, and it's unlikely to reopen soon). The downstairs lobby shows the original torch and flame, which was completed first and used to raise funds for the rest of the statue. Upstairs a small exhibition tells the statue's story with prints, photographs, posters, cuttings, and replicas of bits of the statue and the plaster casts made to build it. There are images of the statue from all kinds of sources – indicative of just how iconic she is. At the top of the pedestal, you can look up into the center of the statue to see its riveted, bolted interior and spiral staircase and take a turn around the balcony outside, where the views are predictably superb.

Ellis Island

Daily 9am–5pm; free; ☎212/363-3200, ⓦwww.ellisisland.org.
Just across the water from Liberty Island sits **Ellis Island**, the first stop for over twelve million immigrants hoping to settle in the US. The island became an immigration station in 1892, processing the massive influx of mostly Southern and Eastern European immigrants. The station closed in 1954; it reopened in 1990 as the **Ellis Island Museum of Immigration** in an ambitious attempt to honor the spirit of the place, with films,

exhibits, and tapes documenting the history of America as an immigrant nation.

Some 100 million Americans can trace their roots back through Ellis Island and, for them especially, the museum is an engaging experience. On the first floor, in the old railroad ticket office, is the excellent "Peopling of America" exhibit that chronicles four centuries of American immigration, offering a statistical portrait of who arrived and where they came from. The huge, vaulted **Registry Room** on the second floor, scene of so much trepidation, elation, and despair, has been left bare, with just a couple of inspectors' desks and American flags. In the side-hall interview rooms, recordings of those who passed through Ellis Island recall the experience, along with photographs and thoughtful, informative explanatory text, while upstairs small domestic artifacts – train timetables and familiar items brought from home – make up the evocative "Treasures from Home" exhibit.

The museum's **American Family Immigration History Center** (⊛www.ellisislandrecords.org) is of great use to genealogical researchers, offering an interactive research database (free) that contains information from ship manifests and passenger lists concerning over twelve million immigrants who passed through the Port of New York between 1892 and 1954. On the fortified spurs of the island, names of immigrant families who passed through the building over the years are engraved in copper, paid for by a minimum donation of $100 from their descendants. This "American Immigrant Wall of Honor," launched in 1990, helped fund the island's restoration and features the names of over 600,000 individuals and families.

2

The Financial District

While most visitors to the southern end of Manhattan journey primarily to Ground Zero, former site of the World Trade Center, the area is also home to some of the city's most historic sights. New York began here, and its development is reflected in the dense, twisted streets of what is now known as the **Financial District**, heart of the nation's business trade. Many of the early colonial buildings that once lined these streets either burned down during the American Revolution or the Great Fire of 1835, or were later demolished by big businesses eager to boost their corporate images with headquarters near **Wall Street**. The explosive commercial development of nearby South Street Seaport and the conversion of old office space to residential units have helped the Financial District shed its nine-to-five aura.

Along Wall Street

The Dutch arrived here first, building a wooden wall at the edge of New Amsterdam in 1635 to protect themselves from the British (who later settled to the north), giving the narrow canyon of today's **Wall Street** its name. Still to this day, the

2

purse strings of the capitalist world are pulled from behind the Neoclassical facade of the **New York Stock Exchange** at 8 Wall St (Map 4, E7). Once a popular tourist attraction, the Stock Exchange has been closed to the public since September 11th, and the surrounding heavy police presence gives the place the feel of a military fortress.

Trinity Church and around

At Wall Street's western end, on Broadway, is **Trinity Church** (Map 4, E6; free guided tours daily at 2pm and free classical music concerts Thurs at 1pm), first built in 1698, though the current version went up in 1846. For fifty years, this was the city's tallest building. Trinity's cemetery is the final resting place for such luminaries as the first secretary of the treasury (and the man on the $10 bill) Alexander Hamilton, steamboat king Robert Fulton, signer of the Declaration of Independence Francis Lewis, and many others.

Further east down Wall Street, the **Morgan Guaranty Trust Building** at no. 23 bears the scars of a mysterious event that happened on September 16, 1920, when a horse-drawn cart exploded in front. The explosion remains unexplained to this day, and the pockmark scars on the building's wall have never been repaired. Formerly in the Standard Oil Building on Broadway near Bowling Green, the **Museum of American Financial History** (@www.financialhistory.org) was, at the time of writing, scheduled to open in the former Bank of New York Building, at no. 48, in October 2007. It is the largest public archive of financial documents and artifacts in the world, featuring such finance-related objects as the bond signed by Washington bearing the first dollar sign ever used on a federal document.

Federal Hall National Memorial
Map 4, E6. 26 Wall St. Mon–Fri 9am–5pm; free; ☎212/825-6888, @www.nps.gov/feha. #1, #2, #4, or #5 to Wall Street.

Across the street from the New York Stock Exchange, **Federal**

Hall National Memorial looks like an Ionic temple that woke up one morning and found itself surrounded by skyscrapers. But the memorial's claim to fame has less to do with the structure – which was built as a Customs House in 1842 – than with the site: in 1789, in a building that used to stand here, George Washington was sworn in as the nation's first president, then addressed a swarming crowd from its balcony. Inside there's an exhibit on Washington's inauguration, including a copy of his surprisingly legible handwritten address, and a fully staffed **visitor center** run by the National Park Service and the city's tourist board.

Ground Zero and around

The former site of the World Trade Center, **Ground Zero** is now a furiously active construction site. There's a viewing platform at Fulton and Church streets, along with a small photographic history of the events of 9/11 and a list of everyone who died that day. But with all the activity, it's hard to get a sense of the enormity of the event. Two nearby sites provide a fuller picture. The oldest church in Manhattan, **St Paul's Chapel** (Map 4, E5; Mon–Sat 10am–6pm, Sun 9am–4pm; free) sat squarely in the shadow of the Twin Towers but miraculously survived the attacks intact. For months, it was the headquarters of the volunteer squad that kept relief workers fed and rested, and when the area reopened to the public, a makeshift shrine of flowers, photos, stuffed animals, letters, and flags accreted along its wrought-iron fence. Pieces of the shrine were saved and are now part of a moving permanent exhibit, which includes videos, inside.

Overlooking the south edge of Ground Zero, the **Tribute WTC Visitor Center**, 120 Liberty St (Mon & Wed–Sat 10am–6pm, Tues noon–6pm, Sun noon–5pm; $10 donation requested; ☎212/393-9160, ⊛www.tributewtc.org), run by victims' families, powerfully evokes the morning of September 11th and its immediate aftermath without straining for sentiment. Video footage and tape recordings of fire fighters

The World Trade Center 1973–2001

On **September 11, 2001**, a hijacked airline slammed into the north tower of the **World Trade Center** at 8.46am; seventeen minutes later another hijacked plane struck the south tower. As thousands looked on in horror – in addition to millions more viewing on TV – the south tower collapsed at 9.59am, its twin at 10.28am. All seven buildings of the World Trade Center complex eventually collapsed, and the Center was reduced to a smoldering mountain of steel, concrete, and glass rubble. Black clouds billowed above, and the whole area was covered in a blanket of dust several inches thick.

The devastation was staggering. While most of the 50,000 working in the towers had been evacuated before the buildings fell, many never made it out; hundreds of firefighters, police officers, and rescue workers who arrived on the scene when the planes struck perished when the buildings fell. In all, **approximately 2600 people died** at the WTC.

In the weeks after the tragedy, Downtown was shut down, and the seven-square-block vicinity immediately around the WTC – soon to be known as **Ground Zero** – was sealed off by the police. New Yorkers lined up to give blood and volunteered to feed and care for the rescue workers (who were mostly firefighters and iron-workers), and vigils were held throughout the city, most notably in Union Square, which was peppered with all manner of candles, missing-persons posters, and makeshift shrines. An acrid haze hung over the city for weeks as underground fires smoldered.

Toiling around the clock for nine months, Ground Zero workers cleared 1.5 million tons of debris from the site, which then stood an open pit for five years awaiting its fate. Finally, in August 2006, construction of the WTC Memorial and Museum began, and in December of that year the foundation of the city's soon-to-be-tallest skyscraper, the 1776-foot-high Freedom Tower, was poured. The memorial is scheduled to open on the eighth anniversary of the attacks; Freedom Tower will open in 2012.

recapture the eerie calm that preceded the towers' collapse (and the deaths of many of those heard and pictured), and hundreds of photographs of the victims remind you of the human tragedy that's been all but overshadowed by the politics of the ensuing "war on terror."

Federal Reserve Bank of New York

Take Liberty Street east to Broadway and you'll find a welcome splash of color in Isamu Noguchi's 1968 **Red Cube**. Across the street is the recently spruced-up **Zuccotti Park** (formerly Liberty Plaza Park), a de facto outdoor café for Financial District workers on sunny days – it's ringed by some decent food-carts. A bit further on stands the original 1924 **Federal Reserve Bank** (Map 4, E6), the most heavily fortified building in the city. Though cash is no longer counted and disbursed here, eighty feet below the somber neo-Gothic interior of the bank is the world's largest accumulation of gold. It is possible – but tricky – to tour; contact the Public Information Department, Federal Reserve Bank, 33 Liberty St (☎212/720-6130, ⓦwww .newyorkfed.org), at least five business days in advance, so tickets can be sent to you (a month's lead-time is recommended).

Bowling Green and around

Map 4, E7. #4 or #5 to Bowling Green.

Heading south along Broadway, a most impressive leftover of the confident days before the Wall Street crash of 1929 is the old **Cunard Building**, at no. 25 (Map 4, D8). Its marble walls and high dome once housed a steamship's booking office – hence the elaborate, whimsical murals of various ships and nautical mythology splashed around the ceiling. Broadway comes to a gentle end at **Bowling Green Park**, originally the city's meat market, but in 1733 turned into an oval of turf used for the eponymous game by colonial Brits on a lease of "one peppercorn per year." In 1626, the green had been the location of one of Manhattan's more memorable business deals, when Peter Minuit, first director-general of the Dutch colony of New

Amsterdam, bought the whole island from the Indians for a bucket of trade goods worth sixty guilders (about $24). The other side of the story (and the part you never hear) is that these particular Indians didn't actually own or even live on the island.

The green sees plenty of office folk picnicking in the shadow of Cass Gilbert's **US Custom House**, a heroic monument to the Port of New York and home of the Smithsonian Institution's **National Museum of the American Indian**, 1 Bowling Green (daily 10am–5pm, Thurs until 8pm; free; ☎212/514-3700, ⊛www.nmai.si.edu). This excellent collection of artifacts from almost every tribe native to the Americas was largely assembled by one man, George Gustav Heye (1874–1957), who traveled throughout the Americas for more than fifty years picking up such works. Highlights include totem poles and other wood carvings from the Pacific Northwest, quilled hides and feathered headdresses from the Great Plains, and thousand-year-old pottery from the mysterious vanished civilization that once thrived around the Grand Canyon in the American Southwest. Built in 1907, the Custom House itself was intended to pay homage to the booming maritime market. The four statues flanking the entrance were sculpted by Daniel Chester French, who also created the Lincoln Memorial in Washington DC. As if French foresaw the House's current use, the sculptor blatantly comments on the mistreatment of Indians in his statues.

Battery Park and Castle Clinton

Map 4, D8. #4 or #5 to Bowling Green.
Just south of Bowling Green, lower Manhattan takes a breath in **Battery Park**, a bright and breezy space with tall trees, green grass, lots of flowers, and views overlooking the panorama of the Statue of Liberty, Ellis Island, and Governors Island. At the park's main entrance at Battery Place and State Street stands the mutilated sculpture **The Sphere**, a representation of Earth created by Fritz Koenig in 1971 as a monument to world peace; this sculpture stood in the World Trade Center plaza until 9/11, when it was heavily damaged – it's an eerie,

immediate reminder of that day's destruction. Various other monuments and statues, ranging from Jewish immigrants to Celtic settlers to the city's first wireless-telegraph operators, adorn the park.

Before a landfill closed the gap, **Castle Clinton**, the 1811 fort on the west side of the park, was on an island, where it served as one of several forts defending New York Harbor; later, it acted as a pre–Ellis Island drop-off point for arriving immigrants. Today, the squat castle is the place to purchase advance tickets for the Statue of Liberty and Ellis Island (see p.29); ferries board nearby.

The free Staten Island Ferry (see p.30) leaves from the new glass terminal on the east edge of Battery Park.

Battery Park City

Map 4, C7. #4 or #5 to Bowling Green.
The hole dug for the foundations of the Twin Towers threw up a million cubic yards of earth and rock; these excavations were dumped into the Hudson River to form the 23-acre base of **Battery Park City**, a self-sufficient area of office blocks, apartments, and parkland that feels a world apart from much of Manhattan.

At its very southern end is the entrance to the peaceful, Zen-like **Robert F. Wagner Jr Park**. In the park, a hexagonal, pale-granite building designed in 1997 by Kevin Roche will catch your eye: **The Museum of Jewish Heritage**, 36 Battery Place (Map 4, C8; Sun–Tues & Thurs 10am–5.45pm, Wed until 8pm, Fri 10am–3pm, closed Jewish holidays; $10, students $5, children free; ℡646/437-4200, @www.mjhnyc.org), was created as a memorial to the Holocaust. Three floors of exhibits feature historical and cultural artifacts ranging from the practical accoutrements of everyday Eastern European Jewish life to the prison garb survivors wore in Nazi concentration camps, along with photographs, personal belongings, and narratives.

Across the street the **Skyscraper Museum**, 39 Battery Place (Wed–Sun noon–6pm; $5, students and seniors $2.50,

☎212/968-1961, ⊛www.skyscraper.org), is lodged on the ground floor of the *Ritz-Carlton* hotel and condominium tower, but makes the most of its small footprint with vertical mini-tower display cases and glass ceilings that convey a sense of soaring height. The museum documents the history of the world's skyscrapers, with rotating exhibits on topics like the construction of the world's tallest building in Dubai, United Arab Emirates, scheduled for completion in 2008. There's a permanent exhibit on the World Trade Center. If you don't want to pony up for admission, drop by to check out the excellent bookstore, which has a superb collection of art and architecture books, guidebooks, and high-rise-related gifts.

Further north, at North End Avenue and Vesey Street, an eye-catching cantilevered wedge of sod forms the base of the **Irish Hunger Memorial**, created in 2002 to honor the one million Irish who died of starvation between 1845 and 1852 as well as the million who immigrated to New York City during that time.

Fraunces Tavern Museum

Retrace your steps through Battery Park to Pearl Street and follow it to Broad Street. On the corner, in the shadow of many skyscrapers, sits the **Fraunces Tavern Museum**, no. 54 (Map 4, F8; Tues–Fri noon–5pm, Sat 10am–5pm; $4, children, seniors, students $3; ☎212/425-1778, ⊛www.frauncestavernmuseum .org), a three-story brick building, parts of which date to the eighteenth century. It's anyone's guess what's original here and what's a reconstruction – its administrators, the Sons of the Revolution, don't really seem interested in the distinction (though architecture critics are, and pan the place accordingly), but the fact remains that George Washington bade farewell to his troops here on December 4, 1783, before returning to his estate at Mount Vernon. The upper floors of the building are now outfitted with early American decor and host rotating exhibits on the colonial era; there's a restaurant and bar on the ground floor.

Stone Street

The best-preserved block of nineteenth-century architecture in the Financial District is narrow, cobblestoned **Stone Street**, between Hanover Square and Coenties Alley – also the Financial District's best place to eat and drink. It's a vast open-air beer garden packed with a party-hardy Wall Street crowd on summer nights, when places like *Ulysses' Bar* and the *Waterstone Grill* cover the street with picnic tables. The rest of the time it's more relaxed, with those places, plus the quaint *Financier* patisserie (see p.195), providing a cozy respite from the traffic and noise of surrounding streets.

South Street Seaport

Map 4, H6. #A, #E, #J, #M, #1, #2, #4, or #5 to Fulton Street–Broadway Nassau.

Centered on Front and Fulton streets, the **South Street Seaport** has long been derided as an outdoor mall, with big, touristy restaurants, chain stores, and a few old boats. But that's not quite fair. Aside from being one of the only truly pedestrian-friendly districts in the city, it has a number of attractive brick buildings dating from the 1800s, when it was still a bustling port. Recently renovated and expanded, the South Street Seaport Museum mounts creative exhibits on the city's history, both maritime and otherwise, and there are the beginnings of some real street life – especially along Front Street between Beekman Street and Peck Slip – as the area gains steam as a trendy residential neighborhood. Finally, one of the best-kept tourist secrets is here: a big TKTS box office (corner of John and Front sts). Like its counterpart in Times Square (p.106), it sells same-day half-price tickets to Broadway shows, but the lines here are usually a fraction of those in Midtown.

The South Street Seaport Museum

Map 4, G5. 12 Fulton St, 209–213 Water St, & piers 15 and 16. April–Oct daily 10am–6pm, Nov–March Fri–Sun 10am–5pm; $8, seniors and students $6, children $4, under-5s free; ☎212/748-8600, ⓦwww.southstseaport.org.

The **South Street Seaport Museum** comprises a number of sites scattered throughout the district. The Schermerhorn Row Galleries, in three linked, early nineteenth-century warehouses at 12–14 Fulton St, hold the bulk of the museum's intriguing collection of art and artifacts, which includes intricate scrimshaw and ship models (at least one made from bones), paintings, and large rotating exhibits. Several historic ships, docked at piers 15 and 16, are tourable with a museum ticket: the 1885 *Wavertree*, the 1908 *Ambrose*, and the magnificent 1911 *Peking*, a four-master with an acre's worth of sails. There are a couple more art galleries at 209 and 213 Water St; in between, at no. 211, Bowne & Company Stationers still turns out wedding invitations and book plates on treadle-operated presses, which workers may demonstrate for you if you ask nicely.

③

City Hall Park and the Brooklyn Bridge

Since New York's earliest days as an English-run city, **City Hall Park** has been the seat of its municipal government. Though many of the original buildings no longer stand, great examples of the city's finest architecture can still be found here. The park itself contains stately City Hall and Tweed Courthouse, and the Woolworth Building stands nearby. Meanwhile, the Municipal Building watches over Police Plaza and the city's main courthouses, and the **Brooklyn Bridge** – which makes for a great walk – soars eastward over the river to the genteel neighborhood of Brooklyn Heights (see p.159).

City Hall

Map 4, E4. Free tours (reservations required in advance) Mon, Wed, Thurs & Fri at 10am; including visits to Tweed Courthouse Tues 10am

& Fri 2pm; ☎212/788-2170, ⓦwww.nyc.gov/artcommission. #R or #W to City Hall, #6 to Brooklyn Bridge/City Hall, or #2 or #3 to Park Place.

Broadway and Park Row form the apex of City Hall Park, a well-groomed triangle of green just beyond the jumble of government offices and courts. This triangular wedge is a mix of contemporary sculpture and old-fashioned gaslights and features a farmers' market each Friday (June–Nov 8am–5pm). Facing City Hall is a statue of the shackled figure of Nathan Hale, who was captured in 1776 by the British and hanged for spying, but not before he'd spat out his famous last words: "I only regret that I have but one life to lose for my country."

At the park's northern head stands **City Hall**, completed in 1812 at what was then the farthest north edge of New York. In 1865, Abraham Lincoln's body lay in state here while 120,000 New Yorkers paid their respects. Later, beginning with a 1927 fete for aviator Charles Lindbergh, the building came to mark the finishing point for Broadway tickertape parades honoring astronauts, returned hostages, and triumphant sports teams. Its interior is an elegant meeting of arrogance and authority, with a sweeping spiral staircase delivering you to the precise geometry of the Governor's Room – but you can see this only by reserving a space on one of the free guided tours.

Park Row and the Woolworth Building

Map 4, E4 & E5. #R or #W to City Hall, #6 to Brooklyn Bridge/City Hall, or #2 or #3 to Park Place.

The southern tip of City Hall Park is flanked on either side by impressive early twentieth-century skyscrapers. **Park Row**, the eastern edge of the park, was known as "Newspaper Row" from the 1830s to the 1920s, when the city's most influential publishers, news services, and foreign-language presses had their offices on this street and surrounding blocks.

At the west side of the park is the 1913 **Woolworth Building**, one of the city's most aesthetically pleasing skyscrapers.

Fringed with Gothic decoration, which seems to have been piled on more as a joke than as a nod to the solemn churches of Europe, the so-called "Cathedral of Commerce" was paid for in cash by the man who brought America the "five-and-dime" store. It displays a good-humored panache that's largely extinct in today's architecture. Unfortunately, the building is closed to the public, but if you're willing to brave the short-tempered guards, take a spin through the revolving door to glimpse the gorgeous blue-and-gold mosaics that carpet the vaulted ceiling.

The Municipal Building and around

On Chambers Street, which runs along the top of City Hall Park, the genteel, marble **Tweed Courthouse** is a monument to the infamous corruption of Tammany Hall boss William Marcy "Boss" Tweed. It now houses the Department of Education, and guided tours (combined with visits to City Hall; see p.43) reveal a beautifully renovated, grand octagonal rotunda soaring upward in a series of arches.

At the east end of Chambers Street, the **Municipal Building** (Map 4, F4) stands like an oversized chest of drawers. Built between 1908 and 1913, it was the first skyscraper by the firm McKim, Mead & White, which also designed Pennsylvania Station. At the building's top, an extravagant pile of columns and pinnacles signals a frivolous conclusion to a no-nonsense structure that houses public records; below, though not apparent, subway cars travel through its foundation.

North along Centre Street is the courts district; the most important ones, the colonnaded **Court of Appeals** and one of the state's supreme courts, face Foley Square. Less attractive but more notorious, the 1939 Art-Deco **Criminal Courts Building**, at 100 Centre St, also contains the Manhattan House of Detention, still nicknamed "the Tombs" after the 1833 Egyptian funereal–style prison that once stood across the street. The courts (and, handily, the buildings' restrooms) are open to the public Monday to Friday 9am to 5pm – just don't expect *Law & Order*–style theatrics.

The Brooklyn Bridge

South along Centre Street from the Municipal Building is the entrance to the **Brooklyn Bridge**, a magnificent piece of engineering that, along with the Staten Island Ferry, is one of the best free vantage points across Manhattan.

Designed by John Roebling and his son Washington, the bridge opened in 1883; for twenty years, it remained the world's largest and longest suspension bridge. To New Yorkers, it was an object of awe, a concrete symbol of the Great American Dream. Italian immigrant painter Joseph Stella called it "a shrine containing all the efforts of the new civilization of America." Indeed, the bridge's meeting of art and function, of romantic Gothic and daring practicality, became a sort of spiritual model for the next generation's skyscrapers.

The bridge's wooden walkway leads across the East River to Brooklyn Heights (see p.159) – though many visitors simply walk halfway, admire the skyline, and walk back. For the most spectacular view, resist the urge to turn around till you're at the midpoint. From there, the Financial District's giants stand shoulder to shoulder behind the spidery latticework of the cables; the East River slips by below as cars hum to and from Brooklyn; and the Statue of Liberty is visible far out in the harbor. It's a spectacular glimpse of the twenty-first-century metropolis, and on no account to be missed.

SoHo, TriBeCa, and NoLita

This triumvirate of acronym'd neighborhoods represents some of the city's most piquant examples of urban renewal and cultural turnaround, having mutated from working-class wholesale and chiefly immigrant areas into artist colonies and then again into super-chic enclaves boasting gourmet eateries, wine and cocktail bars, high-end shopping, and luxury hotel and apartment living. **TriBeCa**, on the rebound from an economic downturn after 9/11, boasts great alternative music venues and several good hotels. **SoHo** has lost most of its galleries to Chelsea, and its trademark cast-iron buildings now play host to a slew of unique stores (as well as many international brand names). Last, it's **NoLita**, with its tiny boutiques, designer ice-cream stores, and cafés crammed with beautiful people that perhaps best exemplifies the fashionable new, moneyed inhabitants of Downtown.

TriBeCa

#1 to Canal Street or Franklin Street, #1, #2, or #3 to Chambers Street.
Just a few blocks' walk northwest from City Hall puts you in **TriBeCa** (Try-beck-ah) – the Triangle Below Canal Street – an

area that was rapidly transformed in the early 1990s from a near ghost town (once a thriving wholesale market district) to an upscale community that mixes commercial establishments with loft residences, studios, art galleries, and chic eateries. Less a triangle than a crumpled rectangle – the area is bounded by Canal and Murray streets, Broadway, and the Hudson River – it takes in spacious industrial buildings whose upper floors have become the apartments of TriBeCa's new gentry.

What was once loft space for renegade artists like Richard Serra now houses galleries, recording studios, computer graphics companies, photo labs, and even film production companies. The Tribeca Film Center production space, 375 Greenwich St (Map 4, C2), for instance, is co-owned by local resident Robert De Niro. So too is **Tribeca Cinemas**, 54 Varick St just south of Canal, an art theatre that also hosts numerous special screenings and the annual Tribeca Film Festival; founded to encourage economic recovery in Lower Manhattan after 9/11, the festival brings together international directors, actors, and audiences every spring.

Exploring TriBeCa

To get a feel for TriBeCa's mix of old and new, go to **Duane Park**, a sliver of green at Duane, Hudson, and Greenwich streets. Around the park's picturesque perimeter, you'll see the former depots of New York's egg, butter, and cheese wholesalers wedged between new residential apartments. The ornate tops of the Woolworth and Municipal buildings guard the skyline.

Head north out of Duane Park on **Greenwich Street toward Canal Street**, a main strip, where you'll find a slew of affordable-to-expensive restaurants. Parallel to Greenwich is **Hudson Street**, which catches the overflow of fancy restaurants before, in sharp contrast, petering out into a few still-active warehouses, whose denizens do the same work they have for decades. See p.210 for TriBeCa restaurant reviews.

West Broadway is one of TriBeCa's major thoroughfares and has a few interesting, if nonessential, sites to check out.

On its northeast corner with White Street stands one of the city's rare remaining Federal-era stores, in continuous use since 1809. But the most poignant spot is **Hook and Ladder Company #8**, between Varick and North Moore streets, a turn-of-the-nineteenth-century brick-and-stone firehouse dotted with white stars. The closest firehouse to the World Trade Center, it suffered many casualties during the terrorist attacks.

SoHo

#N, #R, or #W to Prince Street, #B, #D, #F, or #V to Broadway–Lafayette, #C or #E to Spring Street.

From the mid-1960s to the late 1980s, **SoHo**, the grid of streets that runs south of Houston Street, meant one thing: art. As the West Village increased in price and declined in hipness, artists moved into SoHo's industry-vacated loft spaces. Galleries were established, quickly attracting the city's art crowd, as well as trendy clothing shops and some of the city's best restaurants. Soon the artists who'd settled the district were priced out and moved on to Chelsea, Brooklyn, and beyond. What remains is a mix of chichi antiques shops, often overpriced art galleries, and chain clothiers from around the world.

   Although SoHo now carries the veneer of the establishment – a loft in the area means money (and lots of it) – no amount of gloss can cover up the neighborhood's distinctive appearance: sunlit alleys between former garment factories peeling paint and fronted by some of the coolest cast-iron facades in the country. **Houston Street** (pronounced Howston rather than Hewston) marks the top of SoHo's trellis of streets, any exploration of which entails crisscrossing and doubling back. **Greene Street** is a great place to start, highlighted all along by the historic nineteenth-century cast-iron facades that spared SoHo from the bulldozers during the Robert Moses era of massive urban upheaval. Prince Street, Spring Street, and West Broadway hold the best selection of shops and galleries in the area.

4

SoHo's cast-iron architecture

In vogue from around 1860 to the turn of the twentieth century, **cast-iron architecture** ushered in the age of prefabricated buildings. With mix-and-match components molded from iron, which was cheaper than brick or stone, a building of four stories could go up in as many months. The heavy iron crossbeams carry the weight of the floors, allowing more space for windows. Almost any style or whim could be cast in iron and pinned to a building, yielding instant facelifts for SoHo's sweatshops and creating a whole new generation of beauties.

One of the largest collections of this building style in the world, the **SoHo Cast-Iron Historic District**, runs roughly north–south from Houston to Canal and east–west from West Broadway to Crosby. Have a look at **72–76 Greene St**, an extravagance with a Corinthian portico that stretches its entire five stories, and at the elaborations of its sister building at **nos. 28–30**. Elsewhere on Greene, you'll see similarly vivacious facades, which may not be quite as splendid, but they do make excellent display cases for the retail offerings inside.

At the northeast corner of Broome Street and Broadway is the magnificent 1857 Haughwout Building (Map 5, G7), perhaps the ultimate in cast-iron architecture. Rhythmically repeated motifs of colonnaded arches are framed here behind taller columns in a thin sliver of a mock-Venetian palace. In 1904, Ernest Flagg took the possibilities of cast iron to their conclusion in his "Little Singer" Building, 561 Broadway, at Prince (Map 5, F6), where the use of wide window frames points the way to the glass-curtain wall of the 1950s.

North from Canal Street

Loosely speaking, SoHo's diversions start out grittier down south and get nicer as you move north. Still, **Broome and Grand streets**, formerly full of dilapidated storefronts and dusty windows, are home to a small band of boutiques, galleries, cafés, and eclectic restaurants. The ultra-chic (and ultra-expensive) **SoHo Grand Hotel** occupies the corner of Canal and West Broadway.

If you don't want to fork out the dough for a room, at least check out the lobby or have a cocktail at the bar, where there's often a live DJ playing. Marking SoHo's southern entrance and border with TriBeCa, **Canal Street** links the Holland Tunnel with the Manhattan Bridge, though in truth the street is, in look and feel, more a part of Chinatown than anything.

Prince Street

At 112 Prince St, near the corner of Greene Street, SoHo celebrates its architecture with Richard Haas's mural, a self-referential *trompe l'oeil* affair that reproduces the building's cast-iron facade. Many of the clothing and antiques shops around here are beyond reasonable budgets, but **Prince Street** and the other SoHo streets have their fair share of the chain clothing stores you'd find in any mid-sized American city, plus there's an open-air market at the corner of Spring and Wooster streets. See Chapter 27, "Shopping," for further options.

What you'll find in SoHo's few remaining **galleries** is similarly high-end, but no one minds you taking a look. Most spaces are concentrated on West Broadway and Prince Street, with some on Grand between West Broadway and Broadway. Deitch Projects, 76 Grand St, is certainly the edgiest; the rest are relatively staid in their offerings. They're generally open Tuesday to Saturday 11am to 6pm, with Saturdays being the liveliest days. For a greater selection of galleries, see Chapter 28, "Art galleries."

Two pieces of installation art are very solid remnants of SoHo's avant-garde era: *Broken Kilometer*, which inhabits 393 W Broadway, and *The New York Earth Room*, on the second floor of 141 Wooster St; both are open Wednesday through Sunday. If nothing else, these massive works by Walter de Maria are a defiant use of highly valuable real estate and a fine counterpoint to standard window-shopping.

NoLita

Map 5, G6. #N, #R, or #W to Prince Street, #6 to Spring Street, #B, #D, #F, or #V to Broadway–Lafayette.

Just east of Broadway and south of Houston, fashion, style, and nonchalant living have found fertile breeding ground. Referred to as **NoLita**, this area north of Little Italy, which extends east from Lafayette, Mott, and Elizabeth streets between Prince and Houston, is great for hip, only-in-New-York shopping (and it can be marginally less expensive than SoHo). Its streets are lined with shops that showcase, for instance, handmade shoes, custom swimwear, and items with vintage flair, often sold by the designers themselves. Moreover, the young, artsy, and restless who hang around the nabe's cozy bars and restaurants make it an excellent place for a late-afternoon drink and a perfect spot for gazing at some of the city's most fashionable people.

5

Chinatown and Little Italy

With more than 200,000 residents (over half of them of Chinese descent and the rest of other Asian heritage), seven Chinese newspapers, a dozen Buddhist temples, around 500 restaurants, and hundreds of garment factories and shops, **Chinatown** is Manhattan's most populous ethnic neighborhood. In the late 1800s, this area contained the notorious Five Points district, home to the Irish immigrant and Nativist clans celebrated in Martin Scorsese's *Gangs of New York*, but Chinese culture has predominated here for the last century. Since the 1980s, Chinatown has also pushed its boundaries north across Canal Street into what had long been Italian turf; it also sprawls east across Division Street and East Broadway into the nether fringes of the Lower East Side.

The Chinese community has generally preserved its own way of dealing with things, keeping business affairs within families and allowing few intrusions into the culture. And while insularity means that much of Chinatown's character is relatively undiluted – especially on streets such as Pell, Mott, and Bayard – it has also meant sweatshop labor and overcrowded, ill-kept tenements. Tourists and New Yorkers alike see little of this seamier side (which is steadily moving to newer Chinese communities in Queens and Brooklyn) amid all the excellent Chinese **food** and the bargain **vendors** along Canal Street.

Just north of Chinatown is **Little Italy**, one of the city's most storied immigrant neighborhoods. Signs made out of red, green, and white tinsel effusively welcome visitors here, a signal that today's Little Italy is light years from the solid ethnic enclave of old, settled by a huge influx of Italian immigrants in the second half of the nineteenth century. Walk north on Mulberry from Chinatown, and the transition from the throngs south of Canal Street to Little Italy's somewhat forced hoopla – complete with Frank Sinatra blaring out from nearly every restaurant – can be a little difficult to adjust to. Few Italians live here anymore, though a number still visit for a dose of nostalgia and a plate of fully Americano spaghetti with red sauce.

But that's not to advise missing out on Little Italy altogether – the area's fun for a stroll, a schmaltzy kick, and a decent cappuccino on the hoof. Some original **bakeries** and **salumerias** (Italian specialty food stores) do survive, and here, amid the imported cheeses, sausages, and salamis hanging from the ceiling, you can buy hearty sandwiches made with cured meats and slabs of fresh mozzarella or eat slices of homemade focaccia.

The best way to reach Chinatown and Little Italy is to take the #J, #M, #N, #Q, #R, #W, #Z, or #6 train to Canal Street; for the north edge of Little Italy, you could also take the #6 to Spring Street.

Chinese New Year

Chinatown bursts with even more color than usual during the **Chinese New Year Festival**, held on the first new moon in the first lunar month of the year (usually between mid-Jan and mid-Feb). The highlight is the giant cloth-and-papier-mâché dragons that parade down Mott Street to the sound of drums and gongs. The firecrackers that traditionally accompanied the festival are permitted only in a highly controlled twenty-minute show; locals make do with purely decorative strands of firecrackers, and the gutters run with ceremonial dyes and confetti.

Mott Street

Mott Street is Chinatown's main north–south avenue, although the streets around – Canal, Pell, Bayard, Doyers, and Bowery – also host a glut of restaurants, tea and rice shops, and grocers. Cantonese cuisine predominates, but some **restaurants** specialize in the spicier Sichuan and Hunan cuisines, along with Fujian, Suzhou, and Chaozhou dishes. Just remember that most Chinese restaurants start closing at around 9.30pm – best to go early if you want less-frenzied service and atmosphere. If you're looking for specific recommendations (especially for dim sum), some of the best are detailed in Chapter 22, "Restaurants."

Besides wolfing down Asian delights, the lure of Chinatown lies in wandering amid the exotica of the **shops** and absorbing the neighborhood's vigorous **street life**. You can pick up maps, brochures, and coupons at the **visitors' kiosk** at Canal and Baxter streets, but meandering is highly recommended, and there are several interesting, vaguely structured routes to take. Follow Mott Street down from Canal to the corner of Mosco to see a rare edifice that predates the Chinese arrival. It's the early nineteenth-century, green-domed Catholic school and **Church of the Transfiguration** (Map 7, G3), an elegant Georgian building with Gothic details. Masses are held here daily in Cantonese, English, and Mandarin. On the same block, **32 Mott St** operated as a general store from 1891 to 2004, and was the longest-running store in Chinatown. It has reopened as a generic gift shop, but you can still see some of the original wood trim on the windows and inside. The next block over (head north on Mott, then east one block on Pell) is picturesquely crooked **Doyers Street**, once known as Bloody Angle for its reputation as a battleground during nineteenth-century Chinese gang wars.

Museum of Chinese in the Americas

Map 4, G2. Tues–Sat noon–6pm; $2, students and seniors $1; ☎212/619-4785, 🌐www.moca-nyc.org.

One block west of Mott is Mulberry Street, where, at no. 70, you'll find the double red doors of the community center right on the corner. Two floors up lies the tiny but fascinating **Museum of Chinese in the Americas**, which documents the experiences of immigrants from the earliest days of hand laundries and garment work through Chinatown residents' experiences during and after 9/11. Displays include Chinese photographs, cultural artifacts, and a collection of "yellow peril" movie posters and other memorabilia reflecting racial stereotyping of Asians in the US. Take time to explore with the virtual Chinatown CD-ROM tour, or join a group walk ($12; book ahead with the museum's education department). The museum also sells a **Historic Walking Tour Map**, ideal for touring the neighborhood. By late 2008, the museum expects to relocate to a new, larger space designed by Vietnam Veterans Memorial architect Maya Lin at 211–215 Centre St, between Howard and Grand (Map 4, F1).

Canal and Grand streets

One block north of the Chinese Museum is **Canal Street**, at all hours a crowded thoroughfare crammed with jewelry shops and kiosks hawking sunglasses, T-shirts, and fake handbags. At no. 133, the gilded **Mahayana Buddhist Temple** (daily 8am–6pm; ☎212/925-8787) is certainly worth a peek. Drop a dollar in the donation box to grab a fortune, then proceed to the main hall, where candles and blue neon glow around the giant gold Buddha. Despite the ostentatious display, it's a surprisingly peaceful place.

North of Canal, take Mott or Mulberry to **Grand Street**, passing by a wild variety of produce stands, seafood shops, and butchers. This is where visitors will most strongly feel the Chinese culture of today. Snow peas, bean curd, assorted fungi, numerous varieties of bok choi, and dried sea cucumbers spill out onto the sidewalks, while racks of ribs, whole chickens, and lacquered Peking ducks glisten in store windows. Perhaps even more fascinating than the assortment of foodstuffs are the **herbalists**, in whose shops you will find myriad drawers and jars, all filled with roots and powders that are centuries-old remedies for nearly every human ailment – though for those accustomed to Western medicine they may seem no more familiar than voodoo potions.

Mulberry Street

Little Italy's main strip, **Mulberry Street** is an almost solid row of cafés and restaurants – and therefore filled with tourists. The street is particularly lively, if a bit like a theme park, at night, when the lights come on and the sidewalks fill with hosts who shout menu specials at passers-by. None of the **restaurants** around here are particularly notable for their food, but the northwest corner of Mulberry and Hester streets, the former site of *Umberto's Clam House* (now relocated two blocks north), was quite notorious in its time: it was the scene of a vicious gangland murder in 1972, when "Crazy Joey" Gallo was shot dead while celebrating his birthday with his wife and daughter. Gallo, a big talker and ruthless businessman, was alleged to have offended a rival family and so paid the price. For a more tangible Mafia vibe, you can't beat the 1908 **Mulberry Street Bar**, at no. 176 1/2, where the back room – all fogged mirrors and tile floors – has been the setting for numerous Mob movies and episodes of *The Sopranos*.

For anyone here in mid-September, the ten-day **Festa di San Gennaro** is a wild and tacky celebration of the patron saint of Naples. Italians from all over the city converge on Mulberry Street, and the area is transformed by street stalls and numerous Italian food vendors selling *torrone* candy, *zeppoli*, and *cappicola*. The festivities center on the **Church of the Most Precious**

Blood, just off Canal at 109 Mulberry (main entrance on Baxter Street), providing visitors a rare chance to see the inside of this small church, which is normally closed.

St Patrick's Old Cathedral

Map 5, G6. 263 Mulberry St. Masses in English Mon–Fri 9am & noon, Sat 5.30pm, Sun 9.15am & 12.30pm.

Consecrated in 1815, **St Patrick's Old Cathedral** is the oldest Catholic cathedral in the city and the parent church to its more famous offspring on Fifth Avenue and 50th Street (see p.91). Designed by Joseph-François Mangin, the architect behind City Hall, the building is grand Gothic Revival, with an 85-foot vault, a gleaming gilt altar, and a massive pipe organ that was installed in 1868. Mass (the only time you can view the cathedral's interior) is held in English, Spanish, and Chinese, and the services are open to the public (see times above) – unlike the walled cemetery behind, which is, unfortunately, almost always locked.

Old Police Headquarters

Map 5, G7. Centre St at Broome.

Reaction to Little Italy's illicit past can be found at the corner of Centre and Broome streets, where the palatial 1909 Neoclassical **Old Police Headquarters** was meant to cow would-be criminals into obedience with its high-rise dome and lavish ornamentation. It was more or less a complete failure; the blocks immediately surrounding the edifice were some of the most corrupt in the city in the early twentieth century. Police HQ moved to a bland modern building around City Hall in 1973, and the overbearing palace was converted to upmarket condos in the late 1980s.

6

The Lower East Side

H istorically the epitome of the American melting pot, the **Lower East Side** is one of Manhattan's most engaging neighborhoods, with a mix of slick lounges and gritty dive bars, expensive boutiques and kinky fetish shops, timeworn Jewish delis and wallet-emptying restaurants helmed by celebrity chefs.

For a time during the late nineteenth century, the neighborhood was the most densely populated spot in the world, absorbing half a million Jewish immigrants, as well as other refugees from Eastern Europe, who eked out a living in the quarter's sweatshops while living in its cramped tenements. Most stayed just long enough to scrape together money to move to a leafier neighborhood. Once the tide of immigration slowed, though, working-class Puerto Ricans and Chinese moved in and stayed. Students and artists began arriving here en masse in the 1990s, pushed out of the more expensive East Village, and set the new cultural tone for the neighborhood, though the rapid influx of high-rise luxury condo buildings on the heels of the chichi *Hotel on Rivington* (see p.187) have some rightly worried that the neighborhood will lose its edge.

The hippest part of the Lower East Side lies between Allen

and Clinton streets from Houston to Delancey, but there are also some great spots to be found in its southern reaches, around Grand Street, where it begins to merge with Chinatown (see p.53).

To reach the Lower East Side, take the #F or #V to Second Avenue, the #F, #J, #M, or #Z to Delancey/Essex Street, the #B or #D to Grand Street, or the #M15 bus. A staffed **visitor center**, 261 Broome St, between Orchard and Allen streets, has neighborhood maps, directories, and free parking (☎212/226-9010, ⓦwww.lowereastsideny.com).

Along East Houston

In the first half of the nineteenth century, the streets immediately south of Houston were known as Kleine Deutschland ("Little Germany"), home to well-off German merchants and then, as they moved away, the poorest of the Jewish immigrants fleeing poverty and pogroms in Eastern Europe. Even now, **East Houston Street** still holds remnants of its Jewish past, including *Russ & Daughters*, at no. 179, specializing in smoked fish, herring, and caviar; and *Yonah Schimmel* (see p.197), at no. 137, maker of some of the freshest, densest knishes you'll ever taste.

Ludlow and Orchard streets

On the corner of Ludlow Street and East Houston stands **Katz's Deli** (Map 5, K5), a delicatessen famous for its assembly-line counter service, stellar pastrami sandwich, and motto, "Send a salami to your boy in the army!"; it's lauded by locals as one of the best delis in New York. The block of **Ludlow Street** just south of Houston is the spine of the Lower East Side's rocking **nightlife scene**, with places such as the popular *Local 138* (at no. 138, natch) and *Max Fish* at no. 178, sparking the hipster migration to the neighborhood. Along the block you'll see a number of high-end **secondhand stores** offering retro items – mid-century furniture, records, and used clothing – as well as several bar/performance spaces. For more on the Lower East Side's excellent bar and nightlife scene, see p.240.

Just one block west of Ludlow is **Orchard Street**, center of the so-called **Bargain District**, which is filled with stalls and storefronts stuffed with discount clothes and luggage. The best time to visit is Sunday, when the street is turned into an open-air market.

The Lower East Side Tenement Museum

Map 5, K7. 108 Orchard St (visitor center); 97 Orchard St (tenement museum). Mon 11am–5.30pm, Tues–Fri 11am–6pm, Sat & Sun 10.45am–6pm; the tenement museum is accessible only by guided tours ($15), which run every half-hour and begin at the visitor center; advance tickets highly recommended; ☎212/431-0233, Ⓦwww.tenement.org. #F, #J, #M, or #Z to Delancey/Essex Street; #B or #D to Grand Street.

If you haven't got the time to visit the Lower East Side extensively, make sure to schedule a tour of the **Lower East Side Tenement Museum**'s fully intact and wonderfully preserved 1863 tenement. Various apartments within the five-story building have been renovated with period furnishings to reflect the lives of its tenants, from the mid-nineteenth century when there was no plumbing, electricity, or heating, to the mid-twentieth century when many families ran small cottage industries out of their apartments. The museum also runs a popular **walking tour** of the Lower East Side (see p.24).

Delancey, Essex, and Clinton streets

Orchard Street leads to **Delancey Street**, a wide, traffic-choked boulevard whose eastern end feeds into the Williamsburg Bridge, which in turn leads to the eponymous section of Brooklyn (see p.168). On either side of Delancey sprawls the **Essex Street Market**, where you'll find all sorts of fresh fruit, fish, and vegetables, along with random clothing bargains and the occasional trinket. Farther south on **Essex Street**, between Grand and Hester at no. 49, *The Pickle Guys* dole out fresh homemade pickles and olives from barrels of garlicky brine.

East of Essex Street, the atmosphere changes from a smorgasbord of ethnic treats to an edgy melting pot of artsy post-punk white kids and long-established Latin locals; the neighborhood here is traditionally Puerto Rican and Dominican. **Clinton Street** – a mass of cheap Hispanic restaurants, retailers, and travel agents, punctuated by a good number of upscale, trendy eateries like *WD-50* at no. 50 – is in many ways the central thoroughfare of what remains of Loisaida, or the Spanish-speaking Lower East Side.

The Bowery

The Bowery – from *bouwerij*, the Dutch word for farm – spears north from Canal Street and to Cooper Square in the East Village, cleaving the Lower East Side from its western neighbor, NoLita (see p.51), along the way. No longer the city's famous Skid Row, as it was in the nineteenth century, the Bowery – the city's only thoroughfare never to have been graced by a church – is singularly unattractive regardless, lined with restaurant-equipment dealers, light-bulb depots, and the like. Things have changed somewhat in the last few years, however, with the building of new luxury condos and gourmet grocery stores, as well as the anticipation of the shiny **New Museum** (℡212/219-1222, ⊛www.newmuseum.org), a glass-and-metal concoction that looks like a tower of sloppily stacked boxes, due to open in fall 2007. Formerly based in Chelsea, the museum shows work by contemporary artists.

Between Delancey and East Broadway

Although the southern half of **East Broadway** is now almost exclusively Chinese, the street used to be the hub of the Jewish Lower East Side. Just north of here, the 1886 **Eldridge Street Synagogue**, at no. 12 (Map 5, J9), gives a feel for the old quarter: in its day it was one of the neighborhood's grandest houses of worship, with its brick-and-terracotta hybrid of Moorish arches and Gothic rose windows. The facade still possesses a certain grandeur, and the majestic sanctuary has been undergoing a meticulous, volunteer-driven restoration for more than two decades. Tours of the synagogue's beautifully restored interiors are offered Sunday and Tuesday to Thursday, hourly from 11am to 4pm ($5; ☏212/219-0888, ⓦwww .eldridgestreet.org).

East Broadway, Essex, and Grand streets frame the pie-slice-shaped complex that comprises **Seward Park** (Map 5, L8) and its neighboring apartment blocks. Constructed in 1899 by the city to provide a bit of green space in the overburdened precincts of the Lower East Side, the park boasted the first public playground in New York and is still surrounded by benevolent institutions set up for the benefit of ambitious immigrants.

A few blocks west, you'll pass the **Church of St Mary**, at 440 Grand St, the third-oldest Catholic church (1832) in the city. The benches outside are a favorite spot for elderly residents to sit and watch the world go by.

The East Village

L
ike the Lower East Side, which it abuts, the **East Village**,
stretching between Houston and 14th streets and Broadway and Avenue D, was once a refuge of immigrants
and the working class. It became home to New York's
nonconformist intelligentsia in the early part of the twentieth
century, and ever since has hosted its share of celebrated artists,
politicos, and literati – W.H. Auden lived on St Mark's Place
(no. 77), the neighborhood's main artery. In the 1950s, the East
Village was the New York haunt of the Beats – Kerouac, Burroughs, Ginsberg, et al – who would get together at Ginsberg's
house on East 7th Street for declamatory poetry readings.

Later the neighborhood became closely linked with rock
and pop music. Promoter Bill Graham's *Fillmore East* club, at
Second Avenue and 6th Street, hosted just about every band
you've ever heard of during its short life (1968–71), from
The Doors to the Velvet Underground. The legendary hole-
in-the-wall club *CBGB & OMFUG* launched the likes of the
Ramones, the Talking Heads, Blondie, and Patti Smith in the
Seventies and Eighties but was shuttered in 2006 after 33 years;
Smith performed last rites.

During the Nineties, escalating rents forced many people out,
and today the East Village is no longer the hotbed of dissidence
and creativity it once was. Nevertheless, the area remains one of
downtown Manhattan's most vibrant neighborhoods, with boutiques, thrift stores, record shops, bars, and restaurants aplenty.
And despite the vaudevillian circus of St Mark's Place and cor-

porate attempts to turn the whole neighborhood into a *Starbucks*, principled resistance to the status quo can still be found.

To reach the East Village, take the #6 train to Astor Place, or the #N or #R to 8th Street/NYU, and walk east; you can also take the #F or #V to Second Avenue and walk north.

St Mark's Place, Cooper Square, and around

Most begin their tour of the East Village on **St Mark's Place** between Second and Third avenues, where discount record and video stores struggle for space amid hippie-chic clothiers, head shops, and grungy restaurants in a somewhat contrived atmosphere of bohemian cool. Below St Mark's, **7th Street** boasts used-clothing stores as well as several original boutiques, while **6th Street**, between First and Second avenues – also known as "Indian Restaurant Row" – offers endless choices of all things curry.

Cooper Square (Map 5, H3) – a wedge-shaped park formed by the intersection of the Bowery, Third Avenue, and Lafayette Street – serves as the front yard for the seven-story brownstone mass of **Cooper Union**, erected in 1859 by the wealthy industrialist/inventor Peter Cooper as a college for the poor, and the first New York structure to be hung on a frame of iron girders. The building is best known as the place where, in 1860, Abraham Lincoln wowed an audience of top New Yorkers with his so-called "might makes right" speech, in which he criticized the pro-slavery policies of the Southern states, helping to propel himself to the White House later that year.

Astor Place and around

Just west of Cooper Square lies **Astor Place**, named after fur and real-estate magnate John Jacob Astor. Now little more than a bustling five-way intersection flanked by chain stores, an undulating (and unpopular) mirrored condo building, and two *Starbucks*, it was the focal point of one of the city's most desirable neighborhoods during the 1830s – just before high society decamped for Washington Square Park (see p.70). Astor Place's namesake is honored by colorful mosaics of beavers on the #6 train subway-platforms underground, while a far more famous artwork stands above: *Alamo*, by Tony Rosenthal, a fifteen-square-foot black steel cube that's been teetering on one corner here since 1968. Typically surrounded by young punks and daredevil skateboarders, the sculpture can be rotated at its base if you have enough people to give it a push.

Lafayette Street and Broadway

Astor Place is hardly the stuffy, upper-crust residential district that it was during Astor's era. The last real traces of the time when Lafayette Street, which cuts along the edge of the East Village and down into SoHo, was a high-society address is **Colonnade Row**, just south of Astor Place. This strip of four 1832 Greek-Revival houses with a shared Corinthian colonnade is the site of the **Astor Place Theater**, longtime home to the Blue Man Group dance troupe (see p.260). The **Public Theater**, across the street at no. 425 (Map 5, H3), is legendary both as a forerunner of Broadway theater and as the original venue of hit musicals like *Hair*. For years it was overseen by the director Joseph Papp, who pioneered the free summer festival Shakespeare in the Park (see p.118). On the ground floor you'll find the cabaret club *Joe's Pub*, named in Papp's honor; for details on seeing a show at the Public or *Joe's*, see p.261 and p.268, respectively.

Head one block west to Broadway and look north: filling a bend in the street is the lacy marble of **Grace Church**, on the corner of 10th Street (Map 5, G2), which was built and designed in 1846 by James Renwick (of St Patrick's Cathedral fame) in a delicate neo-Gothic style. Dark and aisled, with a flattened, web-vaulted ceiling, it's one of the city's most successful churches – and, in many ways, one of its most secretive escapes. The grounds and sanctuary are open to all during daylight hours, and there are frequent choral concerts here throughout the year (see ⓦwww.gracechurchnyc.org for schedule).

East toward Tompkins Square Park

Head east along 10th Street until you reach **St Mark's-in-the-Bowery** (Map 5, I2), a box-like church on the corner of Second Avenue. It was built in 1799 on the site of Dutch colonial governor Peter Stuyvesant's family chapel, which dated from 1660; seven generations of Stuyvesants are buried under the church and in the tranquil cemetery out back. The church has a long history of involvement in the arts, hosting readings and performances by Kahlil Gibran, Isadora Duncan, William Carlos Williams, W.H. Auden, and, later, all the Beat poets; Sam Shepard had his first plays produced here in 1964. Today, it has three resident art companies, including Richard Foreman's experimental Ontological-Hysteric Theater (see p.262); unfortunately, the interior isn't much to look at, as it was gutted by fire in 1978.

Continue along 10th Street, past the old redbrick **Tenth Street Russian and Turkish Bath**, at no. 268 (☎212/473-8806, ⓦwww.russianturkishbaths.com), whose steam rooms have been active since the nineteenth century; you can stay all day for $30, but it's extra to get beaten with an oak-leaf broom or chow down on some borscht or herring. Venture further east and you'll catch up with Avenue A, which will lead you south to **Tompkins Square Park** (Map 5, K3), the East Village's largest and most scenic green-space. A concert venue in the 1970s (Jimi Hendrix played here), it was better known in the 1980s as a place to buy drugs and sleep off hangovers. Riots broke out in 1990 when, as a part of the cleanup of Alphabet City (see p.68), the city closed the park, tore down the bandshell, and undertook a major redesign. However heavyhanded it may have been, the move worked, and the park is generally pleasant and safe, with large shade trees, bench-lined paths, and two dog-runs. It's edged with bars and sidewalk cafés, especially along Avenue A.

Alphabet City

In the late 1980s and early 1990s, the lettered avenues forming **Alphabet City** made up a notoriously unsafe corner of town, run by drug pushers and gangsters. Most of this was brought to a halt with "Operation Pressure Point," a massive police campaign to clean up the area and make it a place where people would want to live. Today, crime is way down, rents are up, and avenues A, B, and C have some of the coolest bars, cafés, restaurants, and shops in the city, with a clientele of wealthy twentysomethings, New York University students, and young tourists. One definite cultural highlight is the **Nuyorican Poets Café**, 236 E 3rd St (☏212/505-8183, ⓦwww.nuyorican.org), where you can catch some of the biggest stars of the spoken-word scene.

Community gardens

Over the past three decades, East Village residents have reclaimed neglected and empty lots of land, turning burnt-out rubble into some of the prettiest and most verdant **community gardens** in lower Manhattan and providing a focus for residents in what was traditionally a down-at-heel part of town. Though the city decreed that these spaces should be used for real estate, several have survived. In summer, there is no nicer way to while away an evening than to relax, eat a sandwich, or read a book surrounded by lush trees and carefully planted foliage.

Of particular note is **the 6th Street and Avenue B** affair, overgrown with wildflowers, vegetables, trees, and roses, and home to a spectacular four-story-high sculpture (which will be familiar to those who have seen the East Village–set Broadway musical *Rent*). Other gardens nearby include the very serene **6BC Botanical Garden**, on 6th Street between B and C; **Miracle Garden**, on 3rd Street between A and B; **El Sol Brillante**, on 12th Street between A and B; and the **Liz Christy Garden**, on Houston Street and 2nd Avenue.

The West Village

When the *Village Voice*, NYC's venerable alternative weekly newspaper, began life as a chronicler of Greenwich Village nightlife in 1955, "the Village" had a dissident, artistic, and vibrant voice, one that reached back more than a century, when Edgar Allan Poe wrote his famous poem "The Raven" on what's now West 3rd Street. Poe and his literary successors (Edna St Vincent Millay, Edward Albee, Eugene O'Neill, Theodore Dreiser, and many others) were drawn to the neighborhood's cheap rooms and cozy atmosphere; only the latter remains. You'll see why it's become so exclusive: the tree- and townhouse-lined cobblestoned streets of the **West Village** – the area west of Seventh Avenue – twist and turn in contempt of Manhattan's thrumming street grid, allowing for that rare thing in New York: a quiet stroll. There are more restaurants per capita here than any other neighborhood, and stylish bars and cute local eateries serving super-fresh cuisine, though rarely cheap in these moneyed reaches, abound.

The part of the Village between Broadway and Sixth Avenue conforms to the grid but still has a slightly bohemian air. **Washington Square** – immortalized in Henry James's novel by the same name – is a hub of enjoyably aimless activity throughout the year, with its fountain, street musicians, speedchess players, and famous triumphal arch. It's a good place to start an exploration of the Village. If you venture a couple blocks south down MacDougal Street from the park, you'll find yourself smack in the middle of the Village's student quarter – a mix of cheap bars and restaurants, incense shops, folk clubs, and Italian cafés. Turning west (right) on **Bleecker Street** will take you into the more historic part of the Village: first through the gourmet alley between Sixth and Seventh avenues, then to **Christopher Street**, the historic main artery of gay New York, then through the upscale shopping district around 11th Street. North of here – wedged between the West Village and Chelsea – is the cobblestoned **Meatpacking District**, where bloody aprons are far less in evidence than designer duds, both in the rapidly proliferating ateliers and the vast, velvet-roped clubs.

The West Village is easily reached by taking the #1 to Christopher Street/Sheridan Square or the #A, #C, #E, #D, #B, #F, or #V to West 4th Street/Washington Square.

Washington Square

Map 5, E3.

The Village's biggest public park, **Washington Square** has been through many incarnations over the years: a favorite hunting ground of the early colonists, it was later a potter's field and public gallows; the notorious "Hanging Elm," reputed to be one of the city's oldest trees, still stands in the northwest corner. In the 1830s, New York's old money drifted westward from Astor Place (see p.65) and built the attractive row of redbrick Greek-Revival townhouses on Washington Square North; painter Edward Hopper, novelist John Dos Passos, and Henry James's grandmother all lived in them at one time or another.

Across from the row rises architect Stanford White's impossible-to-miss **Triumphal Arch**, built in 1892 to commemorate the centenary of George Washington's inauguration as president; it's recently been renovated and jazzed up with fancy lighting. If city planners have their way, the whole square will be treated to a makeover in the coming years, with the fountain being shifted into alignment with the arch (and Fifth

Avenue) and the plaza shrunk to make room for more plant-ings. Whatever these niceties may do in terms of aesthetics, it's unlikely they'll increase the park's overwhelming charm: as soon as the weather gets warm, the place boils over with life as skateboarders flip, dogs run, and acoustic guitar notes crash through the urgent cries of performers calling for the crowd's attention. At such times, there's no better square in the city.

Around Washington Square

At Washington Square East and Washington Place lies the **Grey Art Gallery** (Map 5, F4; Tues, Thurs & Fri 11am–6pm, Wed 11am–8pm, Sat 11am–5pm; $2.50; ℡212/998-6780, ⒲www.nyu.edu/greyart), an excellent example of New York University – the major landowner in the vicinity – putting their real estate to good use. The world-class exhibitions here usually last a couple of months and range from investigations of Eastern European Modernism to a survey of illustrations for sixteenth-century books.

From the southwest corner of the park, follow MacDougal Street south until you hit **Bleecker Street**, a vibrant junction with mock-European sidewalk cafés that have been literary hangouts since the 1920s. *Café Figaro*, made famous by the Beats in the 1950s, is always thronged: it's still worth the price of a cappuccino to people-watch for an hour or so. Afterward, follow Bleecker Street west through the hubbub of West Village life.

Sixth Avenue and west

Sixth Avenue itself is mainly tawdry stores and fast-food joints, but on its west side, across Father Demo Square and up Bleecker, are some of the Village's prettiest residential streets. Bleecker between Sixth and Seventh is a fine place to grab a sandwich, either at *Murray's Cheese Shop* at no. 254, or *Amy's Bread* at no. 250. Turn left on **Leroy Street** and cross over Var-ick Street, where, confusingly, Leroy Street becomes St Luke's

Place for a block. The houses here, dating from the 1850s, are among the city's most graceful, one of them (recognizable by the two lamps of honor at the bottom of the steps) is the former residence of Jimmy Walker, mayor of New York in the 1920s. Walker was for a time the most popular of mayors, a big-spending, wisecracking man who gave up his work as a songwriter for the world of politics and lived an extravagant lifestyle that rarely kept him out of the gossip columns.

Bedford and Grove streets

Retrace your steps across Varick Street and take a left on **Bedford Street**, pausing to peer into **Grove Court**, a typical secluded West Village mews. Along with nearby Barrow and Commerce streets, Bedford is one of the quietest and most desirable Village addresses – Edna St Vincent Millay, the poet and playwright, lived at no. 75 1/2, said to be the narrowest house in the city, nine feet wide and topped with a tiny gable. The clapboard structure next door, built in 1799, claims to be the oldest house in the Village; it's been much renovated since and probably worth a considerable fortune now. Further down Bedford, at no. 86, the former speakeasy *Chumley's* (see p.241) is recognizable only by the metal grille on its door – a low profile useful in Prohibition years that makes it hard to find today.

Turn right off Bedford onto **Grove Street**, following it towards Seventh Avenue and looking out for *Marie's Crisis Café* (see p.274) at no. 59. Now a rollicking, gay piano bar, it was once home to Thomas Paine, English by birth but perhaps the most important and radical thinker of the American Revolutionary era, and from whose *Crisis Papers* the bar takes its name. Grove Street meets Seventh Avenue at one of the Village's busiest junctions, **Sheridan Square** (Map 5, C3) – not in fact a square at all unless you count Christopher Park's slim strip of green, but simply a wide and hazardous confluence of several busy streets. The square was named after General Sheridan, cavalry commander in the Civil War, and holds a pompous-looking statue to his memory.

Christopher Street and around

Leading off from Sheridan Square, **Christopher Street** is one of the most visible and historic touchstones of the city's gay community, with many of its shops, cafés, and bars catering to men. Violence erupted here on June 28, 1969, when police raided the *Stonewall Inn*, a gay bar at no. 53, and started arresting those inside – some for not having IDs, others for dressing in drag, and the employees for running the place without a liquor license. Word of the arrests quickly spread through the neighborhood, and soon gay men and lesbians from surrounding bars, as well as local residents, had gathered in front of the *Stonewall* to face down the police. Some protesters simply shouted taunts, others threw bottles and rocks, and the police fought back with billy clubs and more arrests. The standoff sparked up again the next two nights, resulting in a number of injuries on both sides, but it formally inaugurated the gay rights movement. Both this clash and the gay rights movement are honored by the annual **Gay Pride March** (held on the last Sunday in June). You can still visit the *Stonewall*, a friendly, mostly gay watering hole with nightly dancing under spinning disco balls. See Chapter 26, "Gay and lesbian New York," for more nightlife options.

Bleecker Street and around

The bit of Bleecker Street from Christopher to Hudson has become one of the most pleasant stretches for **shopping** in the West Village, with an appealing mix of antiques shops, bookstores, and designer clothing boutiques like Marc by Marc Jacobs, no. 403, the New York native's wildly popular "cheap" line. Next door is tiny *Magnolia Bakery*, at no. 401, the pioneers of the buttercream-frosted cupcake craze that seized New York a decade ago and shows no signs of abating. The bakery's cameo on *Sex and the City* didn't hurt its popularity; some tour buses include a stop on their itineraries. All the sidestreets around here are worth exploring: Perry Street is particularly pretty, anchored by one of the area's most popular **cafés**, *Doma* (see p.199), on its east end and an excellent nouvelle-cuisine restaurant, *Perry Street* (see p.216), on its west end. There's a sprinkling of cute boutiques in between.

8 The Meatpacking District

Stretching from Eighth Avenue to the Hudson River and from West 14th Street to Gansevoort, the **Meatpacking District** is an atmospheric neighborhood of wide cobblestoned streets, with warehouses full of beef carcasses, nightclubs packed with a jet-setting crowd, and high-end boutiques selling expensive frocks – and all three are often represented on most blocks. Those odd juxtapositions are part of what gives the district its undeniable appeal, though the variety is likely to diminish in coming years. Only about thirty (down from more than a hundred) meat dealers remain, most having decamped for the Bronx, and new construction is going up at a furious pace. Most new projects, like celebrity chef Mario Batali's *Del Posto* restaurant and designer Diane von Furstenburg's flagship store, are shamelessly exclusive, but there's plenty for those of more modest means: perched on a rusty train trestle along the river, the **High Line** park (see p.79) will offer a welcome respite from the urban grit and glamour when it opens in 2008, and a couple of new venues, such as *Comix* (see p.268), for stand-up and sketch comedy, and the *Highline Ballroom* (see p.251), for indie rock, are well worth seeking out.

9

Chelsea

A large and varied district of brick townhouses, gleaming glass high-rises, "big box" stores, and warehouse galleries between 14th and 29th streets to the west of Broadway, **Chelsea** has lately come of age, with tons of new construction, the promise of more green space, and a vibrant cultural scene. But it wasn't considered an interesting or desirable neighborhood until the 1990s, with the arrival of affluent gay and artistic communities from the Village and SoHo, respectively – followed by the inevitable wave of yuppies. It continues to sport one of the most rapidly changing skylines in the city, with luxury condo buildings going up at breakneck speed, and work on the much-anticipated **High Line** park continuing along the river. In between, you'll find more than three hundred art **galleries**, a small historic district that boasts a row of beautiful nineteenth-century townhouses, and the storied *Chelsea Hotel*, in which many artists, musicians, and writers have holed up to live – or, in many cases, burn out – in New York. Chelsea's also the sight of the **Rubin Museum of Art**, featuring the art of the Himalayas, and Manhattan's largest indoor sports complex, **Chelsea Piers**.

Chelsea can be reached by taking the #F or #V to 23rd Street (at Sixth Ave); the #1 to either 18th Street or 23rd Street (both at Seventh Ave); or the #C or #E to 23rd Street (at Eighth Ave).

Fifth and Sixth avenues

Though not as trendy as SoHo or as grand as Midtown, the wedge-shaped area between Broadway and Sixth Avenue, from 14th to 23rd streets, is a great place to **shop** if you don't like crowds, with many of the bargain and mid-tier clothing chains (H&M, Esprit, J. Crew, Old Navy, Zara, and the like) opening here in recent years, and tourists fairly oblivious to the fact. The trend isn't without precedent: the area was known as "Ladies' Mile" in the late nineteenth century because of its profusion of department stores – the original Macy's opened at Sixth Avenue and 14th Street in 1858.

Seventh and Eighth avenues

Unlike Fifth and Sixth avenues, **Seventh Avenue** has a genuine neighborhood feel, with small, owner-run restaurants and stores, and a more local clientele. Still, most consider Chelsea's main drag to be **Eighth Avenue**, a broad, busy road lined with bars, restaurants, cafés, and stores – many catering to the neighborhood's large gay population.

Rubin Museum of Art

Map 6 150 W 17th St at 7th Ave. Closed Tues; $10, $7 students and seniors, free Fri 7–10pm; ☎212/620-5000, ⓦwww.rmanyc.org.
Quietly opened in 2004 in what used to be Barney's department store, the **Rubin Museum** is a large and impressive space, with six floors of art from Bhutan, Tibet, and Nepal spanning two millennia, as well as an excellent ground-floor shop and tearoom. Most of the roughly 900 works on permanent display have some connection to Hinduism or Buddhism and reflect the vitality and unique cultural heritage of the Himalayan region.

The Chelsea Hotel

Map 6, F7. 222 23rd St. ☎212/243-3700, ⓦwww.hotelchelsea.com.
Constructed in 1883 (at the time the city's tallest building), the

Chelsea Hotel occupies a rather grubby stretch of 23rd Street but has a certain down-at-the-heel Edwardian grandeur, with its weather-beaten, neon Art-Deco sign and wrought-iron balconies that line the facade. It's a popular place to stay (see p.188) but is best known for putting up (or putting up with) an impressive number of **famous artists**: Welsh poet Dylan Thomas famously collapsed from alcohol poisoning while climbing the hotel's front steps, expiring later at a local hospital; Jack Kerouac, armed with a specially adapted typewriter (and a lot of Benzedrine), typed the first draft of *On the Road* here onto a 120-foot roll of paper; William Burroughs completed *Naked Lunch* here, and Arthur C. Clarke wrote *2001: A Space Odyssey* while in residence.

In the 1960s, the *Chelsea* entered a wilder phase. Andy Warhol and his doomed protégées Edie Sedgwick and Candy Darling walled up here and made the film *Chelsea Girls.* In 1978, Sex Pistols frontman Sid Vicious stabbed his lover Nancy Spungen to death in their *Chelsea Hotel* suite. Between those events, the Chelsea served as a way station for some of the world's most influential musicians: Patti Smith, Bob Dylan, Janis Joplin, Leonard Cohen, and Nico called it home for extended periods, and Jimi Hendrix, Frank Zappa, and Pink Floyd passed through as well.

Ninth and Tenth avenues

Once considered the gritty fringe of Chelsea, **Ninth and Tenth avenues** are undergoing rapid gentrification, with a number of trendy restaurants and bars willing to put up with the roaring four-lane traffic outside in order to cater to affluent locals, gallery mavens, and the glamorous hordes headed to or from clubs in the adjoining Meatpacking District. But there are daytime attractions in the vicinity as well. Housed in the old Nabisco headquarters, where the world's first Oreo cookie was made, **Chelsea Market** (Map 6, C9) occupies the whole block between Ninth and Tenth avenues, as well as the one between 15th and 16th streets; the market is a warren of gourmet shops, cafés, and restaurants, and the Food Network also has its studios here.

Taking up the block between 20th and 21st streets is the **General Theological Seminary** (Map 6, D7), a harmonious assembly of ivy-clad Gothicisms around a lush green lawn. Though the buildings, most of which were completed in the nineteenth century, still house a working seminary, it's possible to explore the park on weekdays and Saturday lunchtimes, as long as you sign in and keep quiet (the entrance is via the modern building on Ninth Avenue). The **Chelsea Historic District**, on 20th, 21st, and 22nd streets, boasts a great variety of predominantly Italianate and Greek-Revival row houses in brick and various shades of brown stone; the oldest ones, built in 1840, stand across from the seminary at 406–418 W 20th St. At the corner of 22nd Street and Tenth Avenue, the nineteenth century meets the Art-Deco era in the *Empire Diner*, built in the 1930s and resembling an old-style railroad dining car done up with metal siding pilfered from the Chrysler Building.

The Gallery District

By far the largest of its kind in the United States, Chelsea's **gallery district** is densely concentrated in the warehouses between Tenth and Eleventh avenues, from 19th to 29th streets. And there are few things more fun for art lovers than spending an afternoon zipping up and down the blocks popping into one after another. Come on a Thursday or Friday and you'll be rewarded with at least a handful – sometimes more than a dozen – openings, usually held from 6 to 8pm and celebrated with free wine and beer. See Chapter 28, "Art galleries," for listings and information.

Chelsea Piers

Map 6, A8. ☎212/336-6666, ⓦwww.chelseapiers.com.

One of Manhattan's most ambitious waterfront projects, the massive **Chelsea Piers** sports complex was built in the

The High Line

The most eagerly anticipated public park in more than a century, the **High Line** falls squarely into a trend in cities around the world to turn obsolete structures into public space. In this case, the structure is a mile-and-a-half-long rusted train trestle along the Hudson River that used to run boxcars to (and through) Chelsea's warehouses. Abandoned in 1980, the elevated tracks soon gave rise to a mini-ecosystem of wildflowers and prairie grasses that urban explorers loved but no one else knew about. Finally in 2002, the city agreed to refurbish it for public use. The design calls for paved pedestrian-only pathways, stepped sitting areas, and a naturalistic mix of plantings: wild grasses, flowers, mosses, trees, shrubs, and even a patch of wetland. The section between Gansevoort Street in the Meatpacking District and West 20th Street in Chelsea is scheduled to open in 2008. For more information, go to Ⓦ www.thehighline.org.

mid-1990s on four neglected Hudson River piers around 23rd Street. Today, it has soccer fields, basketball courts, ice-skating rinks, a bowling alley, a golf driving range, and other facilities usually marginalized or nonexistent in places where space is at a premium. Between the complex and the West Side Highway runs the **Hudson River Greenway**, a land-scaped walkway and bike path that forms part of a 35-mile bicycle circuit of Manhattan. See Chapter 29, "Sports and outdoor activities," for more about the Piers and bicycling in New York.

10

Union Square, Gramercy Park, and the Flatiron District

Noisy, traffic-choked **14th Street** forms the northern border of the East and West villages and the southern boundary of several distinct areas. North of the thoroughfare, Broadway forms a dividing line between Chelsea to the west and Union Square, the Flatiron District, and Gramercy Park to the east. Lively **Union Square** anchors a bustling commercial district and is the site of the city's best **farmers' market**. North of Union Square, at Broadway and 23rd Street, is **Madison Square Park**. Dotted with public art and a tremendously popular burger stand, this is the hub of the **Flatiron District** – named after the iconic wedge-shaped Flatiron Building – and the gateway to the skyscrapers of Midtown. Before heading on to those jaw-droppers, like the Empire State Building (see p.85), head east toward the city's last remaining private park, **Gramercy Park**. It's off limits to the public (only nearby residents have a key for entry), but it's surrounded by stately mansions, an Ian Schrager hotel, and a number of top-tier restaurants.

The #L, #N, #Q, #R, #W, #4, #5, and #6 trains all stop at 14th Street–Union Square.

Union Square

Map 6, J9.

Once the elegant center of the city's theatrical and shopping scene, **Union Square**, where Broadway, University Place, and Park Avenue meet between 14th and 17th streets, is a welcome respite from the crazed taxi drivers and rushed pedestrians on its periphery, with winding shady paths, benches, and an array of statuary and flowers. But while it's pleasant enough to sit here for a while if you need a rest, the proliferation of chain cafés and superstores ringing the square makes it impossible to forget you are on the fringes of the most commercial part of

Union Square Greenmarket

On Mondays, Wednesdays, Fridays, and Saturdays from 8am until 6pm, the northern edge of Union Square plays host to the city's best and most popular **farmers' market**. Farmers and other food producers from upstate New York, Long Island, New Jersey, and as far as Pennsylvania Dutch Country sell fresh produce, baked goods, meats, cheeses, fish, and eggs, as well as plants and flowers, wine, honey, and yarn. Buying picnic fodder from the market to concoct a feast is one of the finest things you can do here on a spring or summer's day, and while there are far fewer stalls in winter, you can still find someone selling hot apple cider and doughnuts. For more information on this and other farmers' markets around the city – there are more than forty – visit ⓦwww.cenyc.org.

New York. On the park's southern end there invariably will be an array of street performers, artists, skateboarders, and activists making a ruckus; sitting on the steps and watching the scene is great free entertainment on a sunny day.

Irving Place and around

Just one block east of Union Square, the six graceful blocks of **Irving Place** lead north toward elegant Gramercy Park. The street is named for *The Legend of Sleepy Hollow* author Washington Irving, who lived for a short time here at no. 56. The street has numerous good cafés, bars, and restaurants, as well as one of the city's most popular rock clubs: the newly renamed *Fillmore New York at Irving Plaza* (see p.251). Before reaching the park, turn west down 20th Street, where, at no. 28, you will find **Theodore Roosevelt's birthplace** (Map 6, I8; Tues–Sat 9am–5pm; $3; ☎212/260-1616), or at least a reconstruction of it; in 1923, the house was rebuilt as it would have been when Roosevelt was born there in 1858. The rather somber mansion contains many original furnishings, some of Teddy's hunting trophies, and a small gallery documenting the former president's life, viewable on an obligatory guided tour.

Gramercy Park

Map 6, K7.

Manhattan's clutter suddenly breaks into ordered open space at **Gramercy Park**, a former swamp that lies between 20th and 21st streets and divides Irving Place and Lexington Avenue. Gramercy is one of the city's most elegant squares, its center beautifully planted and nearly empty for much of the day; it is the city's last private park, and the only people who can gain access are those rich or fortunate enough to live around it. Famous past key-holders have included Mark Twain and Julia Roberts, never mind all those Kennedys and Roosevelts.

Have a walk around the square to get a look at the many early nineteenth-century townhouses. The private social club

The Players, at 16 Gramercy Park South, was created in 1888 when actor Edwin Booth – brother of John Wilkes Booth, Abraham Lincoln's assassin – turned his home into a gathering spot for theater types at a time when they were considered morally suspect. Some famous club members were Irving Berlin, Frank Sinatra, and Winston Churchill – women were not admitted until 1989. Next door, the **National Arts Club**, at no. 15, occupies the former home of Samuel Tilden, governor of New York from 1874 to 1876. (In 1876, Tilden ran for president and won the popular vote but lost the Electoral College to Rutherford B. Hayes.) The stunning Victorian interior, replete with stained glass and elaborate carved moldings and furnishings, can be seen only during art exhibits or at public events (☎212/475-3424, ⊛www.nationalartsclub.org).

At the northeastern corner of the square, no. 38 is the mock-Tudor building that John Steinbeck, a struggling reporter at the time, lived in from 1925 to 1926. At 52 Gramercy Park North stands the imposing 1920s bulk of the **Gramercy Park Hotel**, whose early elite residents included Humphrey Bogart, Mary McCarthy, and a very young John F. Kennedy. Once a fairly stodgy, old-fashioned affair, it was recently renovated by entrepreneur Ian Schrager and turned into a minimalist interior-design masterpiece; hotel guests also get access to Gramercy Park. Lastly, lining Gramercy Park West is a splendid row of brick **Greek-Revival townhouses** dating from the 1840s.

Madison Square and the Flatiron Building

Map 6, I7. #N, #R, or #W to 23rd Street.

Northwest of Gramercy Park, where Broadway and Fifth Avenue meet, lies **Madison Square**. Though a maelstrom of cars, cabs, buses, and traffic-dodging pedestrians is all around, the grandiose architectural quality of the surrounding buildings and the newly renovated park-space in the square's center lend it a neat seclusion that Union Square has long since lost. It also has the best park food in the city, at the ridiculously popular **Shake Shack** (see p.221), a low-slung kiosk in the southeast corner of the park that serves to-die-for burgers in addition to creamy milkshakes. According to some sports historians, baseball as we know it was invented in Madison Square in 1845, when the Knickerbocker Base Ball Club played the first game to adhere to Alexander Cartwright's rules.

The lofty, elegant **Flatiron Building**, set on a triangular plot of land on the square's southern side, is one of the city's most well known buildings. It's now hard to believe that this was the city's first true skyscraper, hung on a steel frame in 1902, its full twenty stories dwarfing all the other structures around.

On Madison Square's east side, at no. 1 Madison Ave, stands the tiered, stately **MetLife Building**, which became the city's tallest tower in 1909 and is still visible from blocks away. Just north of the MetLife Building, at no. 27, is the Corinthian-columned marble facade of the Appellate Division of the **New York State Supreme Court**, resolutely righteous with its statues of *Justice*, *Wisdom*, and *Peace*. The grand structure next to that, the **New York Life Building**, is the work of Cass Gilbert, creator of the Woolworth Building downtown (see p.44). It went up in 1928 on the site of the first and second incarnations of Madison Square Garden, heart of the former theater district; the architect Stanford White, designer of Washington Square Arch (p.70), was killed in a duel on the roof of the second one in 1906.

North of Madison Square

Lexington Avenue begins its long journey north at Gramercy Park: if you're heading uptown from here, you'll pass the lumbering **69th Regiment Armory** at 25th Street. This was the site of the celebrated Armory Show of 1913, which brought modern art to New York. It is now a venue for antiques shows and art fairs. North of the armory sprawls the bland neighborhood of Murray Hill; its main draw for the traveler is the cluster of Indian restaurants near the juncture of Lexington and 27th Street – so-called Curry Hill.

Midtown East

R olling eastward from Fifth Avenue, the opulent sight- and store-studded spine of Manhattan, from 34th Street to 57th Street, is the largely corporate and commercial area known as **Midtown East**. Here you'll find the best Art-Deco facades and exemplary Modernist skyscrapers, two of which – the **Empire State Building** and the GE Building at Rockefeller Center – let you zip up to the top for panoramic vistas of the city and beyond.

Anchored by Cornelius Vanderbilt's Beaux-Arts **Grand Central Terminal**, with its soaring turquoise ceiling studded with electric stars, Midtown East is a trove of architectural and cultural treasures. The best museum in the neighborhood is the recently expanded **Morgan Library**, a vault of priceless manuscripts and drawings. Arrayed along the East River, the rambling geometric bulk of the **United Nations Headquarters** feels like a time capsule from the 1950s, when it was built. You can tour the building for a glimpse into the creaky machinery of international diplomacy.

The Empire State Building

Map 6, H4. Daily 8am–2am; last elevator at 1.15am; $18, seniors and kids 12–17 $16, kids 6–11 $12, 5 and under free; express pass $45 (all ages; combined tickets for New York Skyride and the observatory $38, kids 12–17 $26, under-12s and seniors $24; ℡212/736-3100,

With the destruction of the World Trade Center, the **Empire State Building** is once again the city's tallest skyscraper. Occupying a whole city block between Fifth and Sixth avenues and 33rd and 34th streets, it is easily the most potent and evocative symbol of New York, and has been since its completion in 1931. The building's 103 stories and 1454 feet make it the second tallest in the US (behind Chicago's Sears Tower), but its height is deceptive, rising in stately tiers with steady panache.

Standing on Fifth Avenue below, it's easy to walk right past the building without even realizing it's there; only the crowds serve as an indicator of what looms above. The first elevators up whisk you to the 80th floor in under one minute, and then a second set of (rather old and rickety) elevators takes you to the **observation deck** on the 86th floor, summit of the building before the radio and TV mast was added. The views from the outside walkways here are as stunning as you'd expect; on a clear day you can see as far as Connecticut. If you're feeling brave – and can stand the wait for the tight squeeze into the single elevator – you can go up to the building's last reachable zenith, a small cylinder at the foot of the TV mast that was added as part of a harebrained scheme to erect a mooring post for airships. Skip the eight-minute simulated flight New York Skyride (daily 10am–10pm; $27.50, under-12s $19.50, seniors and kids 12–17 $18.50; ☏212/299-4922 or 1-888/SKY-RIDE, ⓦwww.skyride.com), which purports to soar above skyscrapers and among other New York landmarks but will leave the weak-hearted merely dizzy and the strong-willed wondering why they wasted their cash.

It's important to allow at least two hours for visiting the building, as lines can be very long, especially on clear days. Everyone has to queue for the security checkpoint first of all; the second line (for tickets) can be avoided by buying tickets in advance at the website listed above (the $2- to $3-per-ticket surcharge is worth it). The third and fourth lines – one for elevators to the 80th floor, and the other, much longer one for one of the two elevators to the 86th-floor observation deck – are avoidable only for those holding pricey express passes, which put you to the front of all lines. The best times to

Skyscrapers

⑪

Manhattan is one of the best places in the world to view **skyscrapers**, its puckered, almost medieval skyline of towers the city's most familiar and striking image. In fact, there are only two main clusters of skyscrapers, but they set the tone for the city: the Financial District, where the combination of narrow streets and tall buildings forms slender, lightless canyons; and Midtown Manhattan, where the big skyscrapers, flanking the wide, central avenues from the 30s to the 50s, have long competed for height and prestige.

New York's first skyscraper was Madison Square's 1902 **Flatiron Building**, an iconic 22-story wedge made possible by iron-frame construction, a concept then in its infancy. In 1913, the sixty-story **Woolworth Building** on lower Broadway, across from City Hall, gave New York the world's tallest building for seventeen years. In the 1930s, the city produced such Art-Deco landmarks as the **Chrysler Building** and the **Empire State Building**.

Styles have changed over the years, perhaps most influenced by the stringency of the city's zoning laws. The first skyscrapers were sheer vertical monsters that maximized floor space with no regard to how this affected neighboring buildings. But in the early twentieth century, city authorities limited how high a building could extend up before tapering in a series of ever-smaller steps, or setbacks, allowing light to filter down to neighboring buildings and the street. Later developers – such as those who built the **World Trade Center** – were allowed to return to the vertical mold in exchange for creating public parks or indoor plazas, or simply buying "air rights" from surrounding buildings. But for many the golden age remains the time when gentle setbacks – most elegantly seen in the Empire State Building – reigned; you'll see their ziggurat-like profiles all over the city.

visit are very early in the morning and in the mid-afternoon, while sunset and late-night trips tend to be the most crowded, though the relatively new extended hours mean that after-midnight visits can be quite tranquil.

The Morgan Library

Map 6, J3. 29 E 36th St, at Madison Ave. Tues–Thurs 10.30am–5pm, Fri 10.30am–9pm, Sat 10am–6pm & Sun 11am–6pm; $12 (free Fri 7–9pm); ☎212/685-0008, ⓦwww.themorgan.org. #6 to 33rd Street.

One of the city's finest small museums, the **Morgan Library** inhabits a somewhat jumbled new space on Madison Avenue between 35th and 36th streets. Commissioned to expand the facilities, the architect Renzo Piano recently linked the library's three original structures – an 1850s brownstone, the 1906 library built by the esteemed McKim, Mead and White firm, and a 1928 annex – with a vast glass-and-steel atrium that looks like many you've seen in lesser museums (and office buildings), detracting from the historic feel of the structures it sought to preserve.

That said, the new design – unveiled in 2006 – does allow you to see a bit more of the Morgan's 10,000-piece collection of one-of-a-kind and rare manuscripts, illuminated books, drawings, and ancient seals, as well as the lavish interior of the library and study belonging to its namesake and benefactor, legendary financier Pierpont Morgan (1837–1913). Almost all of the exhibits change frequently, so it's impossible to know exactly what you're going to see; likely items include a Gutenberg Bible (the museum owns three out of eleven surviving originals); drawings by Rembrandt, Leonardo, Degas, and Dürer; original scores by Mahler, Beethoven, Schubert, and Gilbert and Sullivan; and handwritten literary manuscripts by Dickens, Twain, Austen, and Thoreau.

The New York Public Library

Map 6, H1. Fifth Ave between 40th and 42nd sts. Tues & Wed 11am–7.30pm, Thurs–Sat 10am–6pm; ☎212/930-0830, ⓦwww.nypl.org. #B, #D, #F, or #V to 42nd Street/Bryant Park or #7 to Fifth Avenue.

Two majestic, marble lion statues guard the entrance to the **New York Public Library**, a Neoclassical behemoth designed by the famed architects Carrère and Hastings, and finished in 1911. It contains 88 miles of books, stored on eight levels of (closed) stacks – a collection that makes this the largest research library with a circulation system in the world. It's worth stepping inside for two reasons: to see the museum-quality literary and historical exhibitions in **Gottesman Hall**, just inside the main entrance, and to glimpse the magnificent **Rose Reading Room**. Nearly two blocks long, the reading room is arguably the most enchanted public space in the city, with intricate woodwork, soaring 51-foot coffered ceilings, and hundreds of amazingly quiet library patrons seated at communal oak tables studded with brass lamps. Free one-hour tours of the building are available Tuesday to Saturday at 11am & 2pm.

Rockefeller Center

Map 7, H8. #B, #D, #F, or #V to 47th–50th streets/Rockefeller Center.
Filling the whole block west of Fifth Avenue between 49th and 51st streets, **Rockefeller Center** was built between 1932 and 1940 by John D. Rockefeller, son of the oil magnate. It's one of the finest pieces of urban planning anywhere – office space with cafés, a concert hall, television studios, shops, underground concourses, public art, and gardens work together with a rare intelligence and grace.

You're lured into the center from Fifth Avenue down the gentle slope of the Channel Gardens to the **GE Building** at 30 Rockefeller Plaza. Rising 850 feet, this monumental Art-Deco structure is softened by symmetrical setbacks. Inside the building's lobby are José Maria Sert's murals, *American Progress and Time*, which, while faded, are eagerly in tune with the 1930s Deco ambiance; you can pick up a Rockefeller Center **visitor's guide** and a walking-tour map at the lobby's front desk. Also in this building is **Top of the Rock**, a seventieth-floor **observation deck** reopened in 2005 after being

NBC Studios

Among the many office ensembles in the GE Building is **NBC Studios**, home of the network's long-established late-night comedy show *Saturday Night Live* (which simply refuses to die), among other programs. Get a backstage look on the hour-long **NBC Experience Tour** (every 15min Mon–Wed 8.30am–5.30pm, Thurs 8.30am–6pm, Fri & Sat 8.30am–6.30pm, and Sun 9.30am–4.30pm; $18.50, seniors and children $15.50, under-6s not allowed on tour; ☎212/664-7174; ⊛www.nbcstudiotour.com), which drops in on the various studios (provided they are not in use) that serve as home for shows such as *SNL*, *Late Night with Conan O'Brien*, the *Today Show*, and *NBC Nightly News*. Tours leave from the NBC Experience Store on 49th Street between Fifth and Sixth avenues; reservations are recommended (☎212/664-3056).

For a free, early-morning TV thrill, you can gawk at NBC's *Today Show*, which broadcasts live from 7am to 10am weekday mornings from glass-enclosed studios on the southwest corner of 49th Street and Rockefeller Plaza. Occasionally the cameras will pan over the crowd, prompting a general frenzy of hometown shout-outs.

shuttered for nearly twenty years. Still squeaky-clean from the renovation, it doesn't have the timeworn appeal of the Empire State Building, but the views are phenomenal and time-stamped tickets mean you don't have to wait all day for your turn on the elevator (entrance on 50th St between Fifth and Sixth; daily 8am–midnight; $17.50; ☎212/698-2000, ⊛www.topoftherocknyc.com).

At the foot of the GE Building, the **Lower Plaza** is linked visually to the downward flow of the building by Paul Manship's sparkling *Prometheus* sculpture. In winter, the plaza becomes an **ice rink**, giving skaters a chance to show off their skills to passing shoppers; in summer, it's covered with the umbrella tables of two concourse-level **restaurants**.

St Patrick's Cathedral

Map 7, H7. Fifth Ave, between 50th and 51st sts. #E or #V to 5th
Avenue/53rd Street.

Bone-white **St Patrick's Cathedral** sits among the glitz of
Fifth Avenue like a misplaced bit of moral imperative, and
seems the result of a painstaking academic tour of the Gothic
cathedrals of Europe. In the peaceful **Lady Chapel** at the back
of the cathedral, however, the graceful, simple altar captures
the spirituality that its big sister arguably lacks. Nevertheless, St Patrick's is an essential part of the midtown landscape,
and perhaps the most important Catholic church in America,
serving as a premier religious contact-point for generations
of Irish, Italian, and other Catholic immigrants. The Gothic
details are impressive and the cathedral is certainly striking
– made all the more so by the sunglass-black **Olympic Tower**
behind, which serves as a dramatically neutral backdrop to this
work of art. Across Fifth Avenue stands Rockefeller Center's
largest public artwork: the two-ton, well-muscled bronze
Atlas, made in 1937. Immediately south of the cathedral is
Saks Fifth Avenue, one of the last of New York's premier
department stores.

North on Fifth Avenue toward Central Park

Cartier (no. 653), **Gucci** (no. 685), and **Harry Winston** (no.
718) are among many gilt-edged storefronts that will jump out
at you along Fifth Avenue between 53th and 59th streets. If
you're keen to do more than merely window-shop, **Tiffany
and Company**, at no. 727, is worth a look; its soothing green
marble and weathered wood interior was best described by
Truman Capote's fictional Holly Golightly: "It calms me down
right away. . . nothing very bad could happen to you there."

Topping all this off is **F.A.O. Schwarz**, a block north at
no. 767, a colossal emporium of children's toys. Fight the kids

57th Street gallery district

Though hardly a secret to art lovers, the sixty-odd **galleries** on 57th Street around Fifth Avenue are virtually unknown to most tourists, mainly because they're tucked above luxury shops, with little or nothing to announce them to passers-by. Some galleries put on full-scale, museum-quality exhibitions, as in PaceWildenstein's recent show, "Picasso, Braque, and Early Film in Cubism"; others represent big names in contemporary art. Best of all, the galleries are often empty, and there's never an admission charge. See p.288 for listings.

off and there's some great stuff to play with: life-sized stuffed animals, a motion simulator, video games, Lego creations, and the piano featured in the Tom Hanks movie *Big* – which can be yours for a mere $250,000. Across 58th Street, Fifth Avenue broadens into **Grand Army Plaza** and the southeast fringes of Central Park. Looming impressively on the plaza is, aptly enough, the copper-edged *Plaza Hotel* (Map 7, H6). Recognizable from its many film appearances and the *Eloise* children's book series, it recently underwent a two and a half year renovation, reopening in October 2007 with half its rooms serving as pieds-à-terre for the fabulously wealthy.

Madison Avenue

Madison Avenue runs parallel to Fifth one block to the east, offering some of its sweep but less excitement. The thoroughfare is a little removed from its 1960s and 1970s prime, when it was internationally recognized as the advertising industry's epicenter. A few good stores – notably those specializing in men's haberdashery, shoes, and cigars – can still be found between 42nd and 57th streets, while Madison's most interesting buildings come in a four-block strip above 53rd Street.

The **Sony Building** (Map 7, H6), between 55th and 56th streets, followed the postmodern theory of eclectic borrowing from historical styles: the work of Philip Johnson, it's a modernist skyscraper sandwiched between a Chippendale top and a Renaissance base. The **IBM Building**, next door at no. 590, has a far more inviting plaza, the calm glass-enclosed atrium and tropical foliage making for a far less ponderous experience; the small **Dahesh Museum** (☎212/759-0606, ⓦwww.dahesh-museum.org), featuring academic art from the nineteenth and twentieth centuries, sits in the building's basement. Across 57th Street, the black-and-white Art-Deco **Fuller Building** is worth a look, then head east along 57th Street to find the swish, 52-story **Four Seasons Hotel**, designed by I.M. Pei. Its foyer and lobby are ostentatious in sweeping marble, and the Bloody Mary was allegedly invented in its bar.

Park Avenue

In 1929 Collinson Owen described **Park Avenue** as being "Where wealth is so swollen that it almost bursts," and things aren't much different today: north of Grand Central, corporate headquarters jostle for prominence across a thickly planted median strip in a triumphal procession to capitalism. Whatever your feelings, Park Avenue is one of the city's most awesome sights. If you look down it from anywhere north of 42nd Street, your eyes will lift to the high altar of the New York Central Building (now the **Helmsley Building**; Map 7, I8), a delicate, energetic construction with an excessive Rococo lobby.

No matter where you placed the solid **Waldorf-Astoria Hotel** (between 49th and 50th streets; Map 7, I8), a resplendent statement of Art-Deco elegance, it would hold its own. Duck inside to stroll through the sweeping marble and hushed plushness. Crouching across the street, **St Bartholomew's Church** is a low-slung Byzantine hybrid that adds immeasurably to the street scene, giving the lumbering skyscrapers a much-needed sense of scale; the church's patio café is the most pleasant place in the area for an alfresco lunch or drink.

Just a bit further north are two of the city's most famous skyscrapers. Designed by Mies van der Rohe (with the ubiquitous Philip Johnson), the **Seagram Building** (Map 7, 17), finished in 1958, was the seminal curtain-wall skyscraper and the supreme example of modernist reason, deceptively simple and cleverly detailed. Its large **plaza**, designed to set the building apart from its neighbors, was such a success as a public space that the city revised its zoning laws to encourage other high-rise builders to supply them. The plaza is now punctuated by Alexander Calder's stabile *Ordinary*, from 1969, while the building's chichi *Four Seasons* restaurant (see p.223) is home to the power lunch.

On the next block, between 53rd and 54th streets, stands **Lever House** (Map 7, I7), the building that set the modernist ball rolling on Park Avenue in 1952, its two right-angled slabs of green glass a radical departure from the staid masonry of the time. Damien Hirst's three-story-tall bronze *Virgin Mother* – pregnant, naked, and stripped of half her skin – livens up the courtyard.

Grand Central Terminal

Map 6, J1. Park Ave and E 42nd. ⓦwww.grandcentralterminal.com. #4, #5, #6, #7, or #S to Grand Central/42nd Street.

A masterful piece of urban architecture, the 1913 **Grand Central Terminal** represents a time when stations were humbling preludes to great cities. Though it now serves a relatively small number of rail travelers – around 150,000 a day – it still thrums with activity, thanks mainly to its position atop a big subway hub in the heart of Midtown, but also because of its popular **shops and restaurants** (see p.202). The most spectacular aspect of the building is its size: the **main concourse** is one of the world's finest and most imposing open spaces, 470 feet long and 150 feet high, the barrel-vaulted ceiling speckled like a Baroque church with a painted astronomical representation of the winter night sky. The Municipal Arts Society sponsors a **free tour** of Grand Central every Wednesday at 12.30pm;

meet at the central information booth on the main concourse. For a self-guided tour, pick up a brochure at the "I Love New York" information window.

The Chrysler Building

Map 6, K1. #4, #5, #6, #7, or #S to Grand Central/42nd Street.

The **Chrysler Building**, just east of Grand Central, on the block between Lexington and Third avenues and 42nd and 43rd streets, was for a fleeting moment the world's tallest building: completed in 1930, it was surpassed by the Empire State Building in 1931. Its car-motif friezes, a spire resembling a car radiator grill, and hood-ornament gargoyles jutting from the setbacks all recall the golden age of motoring. Originally a car showroom, the lobby (Mon–Fri 8am–6pm) has opulently inlaid elevators, walls covered in African marble, and on the ceiling a realistic, if rather faded, mural showing airplanes, machines, and the brawny builders who worked on the tower (which unfortunately is not open to the public).

East of the Chrysler Building

If you're headed east to the United Nations complex (see p.96) on foot, there are some interesting buildings to take in along the way. Across the street from the Chrysler Building, the stainless-steel facade of the weighty **Mobil Building** is deliberately folded in such a manner that it is cleaned automatically by the wind. One block east is the somber yet elegant former **Daily News Building**, whose stone facade fronts a surprising Art-Deco interior. The most impressive remnant of the original 1923 decor is a large globe encased in a lighted circular frame (with updated geography), made famous by the film *Superman*, in which the Daily News Building housed the fictitious *Daily Planet*.

At the east end of 42nd Street, steps lead up to the residential enclave of **Tudor City**, which feels a world apart from the rest of Midtown. Built around 1925 specifically with the middle

-class in mind, these twelve brick buildings with their leaded glass windows and mock coats of arms contain three thousand apartments overlooking a leafy central courtyard.

The United Nations

Map 7, L9. First Ave, at E 46th. One-hour tours leave every 30min from General Assembly Lobby, Mon–Fri 9.30am–4.45pm, weekends & holidays 10am–4.30pm, closed weekends Jan & Feb; $13, $9 seniors, $8.50 students; ☏212/963-8687, Ⓦwww.un.org. #4, #5, #6, #7, or #S to Grand Central Terminal.

Some see the **United Nations** complex as one of the major sights of New York; others, usually those who've been there, are not so complimentary. The complex, designed by ten architects from ten countries, consists of three main buildings: the thin, glass-curtained slab of the Secretariat Building (1950), the sweeping curve of the General Assembly Building (1952), and the low-rise Conference Wing (also 1952).

Yet, whatever the symbolism of the UN, there can be few buildings that are quite so dull to walk around in. Guided tours, which emphasize that the organization's main purpose is to promote dialogue and awareness rather than enforce policies, take in the main conference chambers of the UN and its constituent parts, the foremost of which is the General Assembly Chamber itself. If you're not keen on touring but still want a peek, you can explore the General Assembly Building's vast lobby. Scarcely changed since the 1950s, it has a massive stained-glass window by Marc Chagall as well as temporary art exhibits and some mid-twentieth-century bric-a-brac.

Around the United Nations

Just north of the UN complex, **Dag Hammarskjöld Plaza** fills most of 47th Street between First and Second avenues with benches, fountains, and a small woodland area named after Katharine Hepburn, a longtime resident of the neighborhood. The **Japan Society** (333 E 47th St ☏212/752-3015,

Roosevelt Island Tram

There's nothing much to see on residential **Roosevelt Island** – aside from the eerie ruins of an old smallpox hospital and its colony of feral cats – but a ride there and back on the aerial **tramway** that's featured in Sam Raimi's *Spider-Man* (2002) is an entertaining way to spend a half-hour, taking in great city views. The Swiss-made cable cars ($2 each way or free with unlimited-ride Metrocard) leave every fifteen minutes from the station at 59th Street and 2nd Avenue, arch up over the East River alongside the Queensboro Bridge, and drop down onto the island. The return trip happens a few minutes later.

Wwww.japansociety.org) has its headquarters in a black, low-rise building facing the north side of the plaza; behind the severe facade lies a tranquil bamboo garden and, often, some first-rate art exhibits. Next door, the 72-story bronze-glass **Trump World Tower** is home to exorbitant condominiums owned by the likes of Bill Gates and Yankees shortstop Derek Jeter. The *World Bar* on the ground floor is a glitzy place for a drink.

Beekman Place, from 49th to 51st streets between First Avenue and the East River, is a beguiling enclave of garbled styles. Similar, though not quite as intimate, is **Sutton Place**, a long stretch running from 53rd to 59th between First and the river. Originally built for the lordly Morgans and Vanderbilts in 1875, Sutton increases in elegance as you move north and, for today's crème de la crème, **Riverview Terrace** (Map 7, L5) is a private enclave of five brownstones.

Museum of Modern Art

New York City's **Museum of Modern Art** – MoMA to its friends – reopened in November 2004, just in time for its 75th anniversary, after a massive renovation that took more than two years. The overhaul was clearly necessary: it has doubled the gallery space available, and Yoshio Taniguchi's design has created new and vibrant public spaces while expanding the galleries into larger, more accessible venues for the museum's extraordinary collection. The building is complex and clever, easy to navigate but constantly and deliberately giving glimpses of other levels – down into the sculpture garden, into the lobby and the second-floor landing where Monet's large *Waterlilies* study is displayed.

Yet, those familiar with the museum may wonder what has really changed: it is still divided broadly into the same categories, and the principal exhibits – in the core Painting and Sculpture galleries at least – are displayed in much the same chronological order as before, albeit with some thematic detours. What is different is the museum's ability to display its peripheral material – its drawings, photography, and more – to show more art from the present day, and to mount temporary exhibitions without cutting into the permanent space.

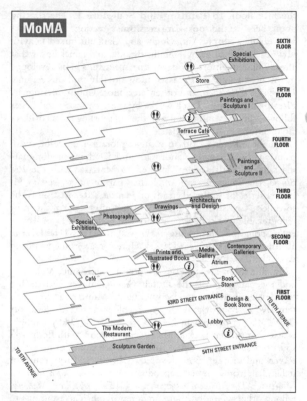

Painting and Sculpture 1

The Painting and Sculpture galleries are the heart of MoMA, and, if these are your priority, you should head straight for the fifth floor, to **Painting and Sculpture 1**. The starting point here is the **post-Impressionist** section, with works by Cézanne, Seurat, Van Gogh, and Gauguin mixed in with vivid early paintings by Derain, Braque, and James Ensor that already hint at a more Modernist perspective. This is developed in the next room by **Picasso**, most notably with his seminal *Demoiselles d'Avignon*, and other later, more Cubist offerings by Picasso and Braque. Later works by these two men and Léger follow, while beyond you'll find the big swirling colors of Boccioni and the Italian Futurists.

Straight on takes you into an exploration of color, with paintings by Chagall, Kandinsky, and Kirchner predominating, and an entire room devoted to **Matisse**, with the *Red Studio*, the *Piano Lesson*, and other paintings, as well as his lumpy series of sculpted heads of *Jeanette*. After Matisse is the so-called "Crossroads" gallery, which houses some of the most recognizable works of the modern age – Picasso's *Three Women at the Spring* and *Three Musicians* as well as Léger's *Three Women*, all painted the same year (1921). Here too are some haunting works by de Chirico.

Off this room are galleries devoted to Duchamp, Malevich, and the paintings of the Dutch *De Stijl* movement, tracing the development of its leading light, **Mondrian**, from his tentative early work to the pure color abstract of *Broadway Boogie Woogie*, painted in New York in 1943. Oddly enough, Matisse's muscular back studies occupy a room with Bonnard's soft domestic scenes, while further on are paintings by Diego Rivera and another room devoted to the **Surrealists** – much of it familiar from popular reproductions: Miró's *Dutch Interiors*, Magritte's *The Menaced Assassin*, and Dalí's *Persistence of Memory*, among others. Finally, there are a few **American** paintings to round things off: Wyeth's *Christina's World*, a couple of typically atmospheric Hoppers, and one of Charles Scheeler's American industrial landscapes.

Map 7, G7. 11 W 53rd St, between 5th and 6th. Wed–Mon 10.30am–5.30pm, Fri open until 8pm, closed Tues, Thanksgiving Day & Christmas Day; $20, seniors $16, students $12, free Fri 4–8pm; tickets can be booked in advance through Ticketmaster on ☏212/220-0505 or ⓦwww.ticketweb.com; general info ☏212/708-9400, ⓦwww.moma.org. #E or #V to Fifth Avenue/53rd Street.

If you need to take a break while touring MoMA, the second-floor *Café 2* serves very good, slickly presented Italian food. There's also a more formal option, *Terrace 5*, on the fifth floor, with nice views over the sculpture garden. The very swanky full-service restaurant *The Modern* runs along the edge of the garden on the first floor. If you don't have (or want) a reservation at *The Modern*, you can still taste the cuisine and have a drink at the adjoining lounge, the *Bar Room*, which makes up for its lack of a view with its cool, airport-lounge decor and impeccable service.

Painting and Sculpture 2

Painting and Sculpture 2, the next floor down, displays work from the 1940s to the 1960s and has a more American feel, starting with works by Pollock, Rothko, and De Kooning. Further on, Dubuffet's challenging paintings sit with Giacometti's sticklike figures and paintings by Bacon (*Study of a Baboon*) and Picasso (*The Charnel Room*), the latter inspired by the horrors of World War II. Beyond here, the Abstract Expressionists hold sway, with vast canvases by Barnett Newman, Rothko, and Pollock – all at the height of their powers in the 1950s, when these paintings were done. Later rooms contain lots of work familiar from the modern canon: Jasper Johns' iconic *Flag*, Robert Rauschenberg's mixed-media paintings, Warhol's soup cans and Marilyn Monroes, Lichtenstein's postmodern cartoons, and Oldenburg's soft sculptures.

Photography, and Architecture and Design

The other parts of the museum are just as impressive as the Painting and Sculpture galleries and shouldn't be missed if you have the time. On the third floor, the **Photography** galleries are also chronological in their layout, and begin with a European slant – photos of Paris by Atget, Brassaï, and Cartier-Bresson – before moving on to Robert Frank's and Robert Capa's stunning pictures of the USA from the 1940s and 50s, their realism mirrored by the hypernaturalism of the later, more contemporary, works in the collection.

Architecture and Design, on the same floor, shows classic designs of the last century: examples of modern buildings and town planning by key innovators like Frank Lloyd Wright; interior design with chairs by Rietveld, Arne Jacobsen, Charles Rennie Mackintosh; and lots of glass and ceramics. There is also a series of neat large-scale objects like a 1946 Ferrari, a British motorcycle, and signage from the New York subway.

Drawing, Contemporary Art, and film

The **Drawing** galleries, also on the third floor, show works on paper by a glittering array of twentieth-century artists – Lucien Freud, Jackson Pollock, Robert Rauschenberg, and his old roommate Willem De Kooning, along with studies by Warhol, Jasper Johns, and Lichtenstein. Finally, the second-floor galleries give MoMA the chance to show its **Contemporary Art** in all media, and basically consist of works from the 1970s onwards, including pieces by Bruce Nauman, Jeff Koons, and other heavyweights. MoMA hosts regular screenings of mainly art-house and foreign-language **films** every evening during the week, and afternoons and evenings on the weekends. Check the website for details; this can be a good opportunity to view some rarely screened gems.

Midtown West

M uch of the midtown Manhattan district that runs between West 30th and 59th streets to the west of Sixth Avenue is an enthralling, noisy, hurly-burly of garish attractions meant to entertain tourists staying in the area's dense concentration of hotels. The southern reaches of **Midtown West** encompass the bustling, business-minded **Garment District** – an area of several blocks filled with fabric store after fabric store, many of them wholesale but others open to the public – whose main attractions are Madison Square Garden and Macy's department store. The real heart of the district, though, is **Times Square**, an exploded version of the east side's more tight-lipped monuments to capitalism. It's at this nexus, where jostling crowds and flashing signs (some many stories high) make for an exhilarating assault on the senses, that New York City reaches its commercial zenith. Just north of the once "naughty, bawdy 42nd Street," the **Theater District** offers the most impressive concentration of live theater in the world.

Head west from Times Square, past Eighth Avenue, and you'll be in **Hell's Kitchen** (or "Clinton," as real-estate folks would like you to call it – though no one does). Formerly one of the most violent parts of town – *West Side Story* was set here – it's now a rapidly gentrifying neighborhood, where shiny open-air eateries far outnumber peep-show pavilions. There aren't many tourist attractions per se in this direction, but Ninth Avenue has many of the best restaurants in the area. If you head all the way over to the Hudson River, you'll come upon the **massive Intrepid Sea-Air-Space Museum**, based in a retired aircraft carrier, as well as the docks for the Circle Line boat tours (see p.22).

Times Square can be reached by taking the #N, #Q, #R, #S, #W, #1, #2, #3, or 7 to Times Square/42nd Street. The Garment District can be reached by taking the #A, #C, #E, #1, #2, or #3 to 34th Street/Penn Station or by taking the #B, #D, #F, #N, #Q, #R, #V, or #W to 34th Street/Herald Square.

The Garment District

Map 6, E4.

Wedged between Chelsea and Times Square, the **Garment District** is a dank, predominantly commercial area whose biggest tourist attraction is the **Pennsylvania Station** and **Madison Square Garden** complex, a combined box-and-drum structure that swallows up millions of commuters into its train-station belly while housing professional sports teams like the Knicks and the Rangers (for ticket info, see p.295), and hosting numerous concerts. There's nothing memorable about the railway station; it has incurred a tremendous amount of resentment because the original Penn Station, demolished in 1963 to make way for it, is now hailed as a lost masterpiece, one that brought an air of dignity to the neighborhood. As 1960s architectural historian Vincent Scully lamented following the passing of the original, "through it one entered the city like a god… one now scuttles in like a rat."

The same architects who built the original Penn Station also designed the **General Post Office** across the street from Madison Square Garden, at 421 Eighth Ave. It's similarly monumental, with a vast Corinthian colonnade and majestic interior spaces that everyone agrees would be put to much better use as a stunning new train station, but the project has been mired in ongoing financial and bureaucratic problems. A new funding plan was announced in March 2007, but it remains to be seen whether the 2010 opening date will be met.

Greeley and Herald squares

One block east of Penn Station, Sixth Avenue collides with Broadway at seedy **Greeley Square**. Perhaps Horace Greeley, founder of the *Tribune* newspaper, deserves better than this triangle. Known for his rallying call to the youth of the nineteenth century to explore the continent ("Go West, young man!"), he also supported the rights of women and trade unions, denounced slavery and capital punishment, and commissioned a weekly column from Karl Marx. His paper no longer exists and the square named after him is one of those bits of Manhattan that looks ready to disintegrate at any moment, despite recent attempts to spruce it up.

Herald Square, two blocks north at the intersection of 34th Street, Broadway, and Sixth Avenue, is perhaps best recognized as the one George M. Cohan asked to be remembered to in his 1904 hit song. The triangular park is a far more pleasant place than it used to be, though it's still a very congested area and the main attraction remains that temple of commercialism, **Macy's** (Map 6, G3), the world's largest department store (see Chapter 27, "Shopping," for more).

Times Square and around

Times Square, tourist destination *ne plus ultra* for many visitors to New York, occupies the streets between 42nd and 47th, where Seventh Avenue and Broadway collide. This is the center of the Theater District, where the pulsating neon suggests a heart for the city itself. Historically a melting pot of debauchery, depravity, and fun, the area used to be quite edgy, a place where out-of-towners supplied easy pickings for petty criminals, drug dealers, and prostitutes. Now, however, almost all of the peep shows and sex shops have been driven out, making Times Square a largely sanitized, family-friendly universe of consumption. This isn't to say that the area is without charm, though; if you've never seen Times Square, plan to visit at night, when the place hums with an excited electricity fueled in large part by tourists oohing and aahing over the bright advertisements they've seen so often on TV and a beguiling array of street characters.

At the square's southernmost edge, the 25-story **Times Tower** was originally the headquarters of the *New York Times*, the city's (and the country's) most respected newspaper. It's here that the alcohol-fueled masses gather for New Year's Eve, to witness the giant sparkling ball drop from the top of the tower.

Dotted around Times Square are most of New York's great **theaters**, such as the majestic 1927 clock-and-globe-topped Paramount Building at 1501 Broadway, between 43rd and 44th streets; it now serves as office space. The New Amsterdam and the New Victory, both on 42nd Street between Seventh and Eighth avenues, have been refurbished to their original splendor, one of the truly welcome results of the massive changes here. The Lyceum, at 149 W 45th St, has its original facade, while the Shubert Theater, which hosted *A Chorus Line* during its twenty-odd-year run, occupies its own small space at 225 W 44th St. At 432 W 44th St is the Actors' Studio, where Lee Strasberg, America's leading proponent of Stanislavski's method-acting technique, taught his students. Among the oldest theaters is the Belasco, on 111 W 44th St, between Sixth and Seventh avenues, which was also the first of Broadway's theaters to incorporate machinery into its stagings.

Tickets for shows at these and other venues can be purchased at the nifty **TKTS booth** located in Duffy Square, at the northernmost island of Times Square. The booth, which sells half-price, same-day tickets for many (though never the newest or most popular) Broadway shows, is always mobbed, though the line moves more quickly than you might think; there's a less-crowded outpost at South Street Seaport (see p.41). The square itself offers an excellent panoramic view of the lights, megahotels, theme stores, and theme restaurants metastasizing daily. Above the square, a lifelike statue of Broadway's doyen George M. Cohan looks on.

Hell's Kitchen

To the west of Times Square lies **Hell's Kitchen**, an area centered on (and really only worth visiting for) the engaging slash of restaurants, bars, and ethnic delis of **Ninth Avenue** and around; for snacking, eating, and drinking reviews in this neighborhood, see pp.202, 224 & 243, respectively. Extending down to the Garment District and up to the mid-50s, this was once one of New York's most lurid neighborhoods, made up of soap and glue factories, slaughterhouses, and the like. Gangs roamed the streets, and though their rule ended in 1910 after a major police counteroffensive, the area remained somewhat dangerous until the mid-1990s, when musicians, Broadway types, and young professionals began moving in.

The tree-lined block of 46th Street between Eighth and Ninth avenues is known as **Restaurant Row**; it's a popular, pleasant, though slightly faded strip of restaurants whose main specialty is getting diners fed and into their theater seats before curtain. A couple of fun-loving piano bars along the strip offer post-theater entertainment, courtesy of waiters and other Broadway-musical hopefuls. The pastoral (or at least less-frenetic) feel only increases on many of the sidestreets between Ninth and Tenth avenues.

Intrepid Sea-Air-Space Museum

Map 7, A8. ☎212/245-0072, ⓦwww.intrepidmuseum.org.

Continue west down 46th Street until you hit the Hudson River at Pier 86 and you'll spot the grey hulk of the USS *Intrepid*, which houses the **Intrepid Sea-Air-Space Museum**. This old aircraft carrier has a long and distinguished history, including hauling capsules out of the ocean following *Mercury* and *Gemini* space missions. It holds an array of modern and vintage air and sea craft including the A-12 *Blackbird*, the world's fastest spy plane, and the USS *Growler*, a guided-missile submarine. At the time of writing the museum is closed while the ship undergoes refurbishment and restoration in a dry dock on Staten Island, but it's set to return and reopen in fall 2008.

North to Central Park

North of Times Square, the **West 50s** between Sixth and Eighth avenues are also emphatically tourist territory. Edged by Central Park to the north and the Theater District to the south, and with Fifth Avenue and Rockefeller Center in easy striking distance, the area has been invaded by overpriced restaurants and cheapo souvenir stores.

A few sights are worth searching out, however. The **Equitable Center** (Map 7, F7), at 757 Seventh Ave, is dapper if not a little self-important, with Roy Lichtenstein's 68-foot *Mural with Blue Brushstroke* poking you in the eye as you enter. Covered with triangular panes of glass, the **Hearst Tower**, 300 W 57th St at Eighth Ave, was designed by Britain's Lord Norman Foster and debuted in October 2006 as New York's greenest office building.

The **Ed Sullivan Theater**, on the other hand, is more famous for what's gone on inside rather than for any particular architectural merit. This 1920s theater, at 1697 Broadway, at West 53rd St, currently serves as the studio for *The Late Show with David Letterman*, and was the site of the Beatles' first television performance in America.

Carnegie Hall

Map 7, F6. 154 W 57th St, at 7th. Tours mid-Sept to June Mon–Fri 11.30am, 2pm & 3pm, Sat 11.30am & 12.30pm, Sun 12.30pm; $9, $6 students & seniors, $3 under-12s; ☎212/903-9765, ⓦwww.carnegiehall.org. #N, #Q, #R, #W to 57th Street/Seventh Ave.

Stately **Carnegie Hall** is one of the world's greatest concert venues, and its superb acoustics ensure full houses most of the year. Tchaikovsky conducted the program on opening night and Mahler, Rachmaninov, Toscanini, Frank Sinatra, and Judy Garland have played here. If you can't attend a performance, try to catch one of the engaging one-hour tours.

Sixth Avenue and around

Sixth Avenue, running along the east side of Times Square, is officially named **Avenue of the Americas**, but no New Yorker calls it that. In its day, the Sixth Avenue elevated train, or "El," marked the border between respectability to the east and shadier areas to the west, and in a way it's still a dividing line separating the glamorous strips of Fifth, Madison, and Park avenues from the brasher western districts. Its broad sidewalks and relative lack of crowds make it a good place to stroll if you're not in the mood to shop. On the west side of the avenue between 47th and 51st streets, across from Rockefeller Center (see p.89), stands a row of impressive skyscrapers: the **Time & Life Building** at 50th Street went up first (in 1959), followed by the three near-identical blocks south of it. Further up Sixth, in the AXA Financial Building, at no. 1290, look out for Thomas Hart Benton's *America Today* murals, which dynamically and magnificently portray ordinary American life in the days before the Depression.

Bryant Park

Map 6, H1. ⓦwww.bryantpark.org. #B, #D, #F, or #V to 42nd Street/ Bryant Park or #7 to Fifth Avenue.

One block east of Times Square, **Bryant Park** lies behind the New York Public Library (see p.88), on the east side of Sixth Avenue between 40th and 42nd streets. It's hands-down Midtown Manhattan's most inviting public space, a lush grassy square lined with slender trees and pebbled *allées* dotted with dainty green folding chairs. Though there's some controversy about the fact that the park is sustained with corporate contributions, it's hard not to be impressed with its elegance and many perks. As well as free jazz, tai chi classes, and outdoor movies in summer months (visit ⓦwww.bryantpark.org for the schedule), there's also a rather aggressive happy-hour singles scene at the pricey **Bryant Park Café**, an antique carousel, free Wi-Fi throughout the park, and – that real rarity – clean public restrooms. Looming over the park at 40 W 40th St, the Radiator Building, designed in

> **Diamond Row**
>
> One of the best things about New York City is the small hidden pockets abruptly discovered when you least expect them. West 47th Street between Fifth and Sixth avenues is a perfect example: **Diamond Row** is a strip of shops chock-full of gems and jewelry, sold at wholesale and retail prices. Stop in to pick up something special, have a piece of jewelry repaired, or simply window-shop.

1924 for the American Radiator Company, commands attention for its Gothic tower and polished, black-granite facade; it's now the somewhat pretentious **Bryant Park Hotel**.

International Center of Photography

Map 7, G9. 1133 Sixth Ave, at 43rd. Tues–Sun 10am–6pm, Friday until 8pm; $12, students $8, free Fri 5–8pm; ☎212/857-0000, ✪www.icp.org.

The glassy confines of the **International Center of Photography**, founded in 1974, are a good place to catch important photography shows, many with a sociological or political bent. Though stretching back to the daguerreotype era, the permanent collection is particularly strong in twentieth-century documentary photography, and boasts more than 100,000 pictures, including classics by the likes of Henri Cartier-Bresson, Weegee, and Robert Capa.

Radio City Music Hall

Map 7, G7. Tours daily 11am–3pm; $17, $14 seniors, children under 12 $10; ☎212/307-7171, ✪www.radiocity.com. #B, #D, #F, or #V to 47th–50th streets/Rockefeller Center.

Radio City Music Hall, at 50th Street, just northwest of Rockefeller Center (see p.89), is by far the most spectacular attraction on Sixth Avenue. This Art-Deco jewel box represents the last word in 1930s luxury: inside, the staircase is regally resplendent with the world's largest chandeliers, and the huge auditorium looks like an extravagant scalloped shell or a vast sunset. Believe it or not, Radio City was nearly demolished in 1970; the outcry this caused resulted in its being designated a National Landmark. Tours here are highly recommended.

Paley Center for Media

Map 7, H7. 25 W 52nd St. Tues–Sun noon–6pm, Friday until 8pm; $10, students $8, under-14s $5; ☎212/621-6800, ⓦwww.mtr.org. #E or #V to 5th Avenue/53rd Street.

Formerly the Museum of Television & Radio, this bicoastal organization holds an archive of 100,000 mostly **American TV shows, radio broadcasts, and commercials**, many of which are available for your personal viewing. The museum's excellent computerized reference system allows you to research news, public affairs, documentaries, sporting events, comedies, advertisements, and other aural and visual selections. There's also a packed roster of **events**, from media panels to sitcom screenings. Note that the place becomes unbearably crowded on weekends, so plan to visit at other times.

Museum of American Folk Art

Map 7, F6. 45 W 53rd St. Tues–Sun 10.30am–5.30pm, Fri until 7.30pm; $9, students and seniors $7, Fri after 5.30pm free; ☎212/265-1040, ⓦwww.folkartmuseum.org. #E or #V to Fifth Avenue/53rd Street.

The **Museum of American Folk Art** stands in an exceptionally intimate, prize-winning building designed by Tod Williams and Billie Tsien. Its highly sculptural eight-floor facade is based on traditional folk-art techniques and clad in tombasil, a white bronze alloy, while a giant skylight atop the structure allows natural light to filter down through all the galleries. Visitors are encouraged to wander freely, and the greatest part of the structure is designed to be public space as well as a gallery. The museum houses interesting (if a little recondite) exhibitions of multicultural folk art from all over the US, with a permanent collection that includes over 3500 works from the seventeenth to twentieth centuries.

14

Central Park

"All radiant in the magic atmosphere of art and taste." So raved *Harper's* magazine on the opening of **Central Park** in 1876, and though that was a slight overstatement, today few New Yorkers could imagine life without it. At various times and places, the park functions as a beach, theater, singles' scene, athletic activity center, and animal-behavior lab, both human and canine. In bad times and good, New Yorkers still treasure it more than any other city institution.

In spite of the advent of motorized traffic, the sense of disorderly nature the park's nineteenth-century designers, Frederick Law Olmsted and Calvert Vaux, intended largely survives, with cars and buses cutting through the park unseen in the sheltered, sunken transverses originally meant for horse-drawn carriages. The Midtown skyline has changed, of course, and buildings thrust their way into view, sometimes detracting from the park's original pastoral intention, but at the same time adding to the sense of being on a green island in the center of a magnificent city.

Getting around and orientation

At 840 acres, Central Park – which runs from 59th to 110th streets and is flanked by Fifth Avenue and Central Park West – is so enormous that it's almost impossible to miss and nearly as impossible to cover in one visit. Nevertheless, the intricate

footpaths that meander with no discernible organization through the park are one of its greatest successes; after all, the point here is to lose yourself . . . or at least to feel like you can. To figure out exactly where you are, find the nearest **lamppost** – the first two digits on the post signify the number of the nearest cross street.

The **Reservoir** divides Central Park in two. The larger and more familiar southern park holds most of the attractions (and people), but the northern park (above 86th St) is worth a visit for its wilder natural setting and its dramatically different ambiance.

As for **safety**, you should be fine during the day, though always be alert to your surroundings and try to avoid being alone in an isolated part of the park. After dark, it's best to stick to high-traffic areas like the Loop Road and the Reservoir track, especially if you're alone. Of course,

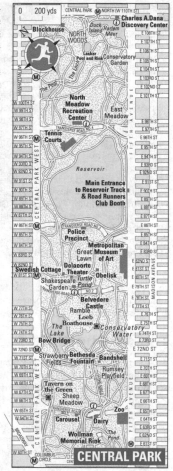

General information

Founded in 1980, the **Central Park Conservancy** (☎212/310-6600, ⓦwww.centralparknyc.org) is a nonprofit organization dedicated to preserving and managing the park. It operates four **visitor centers**, with free maps and other helpful literature, as well as special events. All visitor centers are open Tues–Sun from 10am to 5pm and include The Dairy (mid-park at 65th St; ☎212/794-6564); Belvedere Castle (mid-park at 79th St; ☎212/772-0210); North Meadow Recreation Center (mid-park at 97th St; also open Mon; ☎212/348-4867); and the Dana Discovery Center (110th St off Fifth Ave; ☎212/860-1370).

There are **restrooms** at all of the visitor centers as well as at Heckscher Playground (mid-park at 62nd St), the Merchants' Gate (W 61st St and Central Park West), Mineral Springs House (northwest end of Sheep Meadow), Loeb Boathouse, the Delacorte Theater, and the Conservatory Garden.

In case of emergency, use the **emergency call boxes** located throughout the park and along the crosstown vehicle streets that traverse the park (they provide a direct connection to the Central Park Precinct), or dial ☎911 at any payphone.

you may go deeper into the park for a public evening event such as a concert or Shakespeare in the Park (see p.118); just make sure you leave when the crowds do.

The southern park

If you enter at **Grand Army Plaza** (Fifth Ave and 59th St), you'll find the **Pond** on your left and, a little further north, the **Wollman Memorial Rink**. Sit or stand above the rink to watch skaters and contemplate the view of Central Park South's skyline emerging above the trees. Or **rent skates** of your own, available here in season (Nov–March). In summer, the place plays host to a mini-**amusement park** for kids (entry $6.50 weekdays, $7.50 weekends, plus $1 per ride, or $12/14 for unlimited rides).

The small **Central Park Zoo** lies northeast of the skating rink at 64th Street and Fifth Avenue (April–Oct Mon–Fri 10am–5pm, Sat, Sun & holidays 10am–5.30pm; Nov–March daily 10am–4.30pm; $8, $4 seniors, ages 3–12 $3, under-3s free; ☎212/439-6500). Its collection is based on three climatic regions – the Tropic Zone, the Temperate Territory, and the Polar Circle, and the complex also boasts the **Tisch Children's Zoo**, with interactive displays and a petting zoo geared to children under 6.

The next point to head for is the **Dairy**, at mid-park and 65th Street, a kind of Gothic, toy ranch building constructed in 1870 and originally stocked with cows (and milkmaids) for the purpose of selling milk and other dairy products to mothers with young children. It now houses one of the park's **visitor centers** (Tues–Sun 10am–5pm; ☎212/794-6564), which distributes free leaflets and organizes weekend walking tours.

Just west of the Dairy stands the **Carousel**, at mid-park and 64th Street (April–Oct Mon–Fri 10am–6pm, Sat & Sun 10am–7pm; Nov–Dec daily 10am–dusk; Jan–March weekends & holidays only 10am–dusk; $1; ☎212/879-0244), where kids of all ages can ride on hand-carved jumping horses to the accompaniment of a military band organ. Built in 1903 and moved from Coney Island to the park in 1951, this handmade carousel is one of fewer than 150 left in the country; one of the others is at Coney Island (see p.166).

Straight ahead and north past the Dairy, you'll come to the **Mall**, the park's most formal stretch, where you'll witness every manner of street performer. To the west, between 66th and 69th streets, lies **Sheep Meadow**, fifteen acres of commons where sheep grazed until 1934; today the area is usually crowded with picnickers, sunbathers, families, and Frisbee players.

On warm weekends, an area between Sheep Meadow and the north end of the mall is filled with colorfully attired Rollerbladers and rollerskaters dancing to loud funk, disco, and hiphop music – one of the best free shows around. Meanwhile, just west of Sheep Meadow, at 67th Street and Central Park

West, is the once exclusive (and still expensive) but now rather touristy landmark restaurant *Tavern on the Green*.

At the northernmost point of the Mall lie the 1920s **Naumburg Bandshell**, **Rumsey Playfield** (site of the free Summer-Stage performance series; see box, p.266), and the two-story, excellent-for-people-watching **Bethesda Terrace and Fountain**, at the heart of the park at 72nd Street. Bethesda Terrace overlooks the lake; beneath it is **Bethesda Arcade**, whose Minton-tiled ceilings were recently restored.

Loeb Boathouse

Take a break from your wanderings at the **Loeb Boathouse** (☏212/517-2233), on the east bank of the lake, just off the loop road near 74th Street. Here, you can go for a **gondola ride** or rent a **rowboat**, enjoying the serenity of this beautiful patch of water in the center of the city, with the skyscrapers of Midtown reaching up all around (rowboats and kayaks: March–Nov daily 10am–5pm, weather permitting; $12 for the first hour, $3 each 15min after, with a refundable $30 cash deposit; gondola rides: summer Mon–Fri 5–9pm, Sat & Sun 2–9pm; $30 per half-hour; reservations required). It's also the place to **rent a bike**, one of the most pleasant ways to explore the park. Bikes cost $9–15 an hour and require a (refundable) $250 cash or credit card deposit, along with a passport or driver's license. Finally, the upscale *Central Park Boathouse* restaurant here is your best bet for a meal in the park, with year-round lunch (weekdays) and brunch (weekends), and dinner from April to November; reservations are highly recommended.

The Great Lawn and around

Continuing north will bring you to the backyard of the **Metropolitan Museum of Art**, to the east at 81st Street (see p.120), and the **Obelisk** to the west, an 1881 gift from Egypt that dates back to 1450 BC. Also nearby is the **Great Lawn**, a perfect spot for an early-evening picnic. The Lawn is the site of free summer shows by the New York Philharmonic and the Metropolitan

Strawberry Fields

At 72nd Street and Central Park West, **Strawberry Fields** is a peaceful region of the park dedicated to the memory of John Lennon, who in 1980 was murdered in front of his home at the **Dakota building**, across the street from Central Park (see p.145). Strawberry Fields draws people paying tribute to Lennon, as well as picnickers and seniors who rest on the park benches. Near the West 72nd Street entrance to the area is a round Italian mosaic donated by Yoko Ono; inscribed with the word "Imagine" at its center, it's invariably covered with flowers, photos, and other sentimental knick-knacks. Every year on December 8, the anniversary of Lennon's murder, Strawberry Fields is packed with fans singing Beatles songs and sharing their grief, even after all these years.

Opera, as well as the occasional major rock concert or speech by world-famous dignitaries such as the Dalai Lama. In addition, the Lawn boasts eight softball fields and, at its northern end, basketball and volleyball courts, plus a short jogging track.

Southwest of the Great Lawn is the **Delacorte Theater**, site of the annual free **Shakespeare in the Park** productions (see the box on p.118 for ticket information). Next door, the tranquil **Shakespeare Garden** claims to hold every species of plant mentioned in the Bard's plays. East of the garden is **Belvedere Castle**, a mock medieval citadel first erected in 1869 as a lookout, but now the home of the Urban Park Rangers (who provide walking tours and educational programs). The highest point in the park, and a wonderful viewpoint, the castle also houses the NY Meteorological Observatory's weather center, which provides the "official" Central Park temperature of the day; it makes for a lovely backdrop for the Delacorte's performances.

The northern park

There are fewer attractions, but more open space, north of the Great Lawn. Much of this area is taken up by the **Reservoir**, at mid-park between 86th and 96th streets (main entrance at

Seasonal events and activities

SummerStage concerts are held at the Rumsey Playing Field near 72nd Street and Fifth Avenue (☎212/360-2777, ⓦwww .summerstage.org). **Shakespeare in the Park** takes place at the open-air Delacorte Theater, near the West 81st Street entrance to the park, where free tickets are distributed daily at 1pm for that evening's performance – though you'll probably have to get in line well before then. Tickets are also distributed downtown at the Public Theater (425 Lafayette St) between 1pm and 3pm on the day of the performance. Call the Shakespeare Festival (☎212/539-8750) or visit ⓦwww.publictheater.org for more information.

The **Metropolitan Opera** (☎212/362-6000, ⓦwww.metopera .org) performs a free concert in Central Park in mid-June, with other free concerts at parks around the city. The **New York Philharmonic** (☎212/875-5900, ⓦwww.nyphil.org) performs free in the park in mid-July.

The **Harlem Meer Performance Festival**, 110th Street between Fifth and Lenox avenues ☎212/860-1370 is a fairly intimate and enjoyable free performances of jazz and salsa music outside the Dana Discovery Center on Sundays from 4 to 6pm throughout the summer.

90th St and Fifth Ave), around which disciplined New Yorkers faithfully jog. The raised 1.5-mile track is a great place to get breathtaking 360-degree views of the skyline – just don't block any jogger's path or there will be hell to pay. The reservoir once provided New York City's water but now serves as a steady water supply to three interlaced Central Park water features: the Harlem Meer, the Pool, and the Loch.

If you see nothing else in the park above 86th Street, don't miss the **Conservatory Garden**, between East 103rd and 106th streets along Fifth Avenue. A great spot to pause for a picnic, this pleasing, six-acre space comprises three formal terraced gardens filled with flowering trees and shrubs, planted flower beds, fanciful fountains, and shaded benches. The main iron-gated entrance at 104th Street and Fifth Avenue is a favorite spot for weekend wedding-party photographs.

At the northeast corner of the park is the **Charles A. Dana Discovery Center** (Tues–Sun 10am–5pm, 4pm in winter; ☏212/860-1370), an environmental education and visitor center, with free literature, changing visual exhibits, bird walks every Saturday at 11am in July and August, and multicultural performances (see box, p.118). Crowds of locals fish in the adjacent **Harlem Meer**, an eleven-acre lake that also serves as home to many of the city's swans and grebes. The center provides free bamboo poles and bait, though you have to release whatever you might catch.

(15)

The Metropolitan Museum of Art

The **Metropolitan Museum of Art**, or the Met, as it's usually called, is the foremost art museum in America. It started in a brownstone in Midtown before moving to a larger site in Central Park that Frederick Law Olmsted and Calvert Vaux had initially tagged for a ball field. The building, unveiled in 1880, was designed in Gothic Revival–style brick; as the museum has grown, however, the original structure has become engulfed by many additions, including the magnificent and daunting Beaux-Arts facade, completed in 1902.

The Met owns nearly three million works of art that span the cultures of North America, Europe, Africa, the Far East, and the classical and Islamic worlds. Broadly speaking, the works break down into **seven major collections**: European Art; Asian Art; American Art; Egyptian Art; Medieval Art; Ancient Greek and Roman Art; and the Art of Africa, Oceania, and the Americas. We have also provided an overview of the Met's often overlooked but nevertheless impressive **Modern Art** holdings.

Well worth seeking out but not covered here are the **Arms & Armor collection**, which makes your heart thump for the days

METROPOLITAN MUSEUM OF ART

SECOND FLOOR

- Modern Art
- The American Wing
- The American Wing
- European Paintings
- Musical Instruments
- 19th Century European Paintings & Sculpture
- Drawing, Prints & Photographs
- Japanese Art
- Cypriot Art
- Shop
- Chinese Art
- Asian Art
- Korean Art
- Chinese Art
- Chinese Garden Court
- Ancient Near Eastern Art
- Great Hall Balcony
- South Asian Art
- Islamic Art
- Southeast Asian Art

FIRST FLOOR

- Elevator to roof garden (seasonal)
- The Robert Lehman Collection
- CENTRAL PARK
- Modern Art
- European Sculpture & Decorative Arts
- The American Wing
- Medieval Art
- European Sculpture & Decorative Arts
- Arts of Africa, Oceania & the Americas
- European Sculpture & Decorative Arts
- Arms & Armor
- Temple of Dendur
- Library
- Grace Rainey Rogers Auditorium
- The Sackler Wing
- Shop
- Shop
- Greek & Roman Art
- Great Hall
- Egyptian Art
- Egyptian Art
- FIFTH AVENUE
- MAIN ENTRANCE
- FIFTH AVENUE

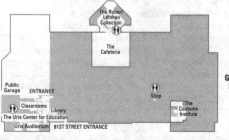

GROUND FLOOR

- The Robert Lehman Collection
- The Cafeteria
- Public Garage
- ENTRANCE
- Classrooms
- Shop
- The Costume Institute
- The Uris Center for Education
- Library
- Uris Auditorium
- 81ST STREET ENTRANCE

of King Arthur, and the **Musical Instruments collection**, best appreciated with the Audio Guide (see below). There are also dozens of **period rooms** packed with European and American furniture and decorative arts, such as Frank Lloyd Wright's *Francis Little Living Room* on the first floor of the American Wing. The **Photographs collection**, long relegated to a dim corridor off the Great Staircase, is finally getting its own gallery in fall 2007, while some of the medieval collection is kept at **The Cloisters** (see p.156), a pastiche of twelfth-century monasteries reconstructed in Fort Tryon Park at 190th Street. The museum also features, at any one time, several **special exhibitions**, usually of very high quality and free with the price of admission. The exhibits range from single-artist retrospectives to surveys of works from the permanent collection.

There is one **main entrance** to the museum, and once you've passed through it you'll find yourself in the **Great Hall**, a deftly lit Neoclassical cavern where, at the main **information desk**, you can get a map, check the day's schedule of events, and pick up information on the Met's excellent lecture and concert series. Directly ahead of the information desk is the **Grand Staircase**, which leads to, for many visitors, the single greatest attraction – the European Paintings galleries. Keep in mind that the museum

Museum practicalities

Map 8, H8. Fifth Ave at E 82nd St, set into Central Park. Tues–Thurs & Sun 9.30am–5.30pm; Fri & Sat 9.30am–9pm; suggested admission $20, seniors $15, students $10 (includes admission to The Cloisters on the same day); ☎212/879-5500 or 535-7710 for recorded information, ⓦwww.metmuseum.org. #4, #5, or #6 to 86th Street. An **Audio Guide headset** ($7) provides recorded expert commentary on hundreds of artworks in both the permanent collection and special exhibitions; free **guided tours** are offered daily but can be crowded and rather broad (ask for the day's schedule at the information desk). There are several **restaurants** and excellent book and **gift shops** scattered around the premises.

is constantly expanding and renovating galleries, so some of the works described below may not be on view when you visit.

European Art

The Met's **European Art galleries**, located on the second floor, are at their best in the Dutch painting section, with major works by Rembrandt (a superb *Self-Portrait*), Hals, and especially Vermeer, whose *Young Woman with a Water Jug* and *A Girl Asleep* display the artist at his most complex. Continue on, and as you loop back to the entrance to the painting galleries you'll pass through another smattering of works by Spanish, French, and Italian painters, most notably Goya and Velázquez. The latter's piercing and somber *Portrait of Juan de Pareja* shouldn't be missed. A whole room is dedicated to the formidable works of El Greco. His extraordinary *View of Toledo* – all brooding intensity as the skies seem about to swallow up the ghost-like town – is perhaps the best of his works anywhere in the world.

The **Italian Renaissance** isn't spectacularly represented, but there's a worthy selection from the various schools; these works consist largely of narrative panels or altarpieces, and gold paint is often used, either for the background or for the haloes of the religious figures. Highlights include an early tempera on wood by Raphael, *Madonna and Child Enthroned with Saints*; a late Botticelli, the crisply linear *Three Miracles of Saint Zenobius*; Filippo Lippi's grandiose, fresco-inspired *Madonna and Child Enthroned with Two Angels*; and Michele de Verona's handsome *Madonna and Child with the Infant John the Baptist*, in which the characters are almost sculpturally rendered.

Impressionist and Post-Impressionist painting

On its second floor the Met has a stunning array of **Impressionist** and **Post-Impressionist** art. Chief works include Manet's *Young Lady in 1866*, an eerie, sepia-toned rendering of a maniacal-looking woman with her parrot; Courbet's crisply pastoral *Young Ladies of the Village*; and one of Degas' beautiful, shadowy ballet works, *Dancers Practicing at the Bar*. Three superb works by Monet – *Rouen Cathedral*, where the same subject was painted at different hours of the day; his rendering of a quintessentially urban Albion, *The Houses of Parliament (Effect of Fog)*; and, done in oils, his watery, ethereal *The Doge's Palace Seen from San Giorgio Maggiore* – show the beginnings of his final phase of near-abstract Impressionism.

Renoir is perhaps the best represented among the remaining Impressionists, though his most important work here dates from 1878, when he began to move away from the mainstream techniques he'd learned while working with Monet. *Mme Charpentier and Her Children* is a likeable enough piece, one whose affectionate tone manages to sidestep the sentimentality of Renoir's later work. Finally, also here is Cézanne's masterpiece *The Card Players*, the second in a series of five paintings all dealing with the same scene. Yet all of this scratches little more than the surface of the galleries. Look out as well for major works by Van Gogh (including *Irises*, *Woman of Arles*, and *Sunflowers*), Rousseau, Bonnard, Pissarot, and Seurat.

Modern Art

The Met's **Modern Art** collection, housed in the Lila Acheson Wallace Wing, is a fascinating group of paintings spread over two floors and a mezzanine. Picasso's *Portrait of Gertrude Stein*,

The Cantor Roof Garden

From May through October, you can ascend to the **Cantor Roof Garden** (accessible by elevator from the first floor) on top of the Wallace Wing, which displays **contemporary sculpture** against the dramatic backdrop of New York's Midtown skyline. In October this is a great place to see the colorful fall foliage in Central Park. Drinks and snacks are available, and while they're a bit on the expensive side, the breathtaking views make up for the stiff prices.

a labor of love that took ninety sittings and almost two years to complete, and his blue-period work *The Blind Man's Meal* are here, alongside works by Klee, Modigliani, Braque, and Klimt. Other highlights include O'Keeffe's sumptuous, erotic *Black Iris* and Pollock's disorienting *Autumn Rhythm (Number 30)*. There are also a number of paintings of nubile young girls by Balthus, along with his wall-sized homage to alpine living, *The Mountain*, from 1936.

Asian Art

The **Asian Art galleries** on the second and third floors gather an impressive and vast array of Chinese, Japanese, Indian, and Southeast Asian sculpture, painting, ceramics, and metalwork, as well as an indoor replica of a Chinese garden. The recently renovated and expanded Chinese Art galleries showcase Chinese painting, calligraphy, jade, lacquer, and textiles, making this collection one of the largest in the world. It has incredible Edo-period works, including a beautiful pair of gold-leaf folding screens by Kôrin (*Eight Planked Bridge*); Sansetu's *The Old Plum*; and Hokusai's *The Great Wave at Kanagawa*, rumored to have been a major source of inspiration for both Debussy and Rilke. Much more ancient beauty is to be found in the fourth-century Buddhist shrine from Pakistan and in the tenth-century Indian *Standing Pavarti* statue.

The highlight is the **Chinese Garden Court**, a serene, minimalist retreat enclosed by the galleries, and the adjacent **Ming Room**, a typical salon decorated in Ming-period style with wooden lattice doors. The naturally lit garden is representative of those found in Chinese homes – a pagoda, small waterfall, and goldfish pond landscaped by limestone rocks, trees, and shrubs conjure up a palpable sense of peace.

American Art

Spread throughout the American Wing, the Met's galleries for **American Art** are in the process of being renovated and reconfigured, so expect a fair number of them to be closed until 2010. Chronologically, the collection begins with eighteenth-century portraits (look out for the heroics of Leutzes's *Washington Crossing the Delaware*) and continues with Benjamin West's allegorical *The Triumph of Love* and the landscape paintings of the nineteenth-century Hudson River School artists. Thomas Cole, the school's doyen, is represented by *The Oxbow*, and his pupil, Frederic Church, by the immense *Heart of the Andes*, combining the mountains' grand sweep with minutely depicted flora. Also here are several striking portraits by John Singer Sargent, including the magnificent *Portrait of Madam X*, and a number of works by Winslow Homer: of his late, quasi-Impressionistic studies of seascapes, the explosive, spuming *Northeaster* is one of the finest.

Medieval Art

Although you could move straight to the **Medieval Art** section from the American Wing, you should instead enter these galleries via the corridor from the western end (or rear) of the Great Hall, to the left of the main staircase. There you'll see displays of sumptuous Byzantine metalwork and jewelry, donated by financier J. Pierpont Morgan. At the end of the corridor is the main sculpture hall, piled high with religious statuary and carvings like the tremendous *St Nicholas Saving Three Boys in the Brine Tub*; it's divided by a 52-foot-high *reja* – a decorative, openwork iron altar screen – from Valladolid Cathedral.

To the right of the hall, the **medieval treasury** has a magnificent and all-embracing display of objects religious, liturgical, and secular. And beyond are the Jack and Belle Linsky Galleries, featuring Flemish, Florentine, and Venetian painting, porcelain, and bronzes.

Ancient Greek and Roman Art

April 2007 marked the triumphant reopening of the Met's **Ancient Greek and Roman Art galleries** (now greatly expanded), showcasing one of the largest collections of its kind in the world. Enter from the southern end of the museum's Great Hall, and you'll soon find yourself in a grand, barrel-vaulted space full of sixth- to fourth-century BC marble sculpture, including several large sphinxes. The gallery is flanked by three rooms on either side, each with exhibits arranged by theme, medium, and chronology. You'll find everything from large funerary monuments to tiny terracotta figures in the same room.

The gargantuan yet finely detailed capital and base of an Ionic column from the Temple of Artemis at Sardis – the shaft, which has been omitted, stood fifty-eight feet tall – marks the beginning of the Roman collection, whose centerpiece is a sun-bathed atrium with a serene fountain and twenty Roman sculptures, almost all of which are copies of Greek originals, attesting to the Romans' intense admiration for Greek art. Two larger-than-life-sized statues of Hercules – one young, one old, both from the first century AD – face off from either side of the court. Around and above the court on the mezzanine and second floor are smaller galleries containing all manner of Roman, Etruscan, Cypriot, and Ancient Near Eastern art. The sheer number of objects is staggering; take care not to try to see too many, or you're likely to get overwhelmed.

Egyptian Art

The **Egyptian Art** collection, to the north end of the Great Hall, holds 36,000 objects, and nearly all are on lavish display. The large statuary are the most immediately striking of the exhibits, but it's the smaller sculptural pieces that hold the attention longest. Look out for the dazzling collection of Princess Sit-hathor-yunet's jewelry, a pinnacle in Egyptian decorative art that dates from around 1830 BC. Most striking of all is the **Temple of Dendur**, a complete fifteenth-century BC temple that's marvelously lit up at night; it was moved here during the construction of the Aswan High Dam in 1965.

Arts of Africa, Oceania, and the Americas

The Rockefeller Wing holds the Met's comprehensive collection of art from **Africa, Oceania, and the Americas**. It's a superb set of rooms, the muted, understated decor throwing the exhibits into sharp and often dramatic focus. The African exhibit has a particularly awe-inspiring display of art from the Court of Benin in present-day Nigeria: tiny carved-ivory statues and vessels, created with astonishing detail. The Oceanic collection – housed in spacious new galleries as of November 2007 – covers the islands of Melanesia, Micronesia, Polynesia, New Zealand, and Australia, and contains a wide array of objects such as wild, somewhat frightening wooden masks with piercing, all-too-realistic eyes. Lastly, highlights of the Americas collection include thousands-of-years-old masks, ancestor figures, and other statues from Mexico, exquisitely crafted pendants from Colombia and Panama, and bottles, drums, and tunics from Peru.

THE METROPOLITAN MUSEUM OF ART

16

The Upper East Side

The defining characteristic of Manhattan's **Upper East Side**, a two-square-mile grid scored with the great avenues of **Madison, Park**, and **Lexington**, is wealth. While other neighborhoods are affected by incursions of immigrant groups, artistic trends, and the like, this remains primarily an enclave of the well-off, with tony shops, clean and safe streets, and well-preserved buildings and landmarks. It also has some of the city's finest museums, many of them in a compact strip on **Fifth Avenue** known as **Museum Mile**: the Metropolitan Museum of Art and the Guggenheim are the best (and best known), though many others, such as the Frick Collection and the Neue Galerie, command attention as well. The Whitney Museum of American Art and the Asia Society stand nearby on Madison and Park avenues, respectively.

Along Fifth Avenue

Fifth Avenue has been the haughty patrician face of Manhattan since the opening of Central Park in 1876, when the Carnegies, Astors, Vanderbilts, Whitneys, and other notable New York capitalists moved from lower Fifth Avenue and Gramercy

Park to build their Neoclassical residences along the park's eastern edge. A great deal of what you see along this stretch, though, is third- or fourth-generation construction. Through the latter part of the nineteenth century, fanciful mansions were built at vast expense, to stand only ten or fifteen years before being demolished for even wilder extravagances or, more commonly – as rocketing land values made the chance of selling at vast profit irresistible – grand apartment blocks.

16 Grand Army Plaza to the Frick Collection

Grand Army Plaza (Map 7, H5), an oval at the junction of Central Park South and Fifth Avenue, marks the division between Fifth as a shopping district (to the south) and as a residential boulevard (to the north). This is one of the city's most dramatic public spaces, boasting a fountain and a gold statue of Civil War victor General Sherman, and flanked by the extended copper-lined chateau of the iconic **Plaza Hotel**. The hotel is currently undergoing an extensive renovation (due to be complete in 2008), with more than half of its storied rooms and suites being turned into luxury condominiums. The darkened, swooping, television-screen facade of the **Solow Building** and two more hotels, the high-necked **Sherry Netherland** and the **Pierre**, luxuriate nearby.

Up six blocks from Grand Army Plaza, on the corner of Fifth Avenue and 65th Street, America's largest Reformed synagogue, the **Temple Emanu-El** (Map 7, H4; Sun–Thurs 10am–noon & 1:30–5pm, Fri 10am–noon & 1.30–4pm, Sat 1:30–5pm; ☏212/744-1400) strikes a sober aspect, a brooding Romanesque–Byzantine cavern that manages to be bigger inside than it seems out. Once within, the interior melts away into mysterious darkness, making you feel very small indeed.

The Frick Collection

Map 7, H3. 1 E 70th St. Tues–Sat 10am–6pm, Sun 11am–5pm; $12, seniors $10, students $5, Sun 11am–1pm pay what you wish; under-10s not admitted; ☏212/288-0700, Ⓦwww.frick.org. A 22min AV

Housed in Henry Clay Frick's eighteenth-century-style mansion, the immensely enjoyable **Frick Collection** comprises the art treasures hoarded by this most ruthless and hated of New York's robber barons. However, the legacy of Frick's ill-gotten gains is a superb collection of works, and as good a glimpse of the sumptuous life enjoyed by New York's early industrialists as you'll find.

Opened in the mid-1930s, the museum has been largely kept as it looked when the Fricks lived there. Much of the furniture is heavy eighteenth-century French, but the nice thing about the place – and many people rank the Frick as their favorite New York gallery for this reason – is that it strives hard to be as unlike a museum as possible. The furnishings and pictures create an intimate interior, making the visitor feel like a high-class voyeur. This intimacy is carried over into the architecture, with Frick's collection stretching from the grandiose, English country-house style of the West Gallery to the airy Fragonard Room and the richly wooded Living Hall, filled with masterpieces by the likes of Titian and Holbein.

There's a magnificent array of works here by Rembrandt (including a set of piercing *Self-Portraits*), Goya, and Whistler, as well as an early (and suggestive) Vermeer, *Officer and Laughing Girl*, and one of Van Eyck's last works, a *Virgin and Child*. The **West Gallery**, where the former two paintings are located, is the Frick's major draw, holding some of its finest works in a truly majestic setting – a long, elegant room with a concave glass ceiling and ornately carved wood trim. Two Turners, views of Cologne and Dieppe, hang opposite one another, each a blaze of orange and creamy tones; Van Dyck is represented with a couple of uncharacteristically informal portraits of Frans Snyders and his wife – two paintings reunited only when Frick purchased them; there are several austere, somewhat generic portraits by Frans Hals; and El Greco dazzles with *Vincenzo Anastagi*, a stunning portrait of a Spanish soldier resplendent in green velvet and armor. Lastly, Piero della Francesca's enormous *St John the Evangelist* presides over the space, framed by the arched entryway to the Enamel Room.

The Neue Galerie

Map 8, H7. 1048 Fifth Ave, at 86th. Sat, Sun & Mon 11am–6pm, Fri 11am–9pm; $15, seniors and students $10, under-12s not admitted; ☎212/423-3500, ⓦwww.neuegalerie.org. #4, #5, or #6 to 86th Street.

The small **Neue Galerie**, opened in 2001, is an elegant, two-tiered celebration of early twentieth-century German and Austrian art and design, housed in a landmark building by architects Carrère and Hastings (who designed the New York Public Library; see p.88). A welcome addition to the city's museums, on the second floor the Neue boasts an exceptional collection of turn-of-the-century Viennese fine and decorative arts, including Klimt's beautifully complex *The Dancer* and Schiele's terrifyingly stark *Self Portrait with Arm Twisted above Head*, as well as works by Hofmann and Wagner. The Germans get their turn on the third floor, where the collection features new objectivist masterworks like Max Beckmann's profound *Self-Portrait in Front of Red Curtain*, which disturbed one contemporary viewer so much he stabbed it with a knife. Rounding out the collection are pieces by Klee, Kandinsky, and Dix, as well as a stunning representation of the various incarnations of Bauhaus.

Off the lobby, **Café Sabarsky**, a Viennese-style coffeehouse, is widely regarded as the best restaurant on Museum Mile; its hours are longer than the museum's, and you don't need to pay admission to get in.

The Guggenheim Museum

Map 8, H7. 1071 Fifth Ave, at 89th. Sat–Wed 10am–6pm, Fri 10am–7.45pm; $18, seniors and students $15, under-12s free, Fri 6–8pm pay what you wish; ☎212/423-3500, ⓦwww.guggenheim.org. #4, #5, or #6 to 86th Street.

Whatever you think of the **Guggenheim Museum**'s collection of paintings, it's the upturned beehive building designed by Frank Lloyd Wright that steals the show, looking wildly out of place amid Fifth Avenue's solemn facades. Based on an inverted ziggurat, or Babylonian temple, the museum was commissioned in 1934 but wasn't finished until 1959, after the architect's death. Whereas most other museums sweep visitors in and immediately barrage them with visuals, ushering them from gallery to gallery, Wright's Guggenheim was designed for the leisurely contemplation of art.

In the first half of the twentieth century, the museum's founder, Solomon R. Guggenheim, was one of America's richest men. A frenetic collector of modern painting, he bought wholesale the works of Kandinsky, Chagall, Klee, Léger, and others, and displayed them at his Museum of Non-Objective Painting to a bemused American public. Subsequent additions include masterworks by Cézanne, Degas, Gauguin, Manet, Toulouse-Lautrec, Van Gogh, and Picasso, greatly enhancing the museum's Impressionist and Post-Impressionist holdings. Much of the Kandinsky is usually on display, along with hefty selections of Picasso, Chagall, and Cézanne.

Since the circular galleries increase upward at a not-so-gentle slope, you should start at the top of the museum and work your way down; most of the temporary **special exhibits** are planned that way.

Cooper-Hewitt, National Design Museum

Map 000, 000. 2 E 91st St, at Fifth Ave. Mon–Thurs 10am–5pm, Fri 10am–9pm, Sat 10am–6pm & Sun noon–6pm; $12, students and seniors $9, under-12s free; ⊤212/849-8400, ⓦ www.cooperhewitt .org. #4, #5, or #6 to 96th Street.

Andrew Carnegie's over-the-top 1902 mansion is the somewhat incongruous setting for the Smithsonian-affiliated **Cooper-Hewitt, National Design Museum**. The museum has more than a quarter million objects and artworks in its **permanent collection** – which ranges from fifteenth-century fine art to the latest in industrial design – but only a fraction of it is on display, as most of the space is taken up by large **temporary**

shows. Even if you don't take in the whole place, step inside to see the lovely foyer or browse the exceptional gift-shop.

The Jewish Museum

Map 8, H6. 1109 Fifth Ave, at 92nd. Sat–Wed 11am–5.45pm, Thurs 11am–9pm, closed Fri; $12, students and seniors $10, under-12s free, Sat free; ☏212/423-3200, ⊛www.jewishmuseum.org. #4, #5, or #6 to 96th Street.

The centerpiece of the **Jewish Museum**, the largest museum of Judaica outside of Israel, is "Culture and Continuity: The Jewish Journey," a **permanent exhibition** of Jewish art and artifacts that covers two floors and spans four thousand years. The museum also mounts large **temporary shows** by major Jewish artists, such as sculptor Louise Nevelson, and co-sponsors (with the Film Society of Lincoln Center) the **New York Jewish Film Festival**, which takes place for two weeks each January; see the website for details.

Museum of the City of New York

Map 8, H3. 1220 Fifth Ave, at 103rd. Tues–Sun 10am–5pm; suggested donation $9, seniors and students $5, families $20, under-12s free, Sun 10am–noon free. ☏212/534-1672, ⊛www.mcny.org. #6 to 103rd Street.

The permanent collection of the **Museum of the City of New York**, housed in a neo-Georgian mansion, provides a thorough, fascinating history of the city from Dutch times to the present. Prints, photographs, costumes, and furniture are displayed across four floors, and a film about the city's history runs continuously. **Permanent exhibits** include "New York Toy Stories," an engaging look at all manner of board games, motion toys, sports equipment, and dollhouses, while the John Golden Archive of theater history comprises an intriguing collection of costumes, screenplays, props, and more. The **short-term exhibits** also tend to be quite good: one recent one dared to question whether urban planner Robert Moses was really the megalomaniac that biographer Robert Caro made him out to be.

Museo del Barrio

Map 8, H3. 1230 Fifth Ave, at 104th. Wed–Sun 11am–5pm, closed Mon & Tues; suggested donation $6, students and seniors $4, Thurs seniors free; ☎212/831-7272, ⓦwww.elmuseo.org. #6 to 103rd Street.

Literally translated as "the neighborhood museum," the **Museo del Barrio** was founded in 1969 by a group of Puerto Rican parents, educators, and artists who wanted to teach their children about their roots and bring wider recognition to artists from the Caribbean and Latin America. Every year the museum puts on five major exhibitions of Latin American painting, photographs, and crafts, by both traditional and emerging artists. You can also expect to see a sampling of the **permanent collection**, which boasts a particularly impressive history of the Puerto Rican print industry, early pre-Columbian Caribbean ceremonial objects, an outstanding collection of *santos de palo* (carved wooden saints used for prayer), and some terrific photographs.

Along Madison Avenue

Immediately east of Fifth Avenue lies **Madison Avenue**, a strip that was entirely residential until the 1920s. Today, it's an elegant shopping street lined with designer clothing stores (Valentino, Jean-Paul Gaultier, and Issey Miyake, among others) and high-end art galleries that cater to the neighborhood's ultra-wealthy residents. The only key sight along its Upper East Side stretch is the Whitney Museum of American Art.

Whitney Museum of American Art

Map 7, I2. 945 Madison Ave, at 75th. Wed, Thurs, Sat & Sun 11am–6pm, Fri 1–9pm; $12, seniors and students $9.50, Fri 6–9pm pay what you wish; ☎212/570-3600, ⓦwww.whitney.org. Excellent free gallery talks Wed–Sun, call for times. #6 to 77th Street.

Located in a heavy, arsenal-like building, the **Whitney Museum of American Art** is a great forum for one of the pre-eminent collections of twentieth- and twenty-first-century American art.

The museum boasts over 12,000 paintings, sculptures, photographs, and films; it's particularly strong on Hopper, and several of his best paintings are here: *Early Sun Morning* is typical, a bleak urban landscape, uneasily tense in its lighting and rejection of topical detail. Other major bequests include a significant number of works by Avery, Demuth, and O'Keeffe (don't miss her spectacular small watercolor *Morning Sky*), and a major collection of Calder, including his perennially popular *Calder's Circus*, a replica of a real circus complete with animals and acrobats, in the artist's typically whimsical wire style. The Abstract Expressionists are featured strongly, with great works such as Pollock's deeply textured *Number 27, 1950*, Louise Bourgeois' haunting postwar sculpture *Quarantania*, and De Kooning's catastrophically coherent *Woman and Bicycle*. Somewhat calmer are pieces by Warhol, Johns (the deceptively simple nationalist dissent of *Three Flags* is a standout), and Oldenburg, whose *Soft Sculptures* are vinyl-type material reconstructions of everyday objects.

Finally, every other year there is an exhibition – the **Whitney Biennial** – designed to give a provocative overview of what's happening in contemporary American art. It is often panned by critics (sometimes for good reason) but always packed with visitors. Catch it if you can between March and June in even-numbered years.

Along Park Avenue

One block east of Madison, the stretch of **Park Avenue** that runs through the Upper East Side is known for the dozens of swish apartment blocks that line each side – look for the uniformed doormen dotting the sidewalk, the sleek black town cars idling with their drivers still inside, and the Chanel-suited women who periodically emerge with their teacup poodles.

Aside from such glimpses of Manhattan's moneyed elite, it's worth wandering down Park for the sweeping view south, where the thoroughfare coasts toward the hulking New York

Central (now Helmsley) and MetLife buildings. In the low 90s, look for the large black shapes of the Louise Nevelson **sculptures** dotted on the traffic islands, while, further south, the hulking, fortress-like **Seventh Regiment Armory** (Map 7, I4) dominates a full square block between 66th and 67th streets. Built in the 1870s with pseudo-medieval crenellations, the armory is the only surviving building from the era before the New York Central's railroad tracks were roofed over and Park Avenue became an upscale residential neighborhood. The building's two surviving nineteenth-century interiors are among the finest in the US: both the Veterans' Room and the Library were designed by a group of artists working under Louis Comfort Tiffany and feature an amalgam of Greek, Moresque, Celtic, Persian, and Japanese influences. Unfortunately, the armory is no longer open to tours, but you can visit the public rooms by attending one of the frequent art and antiques shows held here.

Asia Society

Map 7, I3. 725 Park Ave, at 70th. Tues–Sun 11am–6pm, Fri until 9pm (except July–Sept); $10, seniors $7, students $5, free Fri 6–9pm; ☎212/288-6400, Ⓦwww.asiasocietymuseum.com. #6 to 68th Street.

Founded by John D. Rockefeller III in 1956, the **Asia Society** exhibits both traditional and contemporary art from all over Asia in a bright, airy space. The third-floor galleries hold rotating selections from the **permanent collection**, a relatively small but highly impressive trove of treasures from Korea, Japan, Southeast Asia, China, Mongolia, and the Himalayas. Highlights include late sixth- and eighth-century Buddhas and a first-century Shiva from India, along with Tibetan, Thai, Japanese, and Nepalese Bodhisattvas, sublime Japanese earthenware from the Edo period, and Ming vases from China. The rest of the museum is given over to **temporary exhibits**. The museum also sponsors loads of intriguing performances, political roundtables, lectures, films, and free events in its basement theater.

Lexington Avenue and east

Lexington Avenue – or just "Lex" – is Madison Avenue without the class. Much of the East 60s and 70s now house young, unattached, and upwardly mobile professionals, as the number of boisterous singles bars (and sports bars, for the more resigned) along Second and Third avenues will attest. **Bloomingdale's**, a popular upscale department store, provides retail therapy for those in sartorial need, while culture, of a rarefied kind, can be found under the auspices of the **Mount Vernon Hotel Museum and Garden** and **Gracie Mansion**.

The Mount Vernon Hotel Museum and Garden

Map 7, L5. 421 E 61st St, between York and First aves. Tues–Sun 11am–4pm, Tues in June & July until 9pm, closed Aug; $8, students and seniors $7, under-12s free; ☎212/838-6878, ⓦwww.mvhm.org. #N, #R, #W, #4, #5, or #6 to Lexington Avenue/59th Street.

Several long blocks east of Lex, the **Mount Vernon Hotel Museum and Garden** is a Federal-period structure that has been restored by the Colonial Dames of America, a society founded by women in 1890 to preserve American cultural heritage and history, and to commemorate the original thirteen colonies. The furnishings, knick-knacks, and serene little park out back are more engaging than the house itself, but there's an odd sort of pull to the place if you're lucky enough to be guided around by a chatty Colonial Dame.

Gracie Mansion

Map 8, N7. East End Ave, at 88th. Tours on Wed only; $7, seniors $4, afternoon tea $25; ☎212/639-9675. #4, #5, or #6 to 86th Street.

Much farther north (a good walk from the subway and nearly all the way to the East River), lies **Gracie Mansion**, a 1799 country manor house that remains one of the best-preserved colonial buildings in the city. After serving as a concession stand for the adjoining park for many years, it was restored as the official residence of the Mayor of New York City in 1942, and has housed everyone from Fiorello LaGuardia to Rudy Giuliani. In 2002, however, Mayor Michael Bloomberg – who already owned a multimillion-dollar townhouse on the Upper East Side – declined residency.

The only way to see Gracie Mansion is to take one of the four weekly **guided tours**, offered Wednesdays at 10am, 11am, 1pm, and 2pm. If you manage to secure a spot – book well in advance – you'll be treated to New York lore and detailed information about the design and artisanship of the mansion's many fine examples of nineteenth-century craftsmanship: cabinetry, furniture, lighting fixtures, and so on, mostly in the Federal architectural style.

17

The Upper West Side and Morningside Heights

T he **Upper West Side** has always had a more unbuttoned vibe than its counterpart across the park. It is one of the city's most desirable neighborhoods, and tends to attract what might be called New York's cultural elite and new-money types – musicians, writers, journalists, curators, and the like – though there is also a small but visible homeless presence.

The Upper West Side is bordered by Central Park to the east, the Hudson River to the west, Columbus Circle at 59th Street to the south, and 110th Street (the upper boundary of Central Park) to the north. The main commercial artery is

Broadway and, generally speaking, the further you stray east or west the more wealthy (and residential) things become, until you reach the pinnacle of prosperity, the historic apartment buildings of Central Park West and Riverside Drive. **Lincoln Center**, New York's prestigious performing-arts complex, lies in the region's southern streets; the center, along with the superlative **American Museum of Natural History**, are the Upper West Side's greatest attractions. North of 110th Street finds you in the neighborhood of **Morningside Heights**, home to the stunning **Cathedral Church of St John the Divine** and Ivy League **Columbia University**.

Columbus Circle and around

Map 7, E5. #A, #B, #C, #D, or #1 to 59th Street/Columbus Circle.

Columbus Circle, at the intersection of Broadway, Central Park West, and 59th Street, is a good place to start investigating the Upper West Side. Just a few years ago this area was very dumpy, but an amazing renovation has transformed it into a welcoming public space, with benches, plantings, and a fountain.

One of the first things you'll likely spy here is the glittering bronze *Trump International Hotel* to the north; touted as "The World's Most Prestigious Address," it's just one more example of Donald Trump's extraordinary hubris – though it does house one of the city's top restaurants, *Jean-Georges*.

Soaring skyward from the west side of Columbus Circle is the **Time Warner Center**, the gleaming twin-towered edifice that comprises shops, luxury apartments, a Whole Foods supermarket, Lincoln Center's jazz facilities, Time Warner's HQ, and the *Mandarin Oriental Hotel* (see p.192), whose 35th-floor lobby bar offers one of the best views of Midtown. The building is also home to some of the city's most exclusive restaurants, including *Per Se*, helmed by Thomas Keller (of California's *French Laundry* fame), and the tiny Japanese restaurant *Masa*; both have tasting menus for around $250 to $400.

The recent addition of *Landmarc* (see p.210), a solid bistro known for its affordable wines, appeals to diners on much more modest budgets.

In 2008, the **Museum of Arts & Design**, currently across the street from MoMA (see p.98), will open in its new home on the south side of the circle.

Lincoln Center

Map 7, D4. Ninth Ave, btw 63rd and 66th sts. ☎212/721-6500, Ⓦwww.lincolncenter.org. #1 to 66th Street/Lincoln Center.

Broadway continues north from Columbus Circle to the **Lincoln Center for the Performing Arts**, an imposing group of buildings arranged around a large plaza and fountain. Built in the mid-1960s on a site that formerly held some of the city's poorest slums, Lincoln Center is home to twelve world-renowned arts organizations. Most visible are the **Metropolitan Opera**, the **New York City Ballet**, and the **New York Philharmonic**, whose theaters flank the main plaza; other exceptional groups include the Chamber Music Society of Lincoln Center, the Lincoln Center Theater, and the Juilliard School. A major redesign of the complex by cutting-edge architects Diller Scofidio + Renfro is geared toward giving some of these smaller groups more visibility. Construction will stretch well into the next decade.

Lincoln Center hosts a variety of **free entertainment**, ranging from craft fairs to music concerts throughout the summer; call the phone number listed above or see the website for details. Ticket information is on pp.265–266.

The New York State Theater and Avery Fisher Hall

On the south side of Lincoln Center's plaza, the spare and elegant **New York State Theater** (☎212/870-5570) is home to the New York City Ballet and the New York City Opera, and hosts the famed annual December performances of *The Nutcracker*. The ballet season runs from late November through

February, and from early April through June; the opera season starts in July and runs through mid-November.

   Avery Fisher Hall (☎212/875-5030), on the north side of the plaza, does not possess the magnificence of the auditorium across the way, but its foyer is noteworthy for the huge hanging sculpture that dominates the place. The New York Philharmonic performs here from September through May; the less-expensive "Mostly Mozart" concerts take place here in July and August.

The Metropolitan Opera House

Tours Oct–June Mon–Fri at 3.30pm, also Sun at 10.30am; $15, $5 for students; tour reservations ☎212/769-7020, tickets and information ☎212/362-6000, ⓦwww.metoperafamily.org.

Like the Metropolitan Museum of Art, the **Metropolitan Opera House** – home to one of the best opera companies in the world – is also known as "the Met." The focal point of Lincoln Center's plaza, the Met dazzles with its enormous crystal chandeliers and red-carpeted staircases designed for grand entrances. Behind two of the high-arched windows hang murals by Marc Chagall, adding to the opera house's elegant, opulent appearance.

The rest of Lincoln Center

To the south of the Met lies **Damrosch Park**, a large space with rows of chairs facing the Guggenheim Bandshell, where you can catch free summer concerts and various performances in the Lincoln Center Out of Doors Festival (see p.266). To the north, you'll find a lovely, smaller plaza facing the **Vivian Beaumont Theater**, where top Broadway musicals and plays are performed. Across 66th Street is **Alice Tully Hall** (closed for renovation until winter 2008), a recital hall that houses the Chamber Music Society of Lincoln Center, and the **Walter E. Reade Theater**, which features foreign films and retrospectives and, together with Avery Fisher and Alice Tully halls, hosts the annual New York Film Festival in late September (see p.308). The famed **Juilliard School of Music** is in an adjacent building.

Broadway

On **Broadway** at 72nd, tiny, triangular Verdi Square (featuring a craggy statue in the likeness of the composer) makes a fine place to take a break from Lincoln Center's modernist marvels. From the square, you can fully appreciate the ornate balconies, round corner towers, and cupolas of the **Ansonia Hotel**, 2109 Broadway, at West 73rd. Never actually a hotel (it was planned as upscale apartments, albeit ones without kitchens), the *Ansonia* was completed in 1904; the dramatic Beaux-Arts building is still today the artsy *grande dame* of the Upper West Side.

The turnover of commercial establishments in this neighborhood is often astounding, but one stalwart is **Zabar's**, at 2254 Broadway, between 80th and 81st streets (Map 8, B9). The Upper West Side's principal gourmet shop, this area landmark offers more or less anything connected with food.

A couple of blocks north, at 212 W 83rd St, between Broadway and Amsterdam, the **Children's Museum of Manhattan** (Map 8, C8; Tues–Sun 10am–5pm, children and adults $9, seniors $6, under-1s free; ☎212/721-1234, ⊛www.cmom .org) offers interactive exhibits that stimulate learning, in a fun, relaxed environment for kids (and babies). The Dr. Seuss exhibit and the storytelling room (filled with books from which kids can choose) are perennial winners. For more on what to do with children in New York, see Chapter 31, "Kids' New York."

Central Park West

Central Park West is lined with monolithic, mansion-inspired apartment complexes, mostly dating from the early twentieth century, which rim the edge of the park and hog the best of the views. Between 71st and 72nd streets, you'll find the fittingly named **Majestic** (Map 7, E2). Thrown up in 1930, this gigantic Art-Deco landmark is best known for its twin towers and avant-garde brickwork.

The next block north houses the most famous apartment building of all: the **Dakota**, 1 W 72nd St (Map 7, E2), with its turrets, gables, and other odd details, was built in 1884 to persuade wealthy New Yorkers that life in an apartment could be just as luxurious as in a private house. Big-time tenants over the years have included Lauren Bacall and Leonard Bernstein, and in the 1960s the building was used as the setting for Roman Polanski's film *Rosemary's Baby*. But perhaps the most famous resident of the Dakota was John Lennon, who was murdered outside the building on the night of December 8, 1980, by Mark David Chapman. Lennon's wife, Yoko Ono, still lives here, and Lennon himself is remembered in a memorial plaza just across the street in Central Park (see p.117).

Continue north to the **San Remo**, 145–146 Central Park West, at 74th (Map 7, E2). Another apartment complex, this one dates from 1930 and is one of the most significant components of the skyline here: its ornate twin towers topped by columned, mock-Roman temples are visible from most points in the park. Residents have included Dustin Hoffman, Steve Martin, Steven Spielberg, and Bono.

New-York Historical Society

Map 7, E1. 170 Central Park West, at 77th St. Tues–Sun 10am–6pm; $10, students and seniors $5, children free; ☎212/873-3400, Ⓦwww .nyhistory.org. #B or #C to 81st Street–Museum of Natural History.

The oldest museum in the city, the **New–York Historical Society** was founded in 1804 to preserve the history of the US, not just New York, so the exhibits here are broader than the ones across the park at the Museum of the City of New York (p.134). The **temporary exhibitions** can be quite daring, mixing high and low culture with intelligence and flair; one that garnered a lot of attention recently was a multipart examination of New York's historically underplayed participation in the nation's slave trade.

The fantastic **permanent collection** includes Tiffany lamps, all 432 original paintings of James Audubon's *Birds of America*, and works by the Hudson River School artists – though only fragments are on display at any given time. When visiting, don't miss the fourth-floor **Luce Center**, a mesmerizing room full of floor-to-ceiling glass cases featuring 40,000 historically significant objects.

The American Museum of Natural History

Map 8, E9. Central Park West, at 79th. Museum open daily 10am–5.45pm, Rose Center open Mon–Thurs 10am–5.45pm, first Fri of the month until 8.45pm; suggested donation (including the Rose Center) $14, students/seniors $10.50, children $8; IMAX films, space shows, and certain special exhibits cost extra; ☎212/769-5100, ⊛www.amnh.org. #B or #C to 81st Street–Museum of Natural History.

An enormous complex of buildings full of fossils, gems, skeletons, and other natural specimens, along with a wealth of man-made artifacts from indigenous cultures worldwide, the **American Museum of Natural History** is one of the best and largest museums of its kind

On the first floor, the **Hall of Gems and Minerals** includes some strikingly beautiful crystals – not least the Star of India, the largest blue sapphire ever found. More captivating, however, is the recently renovated **Milstein Hall of Ocean Life**, whose centerpiece is a 94-foot-long model of a blue whale – the largest animal that ever lived – suspended from the ceiling in a dive position. The highlight of the second (entry-level) floor is the **Hall of African Mammals** – don't miss (though how can you?) the life-sized family of elephants in the center of the room.

The fourth floor is almost entirely taken up by the wildly popular **Dinosaur Exhibit**; covering five spacious, well-lit, and well-designed halls, it is the largest collection in the world, with more than 120 specimens on display.

Back on the first floor, across from the Hall of Biodiversity, lies the first installation of the **Rose Center for Earth and Space**: the Hall of Planet Earth, containing the Dynamic Earth Globe, where visitors seated below the globe are able to watch the earth via satellite go through its full rotation.

Don't miss the 400-foot-long Scales of the Universe walkway, which cleverly illustrates the immensity of the universe and our relative insignificance within it. On the floor below is the Hall of the Universe, a permanent exhibition about mankind's astrophysical discoveries.

Lastly, one of the museum's greatest attractions is the **Hayden Planetarium**, which includes a state-of-the-art space theater with highly sophisticated interstellar simulations, narrated by Hollywood stars (Tues–Sun every half-hour 10.30am–4.30pm, first Fri of month last show 7pm; $26, students/seniors $20.50, children $17; includes museum admission). In the space below, the "Big Bang Experience" is a laser and lighting show that illustrates the beginnings of the universe, while the Cosmic Pathway walks you through a study of thirteen billion years of evolution in the skies.

Riverside Park and Riverside Drive

At the western edge of 72nd Street, Riverside Park and Riverside Drive begin. **Riverside Drive** winds north, flanked by palatial townhouses and multistory apartment buildings put up in the early part of the twentieth century by those not quite rich enough to compete with the folks on Fifth Avenue. A number of landmarked districts lie along it, particularly in the mid-70s, mid-80s, and low-100s.

One of only eight designated scenic landmarks in New York City, **Riverside Park** is not as imposing or spacious as Central Park, though it was designed by the same team of architects and took 25 years to complete. The park is at its most narrow between 72nd and 79th, and a delightful place for a break along this stretch is the **79th Street Boat Basin**, with paths leading down to it located on either side of 79th Street at Riverside Drive. There's also a great **café here**, with basic grill food, good beer, and lots of atmosphere (see p.229). It's one of the city's loveliest spots, with views of New Jersey across the Hudson River.

Further north on Riverside Drive, between 105th and 106th streets, is a lovely block of historic apartments. It begins with 330 Riverside Drive, now the **Riverside Study Center**, a glorious five-story Beaux-Arts house built in 1900 – note the copper mansard roof, stone balconies, and delicate iron scrollwork.

Morningside Heights

Morningside Heights, just north of the Upper West Side, is the last gasp of Manhattan's wealth before Harlem. Marked at its eastern edge by the monolithic **Cathedral Church of St John the Divine**, the area is filled with an ethnic hodgepodge of longtime residents and middle-class families of every color, alongside students and professors from the nearby, Ivy-League Columbia University.

The Cathedral Church of St John the Divine

Map 8, D1. Amsterdam Ave, at 112th. Mon–Sat 7am–6pm, Sun 7am–7pm; tours Tues–Sat at 11am, Sun 1pm; tours $5, students and seniors $4; ☎212/932-7347, Ⓦwww.stjohndivine.org. #1 to Cathedral Parkway (110th Street).

The **Cathedral Church of St John the Divine** rises from the urban landscape with a sure, solid majesty; though it's still not finished, it's nevertheless one of New York's most impressive sights.

Work on the Episcopal church began in 1892 to the specifications of a Romanesque design that, with a change of architect in 1911, became French Gothic. Work progressed quickly for a while but stopped with the outbreak of war in 1939 and only resumed again in the mid-1980s. The church declared bankruptcy in 1994, fraught with funding difficulties that led to its controversial decision in 2005 to lease out bits of the property for development – one plot went to Columbia University, the other to a private developer who's building a condominium on the southeast edge of the grounds.

Only two-thirds of the cathedral is finished, and completion isn't due until around 2050 – assuming construction goes on uninterrupted. Still, if finished, St John the Divine will be the largest cathedral structure in the world, its floor space – at 600 feet long and at the transepts 320 feet wide – big enough to swallow both the cathedrals of Notre Dame and Chartres whole.

Walking the length of the **nave**, you can see the melding of the Romanesque and Gothic styles. This blending is particularly apparent in the choir, which rises from a heavy arcade of Romanesque columns to a high, light-Gothic vaulting, the temporary dome of the crossing to someday be replaced by a tall, delicate Gothic spire.

Columbia University and north

Map 9, B9. #1 to 116th Street/Columbia University.

The **Columbia University** campus fills six blocks between Broadway and Morningside Drive from 114th to 120th streets, with its main entrance at Broadway and 116th Street (tours of the campus leave from the information office here Mon–Fri; call ☎212/854-4900 for information). It is one of the most prestigious academic institutions in the country, ranking with the other Ivy-League colleges and boasting a campus laid out in grand Beaux-Arts style. Of the buildings, the domed and colonnaded **Low Memorial Library** (built in 1902) stands center stage at the top of a wide flight of stone steps, a focus for somewhat violent demonstrations during the Vietnam War.

Riverside Church (Map 9, B8), on Riverside Drive between 120th and 121st streets (⊛www.theriversidechurch-ny.org; daily 9am–10pm, free tour following Sun 10.45am service), is one of the city's most progressive churches, with a long history of promoting political dissent and welcoming worshipers of all faiths. At the top of its French Gothic Revival tower is the largest **carillon** in the world, with 74 bells; it offers great views, but it's closed to the public until further notice. You can view the vast **sanctuary**, though, which has lovely Belgian stained-glass windows dating from the fifteenth century.

Up the block from the church at 122nd Street is **Grant's Tomb** (Map 9, B8; daily 9am–5pm; free), a Greek-style memorial and the nation's largest mausoleum, in which conquering Civil War hero and blundering President Grant really is interred with his wife, in two black-marble Napoleonic sarcophogi.

18

Harlem and northern Manhattan

The most famous African-American community in the US (and, arguably, the bedrock of twentieth-century black culture), **Harlem** is known for the 1920s musical and literary explosion referred to as the Harlem Renaissance. Local legends such as Billie Holiday and Langston Hughes were at their prime during this time, and their achievements still linger, inseparable from the place even today. During the postwar years, however, Harlem declined, languishing as a low-rent, high-crime neighborhood, and earning a reputation for racial tension and urban decay. Today, it's a far less dangerous area than its reputation suggests – indeed, pockets of it are among Manhattan's more up-and-coming places.

Continuing northwest, **Hamilton Heights** is largely residential; the old Federalist mansion of Alexander Hamilton is the one sight worth going out of your way to visit here, but call first to make sure it's open, as there's been talk of moving the house to a nearby park. Further uptown, Washington Heights is a Dominican neighborhood with little in the way of attractions. You may still want to pass through it to see The Cloisters, a lovely pastiche of medieval monasteries at the top end of Manhattan that holds some of the Metropolitan Museum's best works of medieval art.

125th Street and below

The working center of Harlem, **125th Street** between St Nicholas and Fifth avenues serves as the neighborhood's main commercial and retail drag. If you take the #2 and #3 trains to 125th Street–Malcolm X Boulevard, you'll be well positioned to take a short walking tour of the area. Head west and you'll soon come to the unmissable **Adam Clayton Powell, Jr. State Office Building**, a looming concrete landmark whose plaza has a small visitor-information kiosk (Mon–Fri 9am–6pm, Sat & Sun 10am–6pm) where you can get advice about what to see and do (and hear and eat) in the area.

Across the street stands the **Studio Museum in Harlem**, at no. 144 (Map 9, D8; Wed–Fri & Sun noon–6pm, Sat 10am–6pm; suggested donation $7, students and seniors $3, under-12s free, first Sat of month free; ☎212/864-4500, ⓦwww.studiomuseum.org), an exhibition space dedicated to contemporary African-American painting, photography, and sculpture. The permanent collection is displayed on a rotating basis and includes works by Harlem Renaissance–era photographer James Van Der Zee, and paintings and sculpture by postwar artists.

A block further on, at no. 253, is the **Apollo Theater** (Map 9, D8; ☎212/531-5300, ⓦwww.apollotheater.com), which, though not much to look at from the outside, was from the 1930s to the 1970s the center of black entertainment in New York City and northeastern America. Almost all the great figures of jazz and blues played here along with singers, comedians, and dancers. Past winners of its renowned Amateur Night have included Ella Fitzgerald, Billie Holiday, The Jackson Five, Sarah Vaughan, Marvin Gaye, and James Brown. The Apollo offers daily one-hour tours (call for times ☎212/531-5337), but it's better to put your tour admission of $16–18 toward seeing a concert here.

South of 125th Street, there's a charming **historic district** full of well-preserved brownstones from 119th to 125th streets between Malcolm X Boulevard (called Lenox Avenue on this strip) and Mount Morris Park West. A number of good **cafés** lie in this – admittedly the most gentrified – section of Harlem, including *Settepani*, 196 Lenox Ave, at 120th St, and *Society*, 2104 Frederick Douglass Blvd, at 114th St (see p.204).

Above 125th Street

Above 125th Street, Seventh Avenue is known as **Adam Clayton Powell, Jr. Boulevard**, a broad sweep pushing north between low-built houses that allow the sky to break through. As with the rest of Harlem, the boulevard shows years of decline in its graffiti-splattered walls and storefronts

Sunday gospel

Gospel music tours are big business in Harlem, and while they're often pricey, they usually cover transportation uptown and brunch afterwards. A reliable company is **Harlem Spirituals** (☎212/391-0900, ⊛www.harlemspirituals.com), whose five-hour gospel brunch tour will set you back $89 per adult and $69 per child. In lieu of an organized excursion, you can easily go it on your own, however. The choir at the **Abyssinian Baptist Church** is arguably the best in Harlem, but others of note include those at the **Metropolitan Baptist Church**, 151 W 128th St, at Powell Blvd (☎212/663-8990), and **Mother AME Zion Church**, 140–146 W 137th St, between Malcolm X and Powell blvds (☎212/234-1544). Keep in mind that worship is taken seriously here, so dress accordingly.

punctuated by demolished lots. However, the recent skyrocketing of real-estate prices throughout Manhattan has led to some renovation along its length.

At 132 W 138th St stands the **Abyssinian Baptist Church** (Map 9, D6), noted primarily because of its long-time minister, the ubiquitous Reverend Powell, who was instrumental in the 1930s in forcing the white-owned stores of Harlem to employ the African-Americans who ensured their economic survival. Later, Powell became the first African-American on the city council, then New York's first black representative in Congress, sponsoring the country's first minimum-wage law.

Strivers' Row

Map 9, D6. #B or #C to 135th Street.

The blocks of 138th and 139th streets between Adam Clayton Powell, Jr. and Frederick Douglass boulevards are lined with what many consider to be the finest **row houses** in Manhattan. They were designed in the 1890s for well-to-do whites by a trio of architects including Stanford White (of Washington Square Arch fame) but got their nickname, **Strivers' Row**, in the 1920s, when they came to be choice residences for ambitious African-American professionals. None of them are open for public viewing, but they're beautiful to see from the outside; past occupants include musicians Eubie Blake ("I'm Just Wild about Harry"), Scott Joplin, and Fletcher Henderson.

Schomburg Center for Research in Black Culture

Map 000, 000. 515 Malcolm X Blvd, at 135th. Mon–Wed noon–8pm, Thurs & Fri 11am–6pm, Sat 10am–5pm; ☎212/491-2200. #B or #C to 135th Street.

The **Schomburg** is by far the best place in the city to learn about New York's African-American history. The center has been part of the New York Public Library since 1926, but the core of its formidable collection of works on paper (prints, books, pamphlets, manuscripts, letters, and the like) was formed during the decades prior to that by Arthur Schomburg, a Caribbean-born bibliophile and historian who was active in the Harlem Renaissance. Works you might see – in sleek new galleries – range from documents signed by eighteenth-century Haitian revolutionary Toussaint L'Ouverture to the personal papers of Malcolm X (one recent exhibit showed what the civil rights leader had in his pockets when he was assassinated at the nearby Audubon Ballroom). Well worth a stop.

Hamilton Heights and Washington Heights

Running along Convent Avenue to City College in the 130s, the **Hamilton Heights Historic District** was populated during the Depression (a period also known locally as the Harlem Renaissance for the flowering of African-American literature and visual art that occurred) by upwardly-mobile black professionals. The Heights' greatest historic lure has long been **Hamilton Grange National Memorial**, the 1798 home of Alexander Hamilton, the country's influential first Secretary of the Treasury (and face on the $10 bill). As of this writing, it's located at 287 Convent Ave, at 142nd St, but it's been closed to the public in anticipation of a move to nearby St Nicholas Park (call ☎212/666-1640 for updates).

Washington Heights is the rather overarching name given to most of the northern tip of Manhattan; though it spans the majority of ground between 145th and 200th streets, it offers only a couple of stopoffs. The **Hispanic Society of America**, on Audubon Terrace between 155th and 156th (Map 9, B4; Tues–Sat 10am–4.30pm, Sun 1–4pm; free; ☎212/926-2234, ⊛www.hispanicsociety.org), contains one of the largest collections of Spanish art outside of Spain, with works by masters such as Goya, El Greco, and Velázquez, and more than 6000 decorative works of art. The **Morris–Jumel Mansion**, at 65 Jumel Terrace, between 160th and Edgecombe (Map 9, C3; Wed–Sun 10am–4pm; $4, students and seniors

$3; ☎212/923-8008, ⓦwww.morrisjumel.org), is another uptown surprise. Cornered in its garden, the mansion, with its proud Georgian outlines faced with a later Federal portico, forms a sharp contrast to the low-end tenement housing that surrounds it.

The Cloisters

Tues–Sun: March–Oct 9.30am–5.15pm, Nov–Feb 9.30am–4.45pm; suggested donation $20, seniors $15, students $10; includes same-day admission to the Metropolitan Museum; ☎212/923-3700. #A to 190th Street.

The Cloisters, a convincing reconstruction of a medieval monastery made from pieces of five European buildings, sits on a hilltop in Fort Tryon Park and holds a number of important pieces from the Metropolitan Museum's collection of **medieval art**. Unequivocally, visiting The Cloisters is a must, and if you're game for riding up on the subway, you'll find an additional reward in the park itself: the stone-walled promenade overlooking the Hudson River and English-style garden makes for a sweepingly romantic spot (and a good place for a bite to eat; see p.232).

Starting from the entrance hall and working counterclockwise, the collection is laid out in roughly chronological order. First off is the simplicity of the **Romanesque Hall**, featuring French remnants such as an arched limestone doorway dating to 1150 and a thirteenth-century portal from a monastery in Burgundy. The frescoed **Spanish Fuentidueña Chapel** is dominated by a huge, domed twelfth-century apse from Segovia and immediately induces a reverential hush. Hall and chapel form a corner on one of the prettiest of the five cloisters here, **St Guilhelm**, ringed by strong Corinthian-style columns that are topped by carved capitals with floral designs from thirteenth-century southern France.

The highlight of the collection, however, is the **Unicorn Tapestries** (ca.1500, Netherlands), which are brilliantly alive with color, observation, and medieval allegory, as all seven have been repaired, restored, and rehung in a refurbished gallery with new lighting. The tapestries depict a hunt for the mythical unicorn that is killed and then magically brought back to life, meant to symbolize both the resurrection of Christ and the courtly transformation of a lover into a bridegroom – presumably after having been hunted down and tamed by his lady.

19

The outer boroughs

Manhattan is a hard act to follow, and the four outer boroughs – **Brooklyn**, **Queens**, **the Bronx**, and **Staten Island** – inevitably pale in comparison. But while they lack the glamour of Manhattan, and life in them, essentially residential, is less overtly dynamic, they all offer unexpected and refreshing perspectives on the city.

Most visitors never set foot off Manhattan, but if you have more than a few days there's much out here to be recommended. Brooklyn has salubrious **Brooklyn Heights** and beautiful **Prospect Park**, along with the evocatively rundown, carnivalesque seaside resort of **Coney Island**. Queens features the bustling Greek community of **Astoria** as well as **Flushing Meadows**, a vast park that played host to the 1939 and 1964 world's fairs. The Bronx has in recent years nearly conquered its reputation as a vast danger zone; the notorious **South Bronx** – whose highlight is **Yankee Stadium** – has been largely rehabilitated, and the borough contains one of the country's best **zoos** and **botanical gardens**. For information on taking a trip on the **Staten Island Ferry**, which affords a grand view of New York Harbor as well as the downtown skyline, see p.22.

Subways and buses

Be warned that the outer boroughs are much larger than Manhattan, and to get to some of the highlights you'll have to take various **subways and buses** in succession. It can be a long haul, but you'll grow to appreciate the MTA's ability to connect vastly separated areas. Make sure you're familiarized with the transit system by studying "City transportation" (see p.17) before you set out. **Taxi cabs** can be taken to and from any borough, though remember they are harder to find the farther you are from Manhattan, when a **car service** might be your best bet. For car service numbers, dial ☏411 or consult ⓦwww.magicyellow.com.

Brooklyn

Brooklyn's most visited and most attractive neighborhood is **Brooklyn Heights**, where the tree-lined streets seem a world away from Manhattan's hustle and bustle, even as they look directly onto the Financial District across the river. More specific reasons to come to Brooklyn are the **Brooklyn Museum** and the **Botanic Garden**, a half-dozen subway stops past Brooklyn Heights to the east. These adjoin Frederick Law Olmsted and Calvert Vaux's **Prospect Park**, which for many is an improvement on their more famous bit of landscaping, Central Park. Aficionados of seedy seaside resorts will love the tacky – and thoroughly fun – **Coney Island**. And anyone visiting New York for contemporary art should head north to gallery-dotted **Williamsburg**, a healthy mix of independent bookstores, boutiques, and restaurants.

Brooklyn Heights

Brooklyn Heights, arguably the most coveted section of the borough, is one of New York City's stateliest neighborhoods, composed of brownstone houses along narrow streets

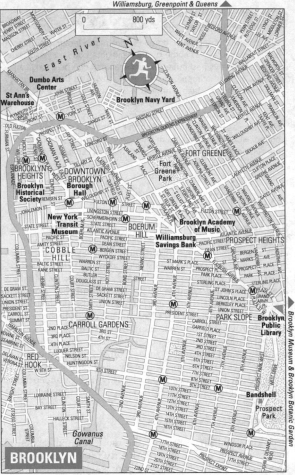

0　　　　800 yds

Dumbo Arts Center

St Ann's Warehouse

Brooklyn Navy Yard

FORT GREENE

Fort Greene Park

BROOKLYN HEIGHTS

DOWNTOWN BROOKLYN

Brooklyn Historical Society

Borough Hall

New York Transit Museum

BOERUM HILL

Brooklyn Academy of Music

Williamsburg Savings Bank

PROSPECT HEIGHTS

COBBLE HILL

CARROLL GARDENS

PARK SLOPE

Brooklyn Public Library

RED HOOK

Gowanus Canal

Bandshell

Prospect Park

160 **BROOKLYN**

19

THE OUTER BOROUGHS

Brooklyn Museum & Brooklyn Botanic Garden

that reveal the occasional cobblestoned mews. Built as a suburb for nineteenth-century bankers, decades later it had a literary cachet to rival that of the West Village, as home to Truman Capote, Norman Mailer, and Arthur Miller; Bob Dylan even named its main thoroughfare, **Montague Street**, in his song "Tangled Up in Blue." The most scenic way to get here is by walking from lower Manhattan over the **Brooklyn Bridge** (see p.46 for directions); the best trains are the #A or #C to High Street or the #2 or #3 to Clark Street.

Lined with Federal-style brick buildings, the streets of Brooklyn Heights are a pleasure to stroll along – particularly **Henry Street**, which leads into the oldest section on the north edge. The unassuming but perfectly preserved wooden house at **24 Middagh St**, at Willow, dates to 1824, making it the district's oldest. Two blocks south, on Orange Street, between Hicks and Henry, the simple **Plymouth Church of the Pilgrims** (Map 4, L7) was the one-time preaching base of Henry Ward Beecher, abolitionist and campaigner for women's rights.

One block further along, on the corner of Pierrepont, the **Herman Behr House**, a chunky Romanesque-Revival mansion, has been, successively, a hotel, a brothel, and a Franciscan monastery (it was the brothers who added the horrific canopy); today it is a private apartment building. East on Pierrepont, stop into the 1844 **First Unitarian Church**, notable for its exquisite neo-Gothic interior. Across the street at no. 128, the **Brooklyn Historical Society** (Map 4, M8; Wed–Sun noon– 5pm; $6, students and seniors $4, under 12 free; ☎718/222- 4111, ⓦwww.brooklynhistory.org) catalogues the borough's fortunes in several moving, well-researched displays.

The Promenade

Walk west on any of the streets between Clark and Remsen and you'll reach the **Promenade** (Map 4, K7; more formally known as the Esplanade), a boardwalk with one of the most

spectacular views in all of New York. It's hard to take your eyes off the skyline, the water, the Brooklyn Bridge, and the Statue of Liberty in the distance, but do turn around and notice between the trees the striking homes set back modestly from the walkway. Were it not for the efforts of locals in the mid-1940s, this would now be another stretch of the Brooklyn–Queens Expressway. Protests forced the highway to run below the neighborhood, just above the waterfront and beneath the Promenade, which was finished in 1951.

Follow State Street back from the Promenade and onto Boerum Place, where, at the corner of Schermerhorn, the **New York Transit Museum** (Map 4, N9; Tues–Fri 10am–4pm, Sat & Sun noon–5pm; $5, children and seniors $3; ℡718/694-1600, ⓦwww.mta.info/mta/museum) occupies an abandoned 1930s subway station. It holds more than one hundred years of memorabilia, including some wonderful trolleys and buses dating from the early 1800s. An exhibition on the city's hundred-year-old subway system offers photographs, maps, refurbished vintage train cars, and a working signal tower. Check out the jewelry and accessories fashioned from old subway tokens in the gift shop.

DUMBO

Following a lightning-speed gentrification process, the streets of the once-desolate warehouse district now known as **DUMBO** (Down Under the Manhattan Bridge Overpass) are a patchwork of asphalt, cobblestones, and railroad tracks, lined with million-dollar condos and a handful of cool **restaurants and bars**. Just north of Brooklyn Heights, directly under the Brooklyn Bridge, **Empire–Fulton Ferry State Park** is a welcome backyard for residents of this area between the Brooklyn and Manhattan bridges. The closest subway is the #F to York Street, which drops you on the northern edge of the neighborhood.

The cultural anchor for the area is the **DUMBO Arts Center** (Map 4, L5), hosting five or six shows yearly; it's typically open Thursday to Monday. It also organizes the huge **Dumbo Art Under the Bridge Festival**, one weekend in September or

October (see p.308). In addition, check out the schedule at **St Ann's Warehouse** (Map 4, K5), an intimate space for avant-garde theater and concerts.

The Brooklyn Academy of Music

30 Lafayette Ave, between Ashland Place and St Felix St. ☎718/636-4100, ⓦwww.bam.org. #B or #Q to Atlantic Ave, #2, #3, #4, or #5 to Nevins Street, or #D, #M, #N, or #R to Atlantic Ave–Pacific Street.

The **Brooklyn Academy of Music** (or just **BAM**, as it's usually called) is the oldest performing-arts center in America, established in 1859. Located on the edge of Fort Greene, a stylish, historically middle-class African-American neighborhood dominated by brownstones, BAM mounts a reliable yet daring program of world-renowned orchestras, dance troupes, and theater companies that draw visitors from all over the city – no small feat, considering Manhattanites' aversion to crossing the river. BAM's four-screen **Rose Cinemas** features new (often independent) releases, as well as rare art-house and foreign films. Check the website for what's on and when.

Prospect Park and around

Brooklyn really surpasses itself – architecturally, at any rate – in the area surrounding **Prospect Park**. A cab ride from downtown Manhattan (about $15; or you can take the #2 or #3 train to Grand Army Plaza) is well worth the price to see some excellent urban planning and a lovely green space in the middle of it all. There's a quality bike path, and lots of spots for a picnic between sightseeing destinations. The playgrounds are crammed with kids from nearby Park Slope, the handsome brownstone neighborhood off the west side that's known for being one of the city's most family-friendly.

Grand Army Plaza

In the 1860s and 1870s, Central Park architects Frederick Law Olmsted and Calvert Vaux designed **Grand Army Plaza** as a dramatic approach to their recently completed Prospect Park; it didn't take on a monumental form, however, until the 80-foot-tall **Soldiers' and Sailors' Memorial Arch** was unveiled in 1892 by John Duncan (the architect of Grant's Tomb), in tribute to the Union victory in the Civil War.

Inside the arch, bronze bas-reliefs of Abraham Lincoln (oddly disproportional) and General Ulysses S. Grant were installed in 1895, and in 1898 the fiery bronze **Victory Quadriga**, at the top of the arch, was added as the finishing touch. An internal **spiral staircase** is open only occasionally, as part of the Open House New York program (ⓦwww.ohny.org).

⑲

Prospect Park

☎718/965-8951, ⓦwww.prospectpark.org.
Energized by their success with Central Park, Olmsted and Vaux landscaped **Prospect Park** in the early 1860s. Its 585 acres are a regular meeting-place for dogs, babies, and their respective parents. There's a lake on the east side; an open meadow on the west side; and a 3.4-mile, two-lane road around the perimeter reserved for runners, cyclists, and Rollerbladers.

From the **Audubon Center** at the Boathouse on the east side (April–Nov Thurs–Sun noon–5pm; Dec–March weekends only noon–4pm; free), visitors can walk a mile-long **nature trail** through the park's restored natural environment. Others can take **electric boat trips** ($5, children $3) on the placid **Lullwater Lake**. The **Prospect Park Zoo** (Nov–March daily 10am–4.30pm; April–Oct Mon–Fri 10am–5pm, Sat & Sun 10am–5.30pm; $6, seniors $2.25, under-12s $2) is not a bad place to while away the time, with its richly restored **1912 carousel** (rides $1). The park's highlight, however, is the ninety-acre **Long Meadow**, which cuts through its center. On warm weekends you can find soccer, volleyball, and even cricket matches, families hosting picnics, and couples reading or romantically entwined.

Brooklyn Museum

200 Eastern Parkway. Wed–Fri 10am–5pm, Sat & Sun 11am–6pm, first Sat of every month 11am–11pm; $8, students and seniors $4; ☏718/638-5000, ⊛www.brooklynmuseum.org. #2 or #3 to Eastern Parkway–Brooklyn Museum.

Though the second-largest art museum in New York City, the **Brooklyn Museum** seems forever doomed to stand in the shadow of the Met (see p.120). That said, it is a jewel in and of itself, notable both for its excellent collection of Egyptian art and its sometimes controversial **contemporary shows**. The first Saturday of every month sees the grand building open till late, with live music and free admission – it's a very popular social scene for a mix of Brooklynites.

A trip through the museum's five floors of exhibits requires considerable selectivity. The **permanent collection** includes ancient relics from the Middle East, traditional African, American, and Pacific crafts, paintings, and sculpture, and six evocative period rooms, ranging from an Art-Deco Park Avenue apartment to a nineteenth-century Moorish smoking room from John D. Rockefeller's estate.

The delicately carved stone "**Brooklyn Black Head**" of the Ptolemaic period, the museum's crown jewel, is one of 1200 objects in the authoritative **Ancient Egyptian Art collection**, one of the largest outside Egypt. The collection is nicely complemented by smaller galleries of Assyrian, Sumerian, and other ancient Middle Eastern art.

One floor up, the **Feminist Art** galleries, opened in 2007, has as its centerpiece Judy Chicago's ceramic and textile installation *The Dinner Party*, which was shown here for the first time in the early 1980s. On the top story, the extremely varied **American painting and sculpture** collection includes Georgia O'Keeffe's sensual 1948 paean to the borough, *Brooklyn Bridge*, bucolic paintings by members of the **Hudson River School**, and works by Winslow Homer and John Singer Sargent. In addition, the museum's Rodin collection, about fifty pieces of vibrant sculpture, is on long-term display in the rotunda.

Brooklyn Botanic Garden

1000 Washington Ave. Mid-March–Oct Tues–Fri 8am–6pm, Sat & Sun 10am–6pm, Nov–mid-March Tues–Fri 8am–4.30pm, Sat & Sun 10am–4.30pm; $8, students and seniors $4, free all day Tues, Sat before noon, and weekdays mid-Nov–Feb; ☎718/623-7200, ⓦwww .bbg.org. #1 or #2 to Eastern Parkway–Brooklyn Museum.

One of the most enticing park spaces in the city, the **Brooklyn Botanic Garden**, just behind the Brooklyn Museum, is smaller but more immediately likeable than its rival in the Bronx (see p.176). Plants from around the world occupy 22 gardens and exhibits, all sumptuous but not overplanted. March brings color to **Daffodil Hill**, while April sees the cherry trees bloom in the **Japanese Garden**, laid out in 1914. The **Rose Garden** opens in the early summer, elaborate **water-lily ponds** are at their best in late summer, and the fall colors in the **Rock Garden** are striking. On a winter visit, enjoy the warmth of the glittering **Palm House**, the **Tropical Pavilion**, and a conservatory filled with orchids and the largest collection of **bonsai trees** in the West. A gift shop stocks exotic plants, bulbs, and seeds.

Coney Island

Accessible to anyone for the price of a subway ride, the beach-front amusement spot of **Coney Island** has long given work-ing-class New Yorkers the kind of holiday they just couldn't get otherwise. Dubbed an "Electric Eden" in the late nine-teenth century and once the home of folk icon Woody Guth-rie, it's now boosted by arts organizations and exudes a certain rickety charm. It's a weird mix of neo–freak shows, blaring hip-hop, and state-of-the-art-circa-1985 rides – though in the future it may have a significantly more modern ambiance, as developers are eyeing the area. See for yourself by taking the subway to the retro-style Stillwell Avenue train station (last stop on the #D, #F, #N, and #Q).

The **beach** can be overwhelmingly crowded on hot days, and it's never the cleanest place in or out of the water. In the off-season, the wind-blown amusements and shuttered hot-dog stands can have a bittersweet, even creepy feel. In short, you have to be in the right frame of mind – one that might appreciate the annual **Mermaid Parade**, for instance, held on the first Saturday of summer (see p.307). It's one of the oddest small-town festivals in the country, where paraders dress (barely) as mermaids, King Neptunes, and other sea-dwellers. Later in the summer, the great indie **Siren Music Festival** draws crowds, as does the 4th of July **hot-dog-eating contest** at *Nathan's*.

Behind the **boardwalk** (where beachgoers promenade in bizarre outfits, whether or not there's a parade going on), the amusement area comprises several independently managed parks. Nearly all the children's rides are in Deno's Wonder Wheel Park, where you might want to buy a pack of ten tickets for $20 (otherwise individual tickets are for sale as well). The 1920 **Wonder Wheel** ($5, plus a free children's ticket to the New York Aquarium; see p.167) is a must; it's surpassed only by the London Eye in height, and it's the only Ferris wheel on which two-thirds of the cars slide on serpentine tracks, shifting position as it makes its slow circle. The most iconic ride at Coney Island, however, is the creaky wooden **Cyclone** roller coaster ($6, $4 for a repeat ride). Built in 1927, it's one of the oldest wooden roller coasters in the US and listed on the National Register of Historic Places. It's not for the faint of heart – as you wait in the snaking line, you can see the cars briefly lose contact with the metal rails.

On the west end of Coney Island, KeySpan Park, the scenic oceanside home of the minor-league **Brooklyn Cyclones** (☎718/449-8497, ⊛www.brooklyncyclones.com), is an intimate, inexpensive place to take in a baseball game.

East down the boardwalk, halfway to Brighton Beach, is the seashell-shaped **New York Aquarium** (hours vary by season; $12, seniors and children 2–12 $8; ☎718/265-FISH, ⊛www.nyaquarium.com). Run by the Wildlife Conservation Society, which also administers New York's four excellent zoos, the aquarium features walruses, sea lions, otters, and seahorses among more than eight thousand creatures from all over the world. It's worth a visit, especially during feeding hours and "animal-enrichment sessions," when zookeepers run games and challenges to keep the animals alert, both physically and mentally.

Brighton Beach

East along the boardwalk from Coney Island, at Brooklyn's southernmost end, is **Brighton Beach**, a formerly affluent seaside resort of its own. Once referred to as "Little Odessa," it's home to the country's largest community of immigrants from Russia and the former Soviet states, who began relocating here in the 1970s.

The main attractions of Brighton Beach are the **restaurants**, which really heat up each evening, becoming a near-parody of a rowdy Russian night out with lots of food, loud live music, glass-clinking, and free-flowing chilled vodka. The most popular spots are *National*, *Oceana*, and *Odessa*, all on Brighton Beach Avenue, at nos. 273, 1029, and 1113, respectively.

Williamsburg

Step off the #L train at the Bedford Avenue stop and you'll be in the heart of **Williamsburg**, a self-consciously hip pocket in north Brooklyn largely populated by artists and various scenesters. Many dilapidated warehouses between North 12th Street and the Williamsburg Bridge have been put to creative use, and the face of the neighborhood changes frequently. Indeed, with easy access to Manhattan and excellent waterfront views, it's not hard to see why this area has exploded.

Williamsburg also boasts more than a dozen **contemporary art galleries**, ranging in ambiance from ultra-professional to makeshift, and run by an international coterie of artists; the most influential is Pierogi, 177 N 9th St (Thurs–Mon 11am– 6pm; ☎718/599-2144, ⊛www.pierogi2000.com).

You can tour the **Brooklyn Brewery**, 79 N 11th St (☎718/486-7422, ⊛www.brooklynbrewery.com), on Saturdays at 1, 2, 3, and 4pm, or hang out in their tasting room for live music at happy hour (Fri 6–11pm). Around 1900, nearly fifty breweries operated in Brooklyn, but the last of these, Schaefer and Rheingold, closed in 1976. Brooklyn Brewery was founded in 1987, but didn't actually set up in its namesake borough until 1996; since then, it's been a major hit.

As waterfront high-rises spring up, a tiny treasure like **Grand Ferry Park** becomes all the more valuable. Look west toward the water and let the old Pfizer smokestack lead you to one of the few waterfront parks left in Brooklyn; here you'll find a great view of the **Williamsburg Bridge**, which, if you so choose, you can walk across into the Lower East Side.

Queens

If Brooklyn, with its strong neighborhood identities and elegant architecture, represents the old, historic city, then aesthetically challenged, sprawling **Queens** puts the "new" in New York. Some 46 percent of the borough's 2.2 million residents hail from more than 150 foreign countries, bringing an incomparable **diversity** and dynamism to the city.

While here, you can travel from industrial Long Island City and Greek Astoria through Irish Woodside to Indian and Latino Jackson Heights and finally Asian Flushing, which can feel as suburban as Long Island on some days and as exotic as Hong Kong on others. You'll find a few underrated **museums** and no shortage of **delicious foods** – just follow the #7 train, aka the "International Express," which chugs through most of the borough: Turkish breads, Romanian sausage, Indonesian noodles, Argentine steak, and Indian roti await.

Finally, in addition to the city's two major airports, **JFK and LaGuardia**, Queens is where baseball fans will find **Shea Stadium**, home to the New York Mets.

Long Island City

Long Island City provides the first view of Queens for most visitors. Here, the #7 (on the south edge, at Vernon Blvd) and the #N and #W (farther north, at Queensboro Plaza) trains cut above ground after crossing from Manhattan; look west for a majestic view of Midtown, particularly in late afternoon, when the sun filters through the skyscrapers. Marked by its elevated trains and highways, Long Island City is not particularly pretty, but it's nevertheless home to some **innovative museums**. Chief among these are the P.S.1 Contemporary Art Center and the Noguchi Museum.

P.S.1 Contemporary Art Center

22–25 Jackson Ave, at 46th Ave. Thurs–Mon noon–6pm; suggested donation $5, students and seniors $2; ☎718/784-2084, ⓦwww.ps1 .org. #7 to 45th Road–Court Square or #E or #V to 23rd Street–Ely Avenue.

Founded in 1971 and now affiliated with MoMa (see p.98), **P.S.1** is one of the most consistently exciting places to see new art in New York; its stately old public-school halls are often filled with site-specific installations, odd videos, and more. Saturday afternoons in July and August, the museum hosts the popular "Warm Up" music series, featuring excellent DJs and live performers; this is also the only time in the summer you can see James Turrell's subtle and mesmerizing light installation *Meeting*, on the top floor.

Fisher Landau Center for Art

38-27 30th St. Mon & Thurs–Sun noon–5pm; free; ☎718/937-0727, ⓦwww.flcart.org. #7 to Queensboro Plaza, #E or #R to Queens Plaza, or #N or #W to 39th Avenue.

The chronically overlooked **Fisher Landau Center** houses an awesome personal collection of late twentieth-century greats and is definitely worth a detour. You'll likely have the place to yourself as you contemplate works by Jenny Holzer, Jasper Johns, Matthew Barney, and others.

Noguchi Museum

9-01 33rd Rd, at Vernon Blvd. Wed–Fri 10am–5pm, Sat & Sun 11am–
6pm; $10, students and seniors $5; ☎718/204-7088, ⓦwww
.noguchi.org. #N or #W to Broadway, #F to Queensbridge–21st
Street, or #Q103 bus from Vernon Blvd west of P.S.1.

The **Noguchi Museum** is devoted to the works of Japanese-
American abstract sculptor Isamu Noguchi, famous for his
memorial in Miami to the astronauts who died in the *Chal-
lenger* explosion, as well as the infamous cube at Astor Place
(see p.65). It's a serene, restful space, built around a garden
filled with Noguchi's stone sculptures, while the surrounding
galleries show off both his familiar furniture designs and more
obscure works, such as proposed playground layouts. On the
downside, getting to the museum can be something of a chore:
check the museum's website for detailed instructions. To make
the trip more worthwhile, walk across the street for a visit to
the funky **Socrates Sculpture Park**, a great agglomeration of
ever-changing work along the waterfront.

Astoria

Astoria is known for two things: filmmaking and the largest
single concentration of Greeks outside of Greece itself. Until
the early 1930s, Astoria was the cinematic capital of the world
– Paramount had its studios here until the lure of Hollywood's
reliable weather left the neighborhood empty and disused.
That's how it remained until recently, when Hollywood's
stranglehold on the industry weakened and interest – in New
York in general and Astoria in particular – was renewed, along
with the likes of the **Kaufman–Astoria Studios**, at 34-12
36th St (closed to the public), where iconic New York shows
like *Sesame Street* and *Law & Order* are produced.

Greek Astoria stretches from Ditmars Boulevard in the
north down to Broadway, roughly from 31st Street (where the
#N and #W trains run) across to Steinway (a stop on the #R
and #V lines). Although new waves of immigrants – Bengali,
Egyptian, Brazilian, Croatian, and more – are adding to the

mix, it's still obvious that some 100,000 Greeks live here, due to the large number of **restaurants** and patisseries. *Agnanti* (see p.235) is one of the best places for a sit-down dinner, while there are numerous places to get good coffee (see p.205).

The American Museum of the Moving Image

35th Ave at 36th St. Wed & Thurs 11am–5pm, Fri 11am–8pm, Sat & Sun 11am–6.30pm; $10, students and seniors $7.50, under-18s $5, Fri free 4–8pm; ☏718/784-0077, ⓦwww.ammi.org. #N or #W to 36th Avenue or #R or #V to Steinway Street.

Part of the old Paramount complex is dedicated to the **American Museum of the Moving Image**, a stellar collection for anyone interested in movie history. See posters, film stills (beginning with Eadweard Muybridge's galloping horse), antiquated equipment, vintage video games, and old adventure serials in "Tut's Fever Movie Palace." On Friday evenings and all day Saturday and Sunday, the AMMI shows classic and occasionally cult films (often included with admission).

Shea Stadium and Flushing Meadows–Corona Park

Take the #7 train to Willets Point for **Shea Stadium** (see p.294), home of the New York Mets. The Beatles famously played here in 1965 (whence the concept of the stadium rock concert), but baseball's the thing between April and October – the Mets have a solid and loyal fan base. See Chapter 29, "Sports and outdoor activities," for ticket details.

South from Shea, you'll easily find your way to **Flushing Meadows–Corona Park**, an enormous swath of green centered on large Meadow Lake, where the beautiful **Dragon Boat Festival** can be witnessed in mid-August every year. The **New York Hall of Science**, 46th Avenue at 111th Street (hours vary by season; $11, seniors and under-17s $8; ☏718/699-0005, ⓦwww.nyhallsci.org), is a concrete and stained-glass structure retained from the 1964 World's Fair (the best remaining structures are deeper in the park). Kids will love the interactive displays, though it can be exhausting for adults. The adjacent **Queens Zoo**, occupying a Buckminster Fuller dome, features exclusively North American animals.

The main reason to visit the park, however, is to see two other World's Fair relics: the Unisphere and the Queens Museum of Art. The **Unisphere** is a 140-foot-high, stainless-steel globe that weighs 380 tons – probably the main reason why it's never been moved. The orb, which you may have seen when you came in from the airport, was declared an official New York City landmark in 1995.

Urban planner Robert Moses's "Versailles of America" vision fans out from the Unisphere in a rather severe array of paths, pools, and blockish buildings. The scenery, however, is softened a bit on sunny days, when the park is swarming with kids on bikes and Rollerblades; you can rent a bike yourself (from kiosks at the north and east entrances) to get around the vast space.

Queens Museum of Art

In Flushing Meadows–Corona Park. Sept–June Wed–Fri 10am–5pm, Sat & Sun noon–5pm, July & Aug Wed, Thurs, Sat & Sun noon–6pm, Fri noon–8pm; suggested donation $5, seniors and children $2.50; ☏718/592-9700, ⓦwww.queensmuseum.org. #7 to 111th Street or Willets Point.

Housed in a 1939 World's Fair building that served briefly as the first home of the United Nations, the **Queens Museum of Art** mixes modern art with vintage photos and other items from the borough's history. The must-see here, though, is the **Panorama of the City of New York**, which was built for the 1964 fair. With a scale of one inch to one hundred feet, the panorama is the world's largest architectural model; its 895,000 buildings – as well as rivers, harbors, bridges, and even tiny planes buzzing into the airports – were scrupulously overhauled and updated in 2006.

Guided tours of the museum (Sat & Sun 3.30pm, included with museum entrance) show off some nifty new sound and light effects.

The Bronx

The city's northernmost borough, **the Bronx**, for a long time held the prize as New York's toughest and most crime-ridden district. After a wave of arson in the slums in the 1970s – followed by hard-core images in popular books and movies (*Fort Apache, the Bronx*; *Bonfire of the Vanities*) – outsiders considered it a no-go zone, even after urban renewal was under way. Its poorer reaches still suffer from urban deprivation, but almost all of the borough has undergone a civic and economic transformation. Part of the rough-and-tumble South Bronx has even earned the realtor-approved neighborhood sobriquet of "SoBro."

The South Bronx and Yankee Stadium

A trip to the borough on the elevated #4 train affords a good general view of the **South Bronx**, if you haven't got time to go visiting individual neighborhoods – and there's not much reason to do so in any case. The area consists of the segment of the Bronx south of Fordham Road, yet most visitors come here for **Yankee Stadium** (first stop on the #B and #D subways after leaving Manhattan, and the third such stop on the #4), home to the New York Yankees baseball team. Baseball fanatics can take an hour-long **tour** of the stadium that includes field access, visits to the dugout and press box, and a look at memorials to Babe Ruth, Joe DiMaggio, and other baseball greats (noon daily; $15, seniors and children $8; ☏718/579-4531, ⊛www .yankees.com); a new stadium is scheduled to open in 2009. If you'd rather just **see a game**, there are plenty throughout the spring, summer, and early fall; see Chapter 29 for ticket info.

Central Bronx and Belmont

As far as real Italian flavor is concerned, the **Belmont** section of the Bronx makes Little Italy look like Disneyland. **Arthur**

Avenue is the neighborhood's main thoroughfare, a mixture of tenements and clapboard houses that is home to one of the largest segments of New York's Italian community. There has been a small influx of other ethnic groups – most notably Haitians, Mexicans, and Albanian Slavs – but the staunch Italian community, where everyone knows everyone else (and asks about their mother), is still the dominant force.

There's no better part of the Bronx if you want to eat, particularly if you're on your way to the zoo. But choose **restaurants** on Arthur Avenue with care: swanky *Mario's* (allegedly the real setting of a pivotal scene in *The Godfather*), at no. 2342, is popular but pricey; you're better off around the corner at *Roberto's*, 603 Crescent Ave. For a snack, opt for clams or oysters on the half-shell from one of the seafood stores, or get a sandwich at the *Arthur Avenue Retail Market*, no. 2331.

The Bronx Zoo

Hours vary by season; $14, seniors $12, children $10, suggested donation on Wed, rides and some exhibits additional; ☎718/367-1010, ⊛www.bronxzoo.org. #2 or #5 to West Farms Square–East Tremont Avenue. Accessible either by its main gate on Fordham Road or by a second entrance on Bronx Park South (near the closest subway stop).

The **Bronx Zoo** – arguably America's greatest zoo and certainly its largest urban one – is probably the only reason many New Yorkers from outside the borough ever travel north. Opened in 1899, it was one of the first zoos to realize that animals both looked and felt better out in the open. Today, various **simulated natural habitats** include the Congo Gorilla Forest (additional fee, varies by season) and the spectacular Tiger Mountain, where Siberian tigers roam. Otherwise, visit in spring to see the new babies (up to a thousand are born each year) or in summer, when most of the animals are on view. A nifty **carousel** with giant bugs rather than horses operates year-round ($2), and a cable car (summer only; $3), a monorail ($3), and a shuttle ($3) provide relief for tired feet – walking the entire complex can be exhausting.

New York Botanical Garden

Tues–Sun: April–Oct 10am–6pm, Nov–March 10am–5pm; $6, seniors $3, students $2, children $1, free all day Wed and Sat 10am–noon; ☎718/817-8700, ⊛www.nybg.org. #B or #D to Bedford Park Boulevard.

Across the road from the zoo's main entrance is the rear turnstile of the **New York Botanical Garden**, which, in its southernmost reaches, is as wild as anything you're likely to see upstate. Its scientific facilities include a museum, library, herbarium, and research laboratory. More cultivated stretches lie further north, near the main entrance. The Garden's centerpiece is the **Enid A. Haupt Conservatory**, a landmark Victorian crystal palace that showcases jungle and desert ecosystems, a palm court, and a fern forest, among other seasonal displays. Prices are for general admission; access to special exhibits can cost more.

Listings

Listings

Accommodation

Accommodation in New York definitely eats up the lion's share of a traveler's budget. Many hotels in the city charge $250–300 a night – some much more – with **taxes** and room charges tacked on to that. With some planning, it is possible to get a decent-sized, clean room for $150 or less, but in truth it's far easier to hunt for splurges than for bargains. Make your **reservations** as far ahead as possible (most hotels cite "supply and demand" as the main determinant of their room rate), and don't even think of calling a day ahead of your visit during the Christmas holidays or peak season (autumn), when you're likely to find everything full. Summer is a busy time as well, but you can get some surprising bargains between June and September, with rooms up to 25 percent cheaper than they are in October.

The best advice regarding **discounts** is simply to ask for them; many hotels run promotional specials or offer corporate rates, or have deals offered only through their websites. The city's official tourism and marketing group, NYC & Company (Ⓦwww.nycvisit.com), lists holiday and summer specials plus pet-friendly hotels online, and several consolidator-type sites – such as Ⓦwww.expedia.com, Ⓦwww.orbitz.com, or Ⓦwww.hoteldiscounts.com – can be good resources as well. Other alternatives include looking into **package vacations**, which offer hotel and airfare deals, or **renting an apartment** through an online listings site (see p.183).

For more extensive hotel listings and a general sense of how much a room will set you back, consult NYC & Company's free *Official Visitor Guide*, available from any of its offices or through its website.

The prices quoted in this chapter are for the lowest-priced double room in high season (autumn).

Hostels and YMCAs

Hostels and YMCAs are just about the only option for cash-strapped backpackers in New York, with dorm beds going for as little as $25 a night. YMCAs are better if you want privacy because they have private single and double rooms, though they tend to have a more institutional feel than hostels and are far more expensive. For a comprehensive listing of hostels in New York and across North America, purchase *The Hostel Handbook* (US and Canada $6, international $10; both prices include shipping) online at Ⓦ www.hostelhandbook.com or by writing to Jim Williams, *The Hostel Handbook*, 730 St Nicholas Ave, New York, NY 10031. The following, meanwhile, is a small selection of the best hostels and YMCAs in the city.

Bowery's Whitehouse Hotel of New York Map 5, H5. 340 Bowery, btw Great Jones and 2nd ☏212/477-5623, Ⓦ www.whitehousehotelofny .com. The latticework roofing on the basic, very small single ($29) and double rooms ($55) makes this place a little too public for those seeking total privacy, but it's perfect for travelers looking for a cheap bed in a great location with better-than-average security.

Center Hostel Eastside Map 6, E5. 313 W 29th St, near 8th Ave

☏212/643-0214, Ⓦ www.chelsea-centerhostel.com. Reputable, safe, and friendly, with dorm beds for $35; amenities include continental breakfast, clean sheets and blankets, and luggage storage. There's a second location on the Lower East Side; the exact address is given out only upon booking. Make reservations well in advance in high season. Cash only.

Central Park Hostel Map 8, E3. 19 W 103rd St, near Central Park West ☏212/678-0491,

Ⓦwww.centralparkhostel.com. This Upper West Side hostel has dorm beds for four, six, eight, or ten people ($26–35) – with clean shared bathrooms – as well as seven lovely studio apartments ($85–139) with kitchenettes and private baths. Lockers are available; bring a padlock. Payment in cash or traveler's checks only (unless the amount is over $100); New York State residents not allowed.

Chelsea Center Hostel & Chelsea Chelsea International Hostel Map 6, F7. 251 W 20th St, btw 7th and 8th ☎212/647-0010, ℱ727-7289, Ⓦwww.chelseahostel.com. Situated in the heart of Chelsea, this hostel is an easy walk from the West Village and Meatpacking District. Dorm rooms sleep four to six and are male- or female-only; beds (350 in all) are $30 a night with shared bath, $34 with private bath. Private rooms for two – either with a bunk bed or double bed – are $70 a night. Rooms are small, but the location is excellent. 24hr check-in. There are security guards plus a sign-in at night. Passport required.

Hosteling International – New York Map 8, C3. 891 Amsterdam Ave, at 103rd ☎212/932-2300, Ⓦwww.hinewyork.org. This historic Upper West Side building has 615 dormitory-style beds in rooms of four to twelve beds each ($30–35), and private rooms that sleep four, with one double and one bunk bed ($135 with bath, $120 without); it's $3 extra per night for nonmembers. Though the place is large, it may be heavily booked; reserve well in advance.

Jazz on the Park Map 8, E2. 36 W 106th St, at Central Park West ☎212/932-1600, ℱ932-1700, Ⓦwww.jazzhostels.com. A groovy bunkhouse, just a stone's throw from the park, with a TV/game room, rooftop barbecues, and the *Java Joint Café*. The rooms, sleeping between two and fourteen, are clean, bright, and air-conditioned. Beds cost $27–32 a night (including linens and a light breakfast); a private room is $90–200. Reservations essential June–Oct and over Christmas and New Year's. There's another Upper West Side location, *Jazz on the City*, at 201 W 95th St, ☎212/678-0323, as well as two *Jazz* hostels in Harlem: *Jazz on Lenox*, 104 W 128th St, ☎212/222-5773, and *Jazz on the Villa*, 12 W 129th St, ☎212/722-6252.

Jazz on the Town Map 6, L9. 307 E 14th St, at 2nd ☎212/228-2780, Ⓦwww.jazzhostels.com. Great location for travelers wanting to spend time in the East Village, with beds in clean, modern, four-, six-, or eight-bed dorms

ACCOMMODATION

with a/c and lockers costing from $29 to $39 a night, including tax, linen, and towels. No curfew, a TV/game room, and rooftop terrace/bar make this a good spot for partiers wanting to live New York life on the cheap.

Vanderbilt YMCA Map 7, J8. 224 E 47th St, btw 2nd and 3rd ☎212/921-2500, 🖷752-0210, 🖳www.ymcanyc.org. Three hundred and seventy clean and quiet single and double rooms with shared baths (no dorms), TVs, a/c, and room service, just five minutes' walk from Grand Central. There's a laundromat and an inexpensive restaurant on the premises, and you get to use some of the sports facilities. Singles $83, doubles $93 (bunk bed) or $110 (double bed). Reservations recommended a month in advance.

Westside YMCA Map 7, E4. 5 W 63rd St, at Central Park West ☎212/875-4100, 🖷875-4291, 🖳www.ymcanyc.org. Wonderfully situated next to Central Park and Lincoln Center, and offering air-conditioned singles and doubles, with shared or semi-private baths, from $89 to $119 per night. Deluxe rooms have new furniture, goose-down comforters, and cable TV. Free use of two pools, saunas, gym, and sports facilities.

Bed-and-breakfasts

Choosing a **B&B** can be a good way to stay right in the heart of Manhattan at a reasonably affordable price. All rooms – except for a few that we've found off the beaten path (see p.184) – are rented via the following official agencies; they all recommend making your reservations as far in advance as possible, especially for the most inexpensive rooms. In cases where landlords prefer that visitors reserve in advance rather than show up on their doorsteps, we have omitted addresses.

B&B and short-term rental agencies

Affordable New York City ☎212/533-4001, 🖳www.affordablenewyorkcity.com. Established network of 120 properties around the city, with detailed descriptions and photos provided on request. B&B accommodations – and by this they mean a bedroom in an apartment with breakfast provided, not a bed-and-breakfast inn – range from $100 to $120 (shared bath) and from $125 to $145 (private); unhosted studios go for $160 and up, one-bedrooms $175–230. Cash or traveler's checks only; four-night minimum for B&B, five for an apartment.

Bed and Breakfast Network of New York Map 5, B4. 130 Barrow St, near Washington ☎1-800/900-8134 or 212/645-8134, ⓦwww.bedandbreakfastnetny.com. Growing network with hosted singles for $75–100, doubles $110–150; prices for unhosted accommodation run

Online apartment rentals and room exchange

Another option when looking for accommodation is to **rent an apartment** directly from the unit's owner or lease holder. The sites below are your best bets.

cyberrentals.com Reputable site for short-term furnished apartment rentals by owner, with about seventy Manhattan listings at any given time and a dozen or so more in Brooklyn. Expect to pay around $2000 a week for a one-bedroom luxury apartment with views, and around $5000 a week for a SoHo loft; some apartments are available by the night, too. All listings have pictures, detailed descriptions of amenities, and calendars of availability.

newyork.craigslist.org New York's branch of the popular international website has scores of short-term apartment rentals posted by owners and lessees daily; housing-exchange offers are also available. Excellent resource for last-minute trips, with some of the hippest, cheapest listings – just be sure to follow all the usual e-commerce precautions.

roomexchange.net Global network of travelers who register to exchange their apartments or rooms for others' in the network ("you at mine and me at yours"), or to host travelers and vice versa ("I'll be your guest, you'll be mine").

vrbo.com Similar to cyberrentals.com, this website, whose name is short for Vacation Rentals By Owner, has about a hundred Manhattan listings at any given time, with a few dozen more in Brooklyn and Queens. Options range from East Village studio apartments from around $125 a night to four-bedroom Upper West Side townhouses from around $450 a night. Most are cheaper by the week. Some take credit cards.

ACCOMMODATION

from $130 to $400. Prices do not include tax. Weekly and monthly rates also available. For an assured booking, write at least a month in advance; make short-notice reservations by phone. Offices open Mon–Fri 8am–6pm. **City Lights Bed & Breakfast** ☎212/737-7049, ⓦwww.city-lightsbandb.com. More than 400 carefully screened B&B and short-term apartment rentals, with many of the hosts involved in theater and the arts. Hosted singles and doubles run from $80 to $175 a night; 95 percent of these properties include private baths. Unhosted accommodation costs $130 for a studio and up to $500 for a penthouse per night, plus tax. Weekly and monthly deals; minimum stay three nights. Reserve well in advance for best selection. Very personable and professional. **CitySonnet.com** Village Station, PO Box 347, NY 10014 ☎212/614-3034, ⒻF425/920-2384, ⓦwww .citysonnet.com. Small, personalized B&B/short-term apartment rental agency with accommodation all over the city, but specializing in Downtown and the West Village. Singles from $135 to $175; doubles $135–175; entire apartments and lofts with kitchen start at $175. Cheaper options available in Brooklyn. All prices include tax.

B&B properties

Bed & Breakfast on the Park 113 Prospect Park West, Brooklyn ☎718/499-6115, ⒻF499-1385, ⓦwww.bbnyc.com. A quiet and secluded 1892 Park Slope limestone townhouse with lavish antique furnishings and views over Prospect Park. Seven double rooms from $165 to $295 a night, plus tax and ten-percent tip, with full gourmet breakfast; three-night minimum in May and Oct; two-night minimum the rest of the year.

🏃 **East Village Bed and Coffee** Map 5, M3. 110 Ave C, btw 7th and 8th ☎212/533-4175, ⒻF979-9743, ⓦwww.bedandcoffee .com. Lovely, tastefully themed twin-, double-, and queen-bedded rooms with a/c and CD players which, along with the wooden floors, open brick walls, garden, and communal kitchen and living areas, make this the best-kept secret in a very happening area of the East Village. All rooms share bathrooms; singles start at $95 a night, doubles at $110, including all taxes.

The Harlem Flophouse Map 9, D8. 242 W 123rd St, btw Powell and Douglass ☎212/662-0678, ⓦwww .harlemflophouse.com. There's an atmosphere steeped in history in this lovely old Harlem brownstone, just steps from the Apollo Theater and boasting four large rooms with fixtures dating from the Harlem Renaissance. Two cats preside over this great Uptown spot. The four rooms share two baths; singles from $100, doubles $150. **Inn at Irving Place Map 6, K8. 56 Irving Place, btw 17th and 18th** ☎1-800/685-1447 or 212/533-4600, ⒲www.innatirving.com. It costs $415–565 a night for one of the twelve lavishly decorated rooms – each named after a famous architect, designer, or actor – in this handsome pair of 1834 brownstones, which ranks as one of the most exclusive guesthouses in the city. The *Inn* offers five-course high teas at *Lady Mendl's*, cocktails at the refined *Cibar Lounge*, Wi-Fi, and a/c.

Hotels

Most of New York's **hotels** tend to be in Midtown Manhattan, which is fine if you want to be close to the Broadway theaters and main tourist sights, but it's hardly the makings of a restful vacation. If you're going to be spending a lot of time in the West Village or SoHo, you might try one of the handful of Downtown or Chelsea hotels. Consider the Upper West or Upper East Side if you're more interested in Central Park, Museum Mile, or Lincoln Center.

Hotel booking services

Should you be uncertain about what you're looking for in an NYC hotel, or if you just don't trust the hotel PR machines, consider using a **hotel booking service**. The various companies listed below offer a selection of rooms at discount prices, tailored to your own criteria.
Central Reservation Service (CRS) ☎407/740-6442 or 1-800/555-7555, ⒲www.reservation-services.com. Phone operators available weekdays only.
Hotel Reservations Network ☎1-800/715-7666 or 214/369-1264, ⒲www.hoteldiscounts.com.
Quikbook ☎1-800/789-9887 or 212/779-7666, ⒲www.quikbook.com. Phone operators available Mon–Sat only.

Taxes will add 13.38 percent to your bill, and there is a $3.50 per night "occupancy tax" as well. Rates given in the following pages are for the lowest-priced double room in high season before tax unless otherwise noted.

At virtually all hotels, **tipping** is expected: unless you firmly refuse, a bellhop will grab your bags when you check in and expect up to $5 (at the more upmarket hotels) to carry them to your room. For housekeeping, figure a minimum of $2 per day for cheaper hotels, more for the nicer establishments.

Below 14th Street

60 Thompson Map 5, E7. 60 Thompson St, btw Spring and Broome ☎212/431-0400 or 1-877/431-0400, ⓦ www.60thompson.com. A stylish spot with 100 modern guestrooms and suites and excellent proximity to SoHo's hip restaurants and chic stores. Has a popular rooftop garden/bar and an in-house DVD library; upstairs rooms overlook SoHo's rooftops. Rooms from $579.

Abingdon Guest House Map 5, A2. 13 8th Ave, at 12th St. ☎212/243-5384, ⓦ www.abingdonguesthouse.com. Cozy pair of nineteenth-century townhouses just a few steps from the coolest part of the West Village, with friendly but hands-off innkeepers. The individually decorated rooms make up in character what they lack in luxury, with antique armoires, iron beds, and bold colors. Each has a private bath, though some are located in the hall. Free local calls and Wi-Fi. From $179; two-night minimum weekdays, four nights weekends.

Best Western Seaport Inn Map 4, H5. 33 Peck Slip (at Front St) ☎212/766-6600, ⓦ www.seaportinn.com. Right in the heart of the South Street Seaport complex (and no longer downwind from the now-departed Fulton Fish Market), this simple place with 72 rooms has a few perks: first, location: though the seaport is admittedly touristy, it's coming into its own as a real neighborhood, with good restaurants, an excellent coffeehouse, and a wine bar, all just around the corner from the hotel in a pleasant pedestrian-friendly zone. Second, the rooms are chain-hotel size, not New York City size. Third, it's a good deal, with doubles from $289.

Hotel Gansevoort Map 6, D9. 18 9th Ave, at 13th ☎212/206-6700 or 1-877/426-7386, ⓦ www.hotel-gansevoort.com. Hugely popular fashionista hangout, with a heated rooftop pool for guests only and an adjacent bar for spectators. Modern rooms are small but lushly appointed, and some have views of the Hudson River. Rooms from $555, suites from $825.

Hotel on Rivington Map 5, K6. 107 Rivington St, btw Essex and Ludlow ☎1-800/915-1537 or 212/475-2600, Ⓦwww.hotelonrivington.com. This controversial monument to modernity is the first real high-rise building to be built in the Lower East Side, but hipsters seem to love it. Every room has floor-to-ceiling windows and steam showers, and most boast balconies and Japanese-style soaking tubs. Doubles from $465.

Larchmont Map 5, E2. 27 W 11th St, btw 5th and 6th ☎212/989-9333, Ⓦwww.larchmonthotel.com. Budget hotel on a beautiful tree-lined street in the heart of Greenwich Village, where hotels are a rarity. Rooms are small but clean and nicely decorated, and all have TV, a/c, phones, and sinks. Small kitchens and bathrooms with showers are on each corridor. Prices include continental breakfast. Very small singles $80–115, doubles $109–135.

The Mercer Map 5, F6. 147 Mercer St, at Prince ☎1-888/918-6060 or 212/966-6060, Ⓦwww.mercerhotel .com. The epitome of "boutique" chic by the guy (Andre Balazs)

behind the *QT Hotel* in Times Square (☎212/354-2323, Ⓦwww.hotelqt.com) and *The Standard*, due to open in the Meatpacking District in 2008. Stylish rooms and suites have simple furnishings, high ceilings, walk-in closets, and oversized bathrooms. The occasional celebrity will share your sofa in the smart lobby, and trendy *Mercer Kitchen* provides room service 24-hours a day. Doubles from $495; studios from $595.

Ritz-Carlton Battery Park Map 4, D8. 2 West St, at Battery Place ☎212/344-0800, Ⓦwww.ritzcarl-ton.com. Incredible views of Lady Liberty, Ellis Island, and the harbor around them can be had from the upper floors of this highly reputable luxury hotel with large quiet bedrooms, a 14th-floor bar with scenic outdoor terrace, three dining options, and a fitness center with spa services. Doubles from $395.

Soho Grand Map 5, E8. 310 W Broadway, at Grand ☎1-800/965-3000 or 212/965-3000, Ⓦwww .sohogrand.com. Great location at the edge of SoHo, with celebrity guests (rock stars, models, actors) and the attitude to match; the staff is surprisingly helpful, though. Small but stylish rooms are accented with classic New York photographs from a local gallery and – if you ask for one –

a goldfish. The hotel also boasts an elegant bar, a restaurant, and a fitness center. Doubles start at $444.

Tribeca Grand Map 4, D2. 2 6th Ave, btw White and Walker ☎1-877/519-6600 or 212/519-6600, Ⓦwww.tribecagrand.com. Unlabeled, and hidden by a brick facade that looks like a brand-new train station, the *Tribeca Grand* is close to its sister hotel, the *Soho Grand*, in location and spirit. Once inside, the striking *Church Lounge* beckons with a warm orange glow. The rooms are stylish yet understated, though each bathroom boasts a phone and built-in TV. Doubles from $444.

Washington Square Map 5, D3. 103 Waverly Place, at MacDougal ☎212/777-9515 or 1-800/222-0418, Ⓦwww.washingtonsquarehotel.com. An ideal location, bang in the heart of Greenwich Village overlooking Washington Square. Rooms are individually decorated and some have good views. Continental breakfast is included, plus there's a fitness room and a romantic lobby bar. Doubles start at $225.

Chelsea and the West Side: West 14th to 34th streets

Chelsea Hotel Map 6, F7. 222 W 23rd St, btw 7th and 8th ☎212/243-3700, Ⓦwww.hotelchelsea.com.

One of New York's most noted landmarks, thanks to its aging neo-Gothic building and long list of former guests, from Dylan Thomas to Bob Dylan (see p.77 for a fuller cast). You used to be able to stay here alongside the artist residents for around $200 a night, but in June 2007 the hotel came under new management, and word has it that there'll be a good deal of renovation in coming years, as well as rate hikes. Call for details.

Herald Square Hotel Map 6, H4. 19 W 31st St, btw 5th and Broadway ☎1-800/727-1888 or 212/279-4017, Ⓦwww.heraldsquarehotel.com. The original home of *Life* magazine, the Beaux-Arts *Herald Square Hotel* still features Philip Martiny's golden *Winged Life* sculpture over the doorway. Inside it's meticulously clean, but somewhat soulless and without much in the way of extras. Very small singles (with shared bathrooms) go for as low as $89 a night, with doubles from $209 and triples and quads from $249. Students with ISIC cards get ten percent off.

Hotel Pennsylvania Map 6, F4. 401 7th Ave, at 32nd ☎1-800/223-8585 or 212/736-5000, Ⓦwww.hotel-penn.com. Standing right across from Madison Square Garden, this hotel offers every possible convenience in its 1705 rooms, though you can't help thinking it once looked better. Decent-sized doubles start around $229. Pet-friendly.

Hotel Stanford Map 6, H4. 43 W 32nd St, btw Broadway and 5th ☎1-800/365-1114 or 212/563-1500, ⓦwww.hotelstanford.com. Rooms here are a tad small, but attractive and very quiet, and the staff is friendly and efficient. Offers free continental breakfast, plus valet laundry, a cocktail lounge, and good Korean cuisine (in the very relaxing surroundings of the *Gam Mee Ok* restaurant). Doubles start at $229.

Wolcott Map 6, H4. 4 W 31st St, btw 5th and Broadway ☎212/268-2900, ⓦwww.wolcott.com. A surprisingly relaxing budget hotel, with a gilded, ornate Louis XVI–style lobby full of mirrors and lion reliefs – even the ceiling is lavish. The rooms, while much more staid, are more than adequate, all with (somewhat old-fashioned) en-suite bathrooms. Doubles and twins from $220, triples from $240.

Union Square to Murray Hill: East 14th to 42nd streets

70 Park Avenue Hotel Map 6, J2. 70 Park Ave, at 38th ☎1-877/707-2752 or 212/973-2400, ⓦwww.70parkave.com. This classy boutique hotel, right in the middle of Midtown, is adorned with re-creations of classical friezes and frescoes, and original lighting and furnishing design featuring rich woods and muted earth tones. Extras include CD/DVD players, flat-screen TVs, Wi-Fi, and a nightly wine reception. Pet-friendly. Doubles from $325.

Carlton Arms Map 6, K6. 160 E 25th St, btw 3rd and Lexington ☎212/679-0680, ⓦwww.carltonarms.com. One of the city's latest bohemian hangouts, with eclectic interior decor by would-be artists, few mod-cons, and a clientele made up of Europeans, down-at-the-heel artists, and long-staying guests. Discount rates are available for students and foreign travelers, plus there's a 10 percent discount if you pay for seven nights in advance. Singles with shared bath from $75, doubles from $99, triples from $120, and quads from $145. Add $10–15 per night for private bath. Reserve well in advance for summer.

Gershwin Hotel Map 6, I5. 7 E 27th St, btw 5th and Madison ☎212/545-8000, ⓦwww.gershwinhotel.com. A twentysomething's hotel just off Fifth Ave in the Flatiron District that also functions as a hostel. Imaginatively decorated with a Pop Art theme, the *Gershwin* has a rooftop deck (where parties are held on the weekend), a small bar, a well-priced restaurant, and a friendly staff. Book well in advance. Double rooms with private baths start around $229 a night.

Hotel Roger Williams Map 6, I4. 131 Madison Ave, at 31st ☎1-888/448-7788 or 212/448-7000, ⓦ www.hotelrogerwilliams.com. At some point during its $2 million "boutique" renovation, this hotel made a turn onto Madison and its prices shot up exponentially. Still, the Scandinavian/Japanese fusion rooms with Aveda bath gels, fluted zinc pillars in the lobby, European breakfast, and 24-hour espresso/cappuccino bar go some way to justifying the extra greenbacks. Doubles from $380.

Library Map 6, I1. 299 Madison Ave, at 41st ☎1-877/793-READ or 212/983-4500, ⓦ www.libraryhotel .com. In this whimsical hotel, each floor is devoted to one of the ten major categories of the Dewey Decimal System, and each room's artwork and books reflect a different pursuit within that group. Only those with a serious sense of purpose could design sixty unique rooms and hand-pick more than 6000 books for the place, and the dedication shows in other ways, notably in the lovely Poet's Garden on the roof. Doubles from $399, with various offers available via the hotel's website.

The Metro Map 6, H3. 45 W 35th St, btw 5th and 6th ☎1-800/356-3870 or 212/947-2500, ⓦ www .hotelmetronyc.com. This very stylish Art Deco-inspired hotel has old Hollywood posters on the walls, a delightful rooftop terrace, spacious communal areas, free continental breakfast, a recently updated fitness room, free Wi-Fi, plush-top beds, and the well-regarded *Metro Grill* on the first floor. Doubles from $365.

Murray Hill Inn Map 6, K5. 143 E 30th St, btw Lexington and 3rd ☎1-888/996-6376 or 212/683-6900, ⓦ www.murrayhillinn.com. It's easy to see why young travelers and backpackers like this affordable spot. Although the rooms are smallish, they all have a/c, telephone, cable TV, and sink; some also have private bathrooms. In addition, the staff is friendly and the residential locale, though a bit dull, offers a breather from the bustle. Doubles from $99 (shared bath), $139 (en suite).

Seventeen Map 6, L8. 225 E 17th St, btw 2nd and 3rd ☎212/475-2845, ⓦ www.hotel17ny.com. A clean and friendly budget hotel, located on a pleasant, tree-lined street. Convenient to the East Village, which is only a few blocks away. Doubles with shared bath start at $150; with private bath at $200.

20

ACCOMMODATION

Thirty Thirty Map 6, J5. 30 E 30th St, at Madison ☎ 1-800/804-4480 or 212/689-1900, ⓦ www.thirtythirty-nyc.com. Small, welcoming hotel with well-appointed, clean, and functional rooms. Standard double rooms start at $299 but are quite small; if you can spare the cash, consider upgrading to a superior double, starting at $340.

W Union Square Map 6, J8. 201 Park Ave South, at Union Square North ☎ 1-877/W-HOTELS or 212/253-9119, ⓦ www.starwoodhotels.com. The only upscale hotel in the area, featuring Todd English's *Olives* restaurant as well as Rande Gerber's *Underbar*. The artificial green grass and cork-screwing bamboo in the lobby are a prelude to the modern rooms decorated with velvet and featuring plush, really comfortable feather beds. Doubles start at around $479.

Midtown West: West 34th to 59th streets

Algonquin Map 7, G9. 59 W 44th St, btw 5th and 6th ☎ 1-800/555-8000 or 212/840-6800, ⓦ www.camberleyhotels.com. New York's classic literary hangout for the past century, as dictated by Dorothy Parker and her associates of the Algonquin Round Table. The *Oak Room* draws some of the best

cabaret acts in the business (with prices to match); the hotel completed a major renovation in July 2004. Doubles from $364.

Broadway Inn Map 7, E8. 264 W 46th St, btw Broadway and 8th ☎ 1-800/826-6300 or 212/997-9200, ⓦ www.broadwayinn.com. Cozy, reasonably priced bed-and-breakfast hotel in the heart of the Theater District. Though on the corner of charmless Eighth Ave, it's just a skip away from Times Square and Restaurant Row. Guests get a twenty-percent discount at the restaurant downstairs, and an excellent staff makes up for the lack of an elevator. Singles from $159 (summer) to $255 (October), doubles $199–325.

Casablanca Map 7, F9. 147 W 43rd St, btw 6th and 7th ☎ 1-888/922-7225 or 212/869-1212, ⓦ www.casablancahotel.com. Moorish tiles, ceiling fans, and, of course, *Rick's Café* are all here in this unusual, thoughtful, and understated theme hotel. While the feeling is 1940s Morocco, the amenities (Internet access, cable TV, work spaces) are more up-to-date. Wine, cheese, and cookies are served in the afternoon, and bottled water and Belgian chocolates are provided at turndown. Doubles from $359.

Jumeirah Essex House Map 7, F5. 160 Central Park South, btw 6th and

7th ☎ 212/247-0300, ⓦ www
.essexhouse.com. A beautiful hotel
for a special occasion. Despite
the excellent service and marble
lobby, the atmosphere is not at
all formal or hushed. The best
rooms have spectacular Central
Park views. Doubles from around
$469.

Le Parker Meridien Map 7, F6.
118 W 57th St, btw 6th and 7th
☎ 212/245-5000, ⓦ www.parker-
meridien.com. Five years of work
and $60 million transformed
the famous *Parker Meridien*,
which now boasts a huge fitness
center, a rare rooftop pool, and
24-hour room service, as well as
gimmicky pluses like cartoon-
playing elevators and glowing
room numbers. *Norma's* restaurant is one of the most acclaimed
brunch spots in the city, and the
incongruously divey but delicious
Burger Joint (see p.225) adds a
nice touch of grit to the scene.
From $415.

Mandarin Oriental New York Map 7,
E5. 80 Columbus Circle, at 60th ☎ 1-
866/801-8880 or 212/805-8800,
ⓦ www.mandarinoriental
.com. Situated on floors 35 to 54
of the Time Warner Center on
Columbus Circle, with some of
the best views in the city, is this
brand-new luxury hotel. Rooms
are a testament to opulence,
featuring cherrywood floors and
original artwork, deep marble

baths, and LCD flat-screen TVs,
with floor-to-ceiling views of Central Park, the Hudson River, or
the Manhattan skyline. Doubles
from $895.

Mansfield Map 7, H9. 12 W 44th
St, at 5th ☎ 1-800/255-5167 or
212/227-8700, ⓦ www.mansfield-
hotel.com. One of the loveliest
hotels in the city, with its clubby
library, copper-domed salon,
and Beaux-Arts details. There's
a charming, slightly quirky feel
about the place – an echo,
perhaps, of its turn-of-the-nineteenth-century role as a pad
for New York's most eligible
bachelors. With the European
breakfast and all-day cappuccino, a great deal at $349 for a
double.

Mayfair Map 7, E8. 242 W 49th
St, btw Broadway and 8th ☎ 1-
800/556-2932 or 212/586-0300,
ⓦ www.mayfairnewyork.com. This
boutique theater-district hotel,
across the street from the St
Malachay Actors' Chapel, has
beautifully decorated rooms, its
own restaurant, and a charming,
old-world feel, emphasized by
the historic photographs on loan
from the Museum of the City of
New York. Doubles from $221.

Paramount Hotel Times Square Map
7, E8. 235 W 46th St, btw Broadway
and 8th ☎ 212/764-5500, ⓦ www
.nycparamount.com. Boutique
hotel popular with creative and

fashionable types, thanks to its sleek Philippe Starck design. Rooms feature silk-screened headboards and fresh flowers, while the *Paramount Bar*, the *Library Bar*, and the *Mezzanine* restaurant are all busy and fun. Doubles from $409.

Warwick Hotel New York Map 7, G7. 65 W 54th St, at 6th ☎212/247-2700, ⓦwww.warwickhotelny .com. Stars of the 1950s and 1960s – including Cary Grant, the Beatles, Elvis Presley, and JFK – stayed here as a matter of course, as it was built by publishing titan William Randolph Hearst to lure celebrities. Although the hotel has lost its showbiz cachet, it's still an attractive spot, from its elegant lobby to the old-fashioned *Randolph's Bar and Lounge* and *Murals on 54* restaurants. Doubles from around $420.

Midtown East and the Upper East Side: East 42nd to 96th streets

Roger Smith Map 7, J8. 501 Lexington Ave, at 47th ☎1-800/445-0277 or 212/755-1400, ⓦwww .rogersmith.com. One of the best Midtown hotels, with very helpful service, individually decorated rooms, a great restaurant, and artwork and sculptures on display. Most rooms have VCRs, and more than 2000 videos are available from the hotel's library. Breakfast is included in the price. Doubles from $349.

San Carlos Map 7, J8. 150 E 50th St, btw Lexington and 3rd ☎1-800/722-2012 or 212/755-1800, ⓦwww.sancarloshotel.com. Well-situated near plenty of bars and restaurants, with perks like free in-room Wi-Fi, bathrobes, and Aveda products. Most of the large rooms have fully equipped kitchenettes. Doubles from $379.

W New York Map 7, J8. 541 Lexington Ave, btw 49th and 50th ☎212/755-1200, ⓦwww .starwoodhotels.com. Usually the least expensive of the city's five *W* hotels, though it still has the usual slick accoutrements, including Egyptian cotton on the feather beds. Other places include the *Whiskey Blue* bar, *Heartbeat* restaurant, and loungy lobby for hanging out. Doubles start at $329.

Waldorf-Astoria Map 7, I8. 301 Park Ave, btw 49th and 50th ☎1-800/WALDORF or 212/355-3000, ⓦwww.waldorf.com. One of the great names in New York hotels, restored to its 1930s glory. Doubles start around $549 in high season ($599 on weekdays) but drop precipitously in summer.

The Upper West Side: Above West 59th Street

Hudson Hotel Map 7, D6. 356 W 58th St, btw 8th and 9th ☎212/554-6000, ⓦwww .hudsonhotel.com. Chic and sleek Philippe Starck and Ian Schrager enterprise near Lincoln Center, with a hoppin' bar scene and a dramatic, futuristic vibe throughout the public spaces. Rooms are small but very attractive, with white furnishings and dark wood-paneled walls. The fifteenth-floor roof deck has sweeping views of the river. Doubles from $490.

Lucerne Map 8, C9. 201 W 79th St, at Amsterdam ☎1-800/492-8122 or 212/875-1000, ⓦwww .thelucernehotel.com. Beautifully restored 1904 brownstone, with an extravagantly Baroque, red terracotta entrance, inviting rooms, and a friendly, helpful staff. Just one block from the American Museum of Natural History and close to the liveliest restaurant stretch of Columbus Ave. Doubles from $400.

Riverside Tower Map 8, B9. 80 Riverside Drive, at 80th ☎1-800/724-3136 or 212/877-5200, ⓦwww .riversidetowerhotel.com. Although the hallways are plain as can be and rooms are ultra-basic, this budget hotel's exclusive location next to Riverside Park, with (on the upper floors) stunning views of the Hudson River, sets it apart from the others. Doubles with private bath, a/c, color TV, kitchenette, and river views from $109.

20

ACCOMMODATION

Cafés, snacks, and light meals

N ew York's **cafés** and **bakeries** run the gamut of its population's ethnic and cultural influences. They can be found in every neighborhood, with the usual French, Italian, and American ones the most visible. The city also has a number of **coffeehouses** and **tearooms**, which, in addition to the obvious fare, usually offer fruit juices, pastries, light snacks, and, on occasion, full meals. There are plenty of **takeout** options as well, with falafel stands, pizzerias, and ice-cream parlors ruling the residential neighborhoods, and salad bars and sandwich shops feeding the lunchtime crowds of Midtown and the Financial District. Places more suitable for sit-down dinners are listed in Chapter 22, "Restaurants."

Financial District

Financier Patisserie Map 4, B4.
62 Stone St, btw Mill Lane and
Hanover Square ☏ 212/344-5600.
Cozy café great for an espresso
and madeleine; also offers a full
complement of breakfast pastries
(scones, brioches) and French
lunch staples (quiche, *croque*

monsieur, salad *niçoise*) at reasonable prices. There are two other locations: 35 Cedar St, btw Pearl and William (☎212/742-7016), and the World Financial Center, Battery Park City (☎212/786-3220).
Jack's Stir Brew Map 5, C3. 222 Front St btw Beekman and Peck Slip ☎212/227-7631. This laid-back, gourmet coffee-shop near South Street Seaport makes an exquisite cappuccino – with organic, shade-grown, free-trade beans no less. Opened in 2006, the original location is at 138 W 10th St, at Waverly Place, in the West Village (☎212/227-7631).

SoHo and TriBeCa

Balthazar Bakery Map 5, G7. 80 Spring St, btw Crosby and Broadway ☎212/965-1414. Wonderful breads and pastries, both simple and ornate, without the attitude of the celebrated *Balthazar* brasserie, next door.
Hampton Chutney Map 5, G6. 68 Prince St, at Crosby ☎212/226-9996. The American sandwich takes a detour through Indian breads and ingredients. Out of the ordinary and quite good.
Snack Map 5, E6. 105 Thompson St, btw Prince and Spring ☎212/925-1040. Fresh Greek food and *mezes* that will set you back about $10 at lunch. The place is thimble-sized, so be prepared to wait for a table – or take your food to go.
Yaffa Tea Room Map 4, C3. 353 Greenwich St, at Harrison ☎212/274-9403. Serves Mediterranean-style dinners, good brunch, and a cozy, if rather expensive, high tea (reservations required). Hidden in an unassuming corner of TriBeCa, next to the *Yaffa Bar*.

Chinatown and Little Italy

Café Gitane Map 5, H6. 242 Mott St, at Prince ☎212/334-9552. Sunny little café that's extremely popular with the fashion crowd; serves coffee and creative, light-lunch fare with a Moroccan slant. Smokers are welcome at the sidewalk tables.
Caffè Roma Map 5, H7. 385 Broome St, btw Mulberry and Mott ☎212/226-8413. Old Little Italy *pasticceria*, ideal for a drawn-

out coffee and pastry. Try the homemade Italian cookies, exceptionally good cannoli (plain or dipped), or gelato at the counter in back.

Ceci-Cela Map 5, H7. 55 Spring St, at Mulberry ☎212/274-9179. Tiny French patisserie serving coffee and delectable croissants and *palmiers*; eat at the stand-up counter or the bench out front. A second location is in TriBeCa, at 166 Chambers St, btw W Broadway and Greenwich (☎212/566-8933).

Chinatown Ice Cream Factory Map 4, G2. 65 Bayard St, btw Mott and Elizabeth ☎212/608-4170. An essential stop after sampling one of the restaurants nearby, though the wondrously unusual flavors make it good anytime. Specialties include green tea, ginger, almond cookies, and lychee ice cream.

Ferrara Map 4, G1. 195 Grand St, btw Mott and Mulberry ☎212/226-6150. The best-known and most traditional of the Little Italy coffceehouses, founded in 1892. Try the cheesecake, cannoli, or *granite* (Italian ices) in summer.

Lower East Side

Il Laboratorio del Gelato Map 5, K7. 95 Orchard St, at Broome ☎212/343-9922. This tiny scoop shop makes the best ice cream in New York. About a dozen of the *Lab's* hundred flavors are offered at one time: some, like honey lavender and lemon basil, are truly unique, but even the basics (dark chocolate) are incredible. Don't miss it.

Kossar's Map 4, I1. 367 Grand St, at Essex ☎212/473-4810. Jewish baker whose bialys may be the best in New York. Closed Sat.

Teany Map 5, K6. 90 Rivington St, btw Orchard and Ludlow ☎212/475-9190. Vegetarian café owned by musician Moby, offering a wide selection of teas and tea sandwiches, baked beans on toast, and Welsh rarebit.

Yonah Schimmel Map 5, J5. 137 E Houston St, btw Forsyth and Eldridge ☎212/477-2858. This old-school Jewish bakery has been turning out knishes – dense baked dumplings stuffed with potatoes, apples, or vegetables – since 1910. There are a few rickety tables where you can sit and eavesdrop on the old men wisecracking in Yiddish.

The East Village

B & H Dairy Map 5, I3. 127 2nd Ave, btw 7th and St Mark's ☎212/505-8065. Tiny luncheonette serving homemade soup, challah, and latkes. Create your own juice combination.

Café Pick Me Up Map 5, K3. 145 Ave A, at 9th ☎212/673-7231. East Village charmer with tiny wooden tables designed for close conversations or a quiet read. Choose from quiche or cake, coffee or wine, and enjoy the owner's varied collection of international music. Snag the sidewalk seating and you can pick up Wi-Fi from Tompkins Square Park, just across the way.

Damask Falafel Map 5, K4. 89 Ave A, btw 5th and 6th ☎212/673-5016. One of the better Middle Eastern snack providers in the area. The usual falafel and hummus are supplemented by exquisite baklavas and similarly rich Mediterranean dessert pastries. Open until 2am.

De Robertis Map 5, J2. 176 1st Ave, btw 9th and 10th ☎212/674-7137. Traditional Italian bakery/café that's been here since 1904 and has since been featured in multiple Woody Allen flicks for its Old New York vibe. Wonderful ricotta cheesecake and espresso. Closed Mon.

Liquiteria Map 5, I2. 170 2nd Ave, at 11th ☎212/358-0300. The best smoothies in Manhattan (try the Orangasm) plus delicious, healthy lunches like oatmeal with fresh fruit and organic PB&Js.

Mud Map 5, I3. 307 E 9th St, at 2nd Ave ☎212/228-9074. A local favorite for its intensely strong fair-trade coffee, which is also sold from orange trucks around town (check for one at Astor Place). You can sit for hours at the café tables or in the garden out back and enjoy the good (if somewhat pricey) veggie fare as well as rocking tunes. Hosts performances and art shows on occasion.

Via Della Pace Map 5, I3. 48 E 7th St, at 2nd ☎212/253-5803. Dark and cozy East Village café with good Argentine pastas and sandwiches, plus a wide selection of coffees and desserts; the tiramisu is especially delicious. Kitchen open until 1am daily.

The West Village

A Salt and Battery Map 5, C2. 112 Greenwich Ave, at W 13th ☎212/691-2713. Run by the Brits from *Tea and Sympathy* next door, this authentic-enough affair serves decent battered cod and plaice, great chips, and mushy peas. However, it may be the most expensive chippie in the world, with a fish supper costing you a good twenty bucks. Try a fried Mars bar for dessert.

Caffè Dante Map 5, D5. 79 MacDougal St, btw Bleecker and Houston ☎212/982-5275. A morning stop-off for many locals since 1915. Popular for its good cappuccino, double espresso, and *caffè alfredo* with ice cream. Often jammed with NYU students and teachers.

Caffè Reggio Map 5, D4. 119 MacDougal St, btw Bleecker and 3rd ☎212/475-9557. One of the first Village coffeehouses, dating back to the 1920s. Always crowded, especially its outside tables when the weather is warm.

Doma Cafe and Gallery Map 5, 2C. 17 Perry St, at 7th Ave ☎212/929-4339. Lively sun-washed corner café where trendy West Villagers tap away on laptops, read, or chat at communal tables. Offers coffee, wine, and beer, and a reasonably priced menu of sandwiches and salads; breakfast is served all day.

Elixir Map 5, A3. 523 Hudson St, btw 10th and Charles ☎212/352-9952. Casual, friendly joint good for juices, smoothies, and seasonal elixirs. Three other locations, including 95 W Broadway, between Reade and Chambers, in TriBeCa (☎212/233-6171).

Magnolia Bakery Map 5, A3. 401 Bleecker St, at 11th ☎212/462-2572. Like you've died and gone to sweets heaven: the specialty here is buttercream-frosted cupcakes. Expect a line out the door on weekends.

Tea and Sympathy Map 5, C2. 108 Greenwich Ave, btw 12th and 13th ☎212/807-8329. Self-consciously British tearoom, serving an afternoon high tea full of traditional staples like jam roly-poly and treacle pudding, along with shepherd's pie and scones.

(21)

CAFÉS, SNACKS, AND LIGHT MEALS

Chelsea

Amy's Bread Map 6, D9. Chelsea Market, 75 9th Ave, btw 15th and 16th ☎212/462-4338. You can find *Amy's Bread* products in gourmet stores citywide but it's freshest here, where people line up for sandwiches like roast turkey on semolina raisin and fennel bread. Two other locations, in Hell's Kitchen and the West Village.

F&B Güdtfood Map 6, F7. 269 W 23rd St, btw 7th and 8th ☎646/486-4441. Cheap, classy joint serving all manner of franks (vegetarian, too) and beignets (awesome with apricot dip) with fries. Eat in or take out.

La Bergamote Map 6, D7. 169 9th Ave at 20th ☎212/627-9010. Local-favorite French café and patisserie that's perfect for fueling up before hitting the galleries or unwinding afterward. Divine, buttery croissants.

Bagels

Theories abound as to the origin of the modern bagel. Most likely, it's a derivative of the pretzel, and its name comes from the German word *beigen*, "to bend." The famous hole in the middle is believed to have made them easy to carry on a long stick, for hawking on street corners. Regardless of where they're from, bagels are a New York institution. They are most traditionally enjoyed with cream cheese and lox (smoked salmon), though of course you can top them with anything you like. A list of some of the better bagel purveyors is below. (If you prefer bialys, a drier, flatter bagel-type bread without a hole, head straight to *Kossar's*; see p.197.)

David's Bagels Map 5, J1. 228 1st Ave, btw 13th and 14th, East Village ☎212/533-8766.

Ess-A-Bagel Map 6, M7. 359 1st Ave, at East 21st, Gramercy ☎212/260-2252.

H & H Bagels Map 7, C1. 2239 Broadway, at W 78th, Upper West Side ☎212/595-8000.

Hot & Crusty Bagel Café Map 8, B7. 2387 Broadway, btw 87th and 88th, Upper West Side ☎212/496-0632.

Murray's Map 5, D1. 500 6th Ave, btw 12th and 13th, ☎212/462-2830, **West Village, and 242 8th Ave, btw 22nd and 23rd, Chelsea** ☎646/638-1335.

Union Square and Gramercy Park

71 Irving Place Coffee and Tea Bar Map 6, K8. 71 Irving Place at 19th St ☎212/995-5252. The kind of genial, all-purpose café you wish you lived next door to. The coffee is roasted on a farm upstate, there are sandwiches and muffins aplenty, and the management lets you linger even when the place is crowded, which is pretty much always.

City Bakery Map 6, I8. 3 W 18th St, btw 5th and 6th ☎212/366-1414. Stylish bakery that turns fresh produce from the Greenmarket (see p.81) into delectable soups, pay-by-the-pound salads, and light breakfast and lunch fare. The specialties, though, are the masterfully delicate tartlets, European-style hot chocolate, and pretzel croissants.

Eisenberg's Sandwich Shop Map 6, I7. 174 5th Ave, btw 22nd and 23rd ☎212/675-5096. This narrow little restaurant is a Flatiron institution. A tuna sandwich and some matzoh-ball soup will cure whatever ails you.

News Bar Map 6, H8. 2 W 19th St, btw 5th and 6th ☎212/255-3996. Tiny, minimalist café with plentiful pastries and periodicals. Draws photographer and model types, making it good for people-watching. There's another branch at 107 University Place, between 12th and 13th streets (☎212/353-1246), with Internet terminals you can use for a fee.

Midtown East

AQ Café Map 6, 2K. 58 Park Ave, at 38th ☎212/879-9779. This spartan, sun-drenched café on the ground floor of Scandinavia House looks a bit like an IKEA store, but is a true find. Run by the folks behind *Aquavit* (p.224), it serves delicious and well-priced Nordic goodies such as smoked-salmon sandwiches and Swedish meatballs. Closed Sun.

Grand Central bites

Midtown East is largely a culinary wasteland when it comes to finding a good café but, thankfully, **Grand Central Terminal**, at 42nd St and Lexington Ave (Map 6, J1), has a number of great options – from its sprawling market with specialty shops on the main concourse level to its various sit-down spots on the dining concourse level below. Some of the best options include the following:

Brother Jimmy's BBQ ☎212/661-4022. Don't miss the Carolina-style yellow barbecue pulled-pork sandwiches here. All BBQ is cooked for 5–12 hours over an open flame before serving.

Café Spice ☎646/227-1300. Quickie high-quality curries. The lamb *vindaloo* is tasty and very hot.

Caffè Pepe Rosso ☎212/867-6054. You can get exceptional panini here – try the prosciutto, tomato, mozzarella, and arugula – as well as fresh, creative salads and basic pasta dishes for around $6.95 each.

Ciao Bella Gelateria ☎212/867-5311. Exceptional Italian treats, including an out-of-this-world blood-orange sorbet and a fine pistachio gelato.

Little Pie Company ☎212/736-4780. The three-berry pies are to die for, while the peach-raspberry, available in summer, has been known to provoke rioting. If you'll be eating solo, pick up a five-inch personal pie.

Two Boots ☎212/557-7992. Beloved Downtown pizza joint with creative pies like the Mr. Pink, dresed with marinated chicken, plum tomatoes, garlic, and mozzarella.

Midtown West

Azuri Café Map 7, D7. 465 W 51st St, btw 9th and 10th. ☎212/262-2920. Service can be gruff at this Hell's Kitchen eight-seater, but it's worth it for the perfectly spiced falafel and super-fresh Israeli salads. Closed Fri night and Sat.

Brasserie Centrale Map 7, F7. 1700 Broadway, at W 53rd St ☎212/757-2233. A Midtown rarity, where you can linger over coffee, freshly baked treats, or a full meal. The menu offers a range of burgers, soups, salads, pastas, and average French-tinged brasserie standards (stick with the simpler items on the menu). Large outdoor seating area. Open 24hrs. **Cupcake Café Map 6, D2. 545 9th Ave, btw 40th and 41st.** ☎212/465-1530. A delightful little joint, offering decent soups and sandwiches at bargain prices, as well as great cakes and pillowy, buttercream-frosted cupcakes. Anything with fruit is a must. The main location is inside the Books of Wonder children's bookstore at 18 W 18th St, in Chelsea.

Upper East Side

Payard Patisserie & Bistro Map 7, J2. 1032 Lexington Ave, btw 73rd and 74th ☎212/717-5252. This is real Parisian pastry – buttery, creamy, and over the top. Cookies, cakes, and *crème brûlée* made to the highest standards. **Serendipity 3 Map 7, J5. 225 E 60th St, btw 2nd and 3rd** ☎212/838-3531. Long-established eatery and ice-cream parlor, adorned with Tiffany lamps. The frozen hot chocolate, a trademarked and copyrighted recipe, is out of this world. Long lines on weekends. **Wildgreen Café Map 8, J7. 1555 3rd Ave, at 88th** ☎212/828-7656. A small-town feel adds to the draw of this shop, "where natural foods become gourmet." It's justly known for its muffins, salads, wraps, and, especially, fresh-blended, exotic smoothies.

Upper West Side and Morningside Heights

Café Mozart Map 7, E3. 154 W 70th St, btw Central Park West and Columbus ☎212/595-9797. This faded old Viennese coffeehouse is the place to go after a night at the opera; it's open until midnight. Double up on dessert and get the apple crumb cake and the iced espresso with chocolate ice cream. **Caffè la Fortuna Map 7, E2. 69 W 71st St, btw Central Park West and Columbus** ☎212/724-5846. The atmosphere here is dark, comfy, and inviting, and the Italian pastries are heavenly. You can sip a coffee all day long in the shade of the peaceful garden, or wind down after a night on the town. Open till midnight weekdays, 1am weekends.

Edgar's Café Map 8, B8. 255 W 84th St, btw West End Ave and Broadway ☎212/496-6126. A pleasant coffeehouse named after Edgar Allan Poe, who once lived at this address, with good (though expensive) desserts and light snacks, spicy hot cider in the winter, and well-brewed coffee and tea all the time.

Gray's Papaya Map 7, C2. 2090 Broadway, at W 72nd ☎212/799-0243. Order two all-beef franks and a papaya juice for a true New York experience. No ambiance, no seats, just good, cheap grub.

Hungarian Pastry Shop Map 8, C1. 1030 Amsterdam Ave, btw 110th and 111th ☎212/866-4230. This simple, no-frills coffeehouse with plentiful outdoor seating is a favorite with Columbia University students and faculty alike. You can sip your espresso and read all day if you like. The pastries are made on the premises.

Levain Bakery Map 7, C2. 167 W 74th St, at Amsterdam. ☎212/874-6080. The huge, heaven-sent chocolate-chip and chocolate-peanut-butter-chip cookies baked in this cheerful basement bakery may be the best you'll ever taste – crispy on the outside, soft and cakey within, and generously strewn with gooey chips. There are a few window stools and benches outside where you can sit.

Harlem

Settepani Bakery and Café 196 Lenox Ave, at 120th St ☎917/492-4806. Great place to get a coffee and a sweet in Harlem, especially in the summer when there's ample sidewalk seating and good people-watching. The chef is a graduate of the French Culinary Institute and it shows in his terrific pastries – éclairs, napoleons, tiramisu, mini-tarts piled high with fruit. Unlike the flagship bakery in Williamsburg, Brooklyn (see p.168), this location also serves light lunches of salads, sandwiches, and pasta.

Society Coffee Lounge 2104 Frederick Douglass Blvd, at 114th. ☎212/222-3323. Popular new coffeehouse in South Harlem with exposed brick walls and communal tables and banquettes good for cozy conversation, reading, or writing. Waffles – the specialty – come with toppings like cinnamon-apple and dark chocolate. Also serves soups and salads and good espresso drinks.

Strictly Roots Map 9, C4. 2058 Adam Clayton Powell Blvd, btw 122nd and 123rd ☎212/864-8699. Harlem health-food café with protein shakes, smoothies, and apple-cider-sweetened sweet-potato pie.

The outer boroughs

Athens Café 32-01 30th Ave, Astoria, Queens ☎718/626-2164. The Greekest of Greek cafés, with spinach pies and sticky desserts. Sidewalk seating, best enjoyed with a foamy coffee frappe.

Bedouin Tent 405 Atlantic Ave, at Bond St, Brooklyn ☎718/852-5555. Fresh, delicious Middle Eastern pita sandwiches, salads, and pitzas; convenient to Brooklyn Heights.

🏃 **Café Bar 32-90 36th St, entrance on 34th Ave, Astoria, Queens** ☎718/204-5273. Vintage furniture crowds this artsy version of a Greek café near the American Museum of the Moving Image. Try the grilled-pork-and-halloumi sandwich.

Egg/Sparky's American Food 135 N 5th St, between Bedford and Berry, Williamsburg, Brooklyn ☎718/302-5151. *Egg's* hearty all-breakfast menu runs 7am–noon; later, *Sparky's* does high-end hot dogs and shakes.

Grimaldi's Map 4, K6. 19 Old Fulton St, between Water and Front sts, DUMBO, Brooklyn ☎718/858-4300. People line up down the sidewalk for the delicious thin-crust pizza. Lunchtime has lighter crowds. Cash only.

Lemon Ice King 52-02 108th St, at 52nd Ave, Corona, Queens ☎718/937-2044. Italian-style fruit ices (in more flavors than just lemon), served in paper cups; close to Flushing Meadows.

Lounge 47 47-10 Vernon Blvd, Long Island City, Queens ☎718/937-2044. See review, p.247.

Nathan's Surf Ave at Stillwell Ave, Coney Island, Brooklyn ☎718/946-2202. The original hot-dog stand – totally irresistible.

Press Café 114 E 157th St, at Gerard Ave, the Bronx ☎718/701-0545. This surprisingly elegant place deals in tasty toasted sandwiches, among other things. Open only on Yankee game days.

22

Restaurants

New York is a rich international city that can get the best foodstuffs from anywhere in the world, and, as a major immigration gateway, it attracts chefs who know how to cook the world's cuisines with flair. As you stroll through the streets of New York, heavenly odors seem to emanate from every corner – it's not hard to work up an appetite.

Outside of **American** and **Continental cuisines** (more or less including New American, which can either dazzle with its inventive fusions or fail miserably and pretentiously), be prepared to confront a startling variety of **ethnic food**. In New York, none has had so dominant an effect as **Jewish food**, to the extent that many Jewish specialties – bagels, pastrami, cream cheese, and lox – are now considered archetypal New York. **Eastern European restaurants** – Russian, Ukrainian, Polish, and Hungarian – are dwindling in number, but those that remain serve well-priced, filling fare. Chinese food includes the familiar Cantonese, as well as spicier Sichuan and Hunan dishes; most restaurants specialize in one or the other. Japanese food is widely available and very good. Other **Asian cuisines** include Indian and a broad sprinkling of Thai, Korean, and Vietnamese restaurants.

Italian cooking is widespread and not terribly expensive, and usually a fairly safe bet. **French** restaurants tend to be pricier, although bistros and brasseries that turn out authentic and reliable French nosh for attractive prices can be found in nearly every neighborhood. **Spanish** tapas bars, where you can assemble your dinner out of appetizer-size dishes or (usually) share a giant paella, have made a resurgence of late, as has modern Spanish cuisine. **Caribbean**, **Central American**, and **South American** restaurants are also on the rise in New York, and usually offer a good deal and a large, satisfying, and often spicy meal. Still, by far the biggest food trend to grip the city in recent years is the passion for **local foods**, especially those grown or raised organically, or without artificial fertilizers or pesticides.

As for where you'll be going for these foods, we've divided our selections below **by neighborhood** (and then cuisine) and have given very brief descriptions for what you might expect to find in those areas. As you'll see, some neighborhoods are dining destinations; others cater mainly to locals, but for the most part you won't have to walk very far to find a decent place in almost any district.

Useful websites

As with anything that elicits strong opinions, New Yorkers love to talk about food. And not just fancy food: there's as much interest in pizza as there is in pork belly, which you'll quickly see if you visit any of the city's **food-centric websites**. Of these, ⓦ www.nymag.com, *New York* magazine's website, is particularly good, with a quick search engine and both professional and amateur reviews. Another great site is ⓦ www.menupages.com, which has up-to-date menus, contact information, user reviews, and prices for more than six thousand New York restaurants. The most chaotic and rabid of the foodie sites, ⓦ www.chowhound.com, features endless threads on both mainstream and arcane eateries and has especially good coverage of spots in the outer boroughs. When you're ready to seal the deal, go to ⓦ www.opentable.com, where you can check availability and make free reservations at eight hundred top restaurants.

Financial District and City Hall

Financial District restaurants have typically revolved around lunch – takeout feeding troughs for the office workers and overpriced steakhouses for the Wall Street crowd – with the area virtually dead at night. But with the sprucing up of Stone Street and the area just north of the South Street Seaport, there are far more options for dinner than there used to be, some of them quite good. See also Chapter 23, "Drinking," as most of the neighborhood's pubs also serve food.

American and Continental

Bridge Café Map 4, G5. 279 Water St, at Dover ☎212/227-3344. This quaint red-painted frame house in the shadow of the Brooklyn Bridge has supposedly held a bar since 1794, but the food is very up-to-the-minute. Buffalo steak with lingonberry sauce and *gnocchi* is a perennial hit, and there are plenty of upscale beers to choose from. Dinner entrees are priced between $20 and $30, lunch between $15 and $25; brunch is $22 and very popular so reserve ahead.

Italian

Gigino at Wagner Park Map 4, D8. 20 Battery Place, at West St. ☎212/528-2228. Your best bet for waterfront dining downtown. This little Italian place is stashed beneath the stone observation deck in Wagner Park, but the interior is bright and modern, with floor-to-ceiling glass windows and a vast back patio overlooking New York Harbor. Brick-oven pizza and homemade pasta are the specialties, but there's lighter fare (arugula salads, various soups), too. The $25 prix-fixe dinner ($22 lunch) is good value.

Latin American

Salud! Map 4, G6. 142 Beekman St, at Front. ☎212/566-2220. Rockin' newcomer that's helping transform Front Street into the Financial District's restaurant row. The tapas menu ($8–15 each) has the usual Spanish dishes (codfish croquettes, *ceviche*) as well as Latin American specialties like mini-Cuban sandwiches and fried plantain. The *mojitos* are spectacular, and there's live Cuban music Tuesday and Thursday nights.

SoHo and NoLita

Though **SoHo** is slowly losing cachet to TriBeCa and other trendy neighborhoods, a number of the city's top restaurants still make their home here. The **NoLita** strip at the east end of SoHo is notable for a couple of wildly popular budget restaurants, while in the district's heart you can expect to pay top dollar for the more sophisticated fare.

Asian

Blue Ribbon Sushi Map 5, D6. 119 Sullivan St, btw Prince and Spring ☎212/343-0404. The focus here is actually more on the outstanding raw bar, but they have excellent sushi as well. The lines for a table can be long, thanks to the no-reservations policy, but have a couple of cocktails and relax – the kitchen is open until 2am.

Lovely Day Map 5, H7. 196 Elizabeth St, btw Prince and Spring ☎212/925-3310. Budget NoLita favorite whose homely interior-decor belies the place's jam-packed, lively atmosphere at all hours. Asian-leaning menu with gently priced pad thai, satay, and curry.

Omen Map 5, E6. 113 Thompson St, at Prince ☎212/925-8923. Named for a noodle shop but with the best sushi in the area by far (try the bluefin sashimi platter, formed in the shape of a rose), with a rotating seasonal menu and extensive *sake* list. If you go to one Japanese restaurant in New York, make it this one.

Prem-on Thai Map 5, D5. 138 W Houston, btw MacDougal and Sullivan ☎212/353-2338. Friendly Thai outpost with a lovely garden dining area. Pad thai is a good bet, but they also have delicious Southeast Asian curries and fish dishes.

Cuban

Café Habana Map 5, H6. 17 Prince St, at Elizabeth ☎212/625-2002. Small, hip, and always crowded, this Cuban/South American eatery features some of the best skirt steak and fried plantain this side of Havana. They also have a takeout window next door with great *café con leche*.

French

Balthazar Map 5, G7. 80 Spring St, btw Crosby and Broadway ☎212/965-1414. The tastefully ornate Parisian decor and surfeit of beautiful people keep your eyes busy until the food arrives; then all you can do is savor the fresh oysters and mussels, exquisite pastries, and everything in between. Great for late dinners, as the kitchen is open until 2am.

Raoul's Map 5, E6. 180 Prince St, btw Sullivan and Thompson ☎212/966-3518. French bistro seemingly lifted from Paris. The food, especially the steak *au poivre* and shrimp risotto, are wonderful – as you'd expect at prices as high as these (entrees run from $18 to $41). Reservations recommended.

Italian

Arturo's Pizza Map 5, E5. 106 W Houston St, at Thompson ☎212/677-3820. The coal-oven pizzas (no slices) in this checkered-tablecloth sauce joint rival some of the best pies in town. While-you-eat entertainment often includes live jazz.

TriBeCa

One of New York's trendiest neighborhoods, there are divine meals to be had in **TriBeCa** – and the people-watching isn't bad either.

American and Continental

Bouley Upstairs Map 4, D3. 130 W Broadway, at Duane ☎212/608-5829. Compared to David Bouley's eponymous restaurant across the street, where the tasting menu runs $90, the $15–20 entrees at this new venture above from his bakery are a bargain. The menu has a startling range of foods, from the signature Bouley burger, on an English muffin, to buttery fresh sushi.

Bubby's Map 4, C2. 120 Hudson St, btw Franklin and North Moore ☎212/219-0666. A relaxed TriBeCa restaurant serving rib-sticking Southern comfort food and gut-busting pies for dessert. A good, moderately priced brunch spot, too – the trout and eggs is killer.

Landmarc Map 4, D2. 179 W Broadway, btw Leonard and Worth. ☎212/343-3883. A popular spot for its buzzy but not over-the-top atmosphere and solid, something-for-everyone menu with particularly well executed steaks (five cuts) and salads, and cute $3 desserts including mini-ice cream cones. Best of all, they sell wines almost at cost. There's a new, much larger location in the Time Warner Center (☎212/823-6123).

Odeon Map 4, D3. 145 W Broadway, at Thomas ☎212/233-0507. *Odeon* has shown surprising staying power, perhaps because the eclectic food choices are actually pretty good and the people-watching can't be beat. Entrees go for around $20–30 and, on the whole, are worth it.

Tribeca Grill Map 4, C2. 375 Greenwich St, at Franklin ☎212/941-3900. Some people come for a glimpse of owner Robert De Niro, when they should really be concentrating on the fine American cooking with Asian and Italian accents. Main courses run around $25, while a prix-fixe Sunday brunch is only $24. The setting is nice, too: an airy, brick-walled eating area around a central Tiffany bar.

Asian

Nobu Map 4, C2. 105 Hudson St, at Franklin ☎212/219-0500. The lavish woodland decor complements superlative Japanese cuisine (especially sushi) with South American influences, all at ultra-high prices. If you can't get a reservation, try the slightly cheaper *Nobu Next Door*, located – wait for it – just next door. Another branch, helpfully called *Nobu 57*, is in Midtown at 40 W 57th St, between 5th and 6th (☎212/757-3000).

Austrian

Danube Map 4, D3. 30 Hudson St, at Duane ☎212/791-3771. Opulent puff-pastry of a restaurant that evokes old-world Viennese dining rooms, with Gustav Klimt–inspired murals and impressively efficient service. Try the port-glazed venison ($32) and top it off with a Middle-European white wine.

French

Chanterelle Map 4, C3. 2 Harrison St, at Hudson ☎212/966-6960. Some say while in New York you should live on stale bread all week and spend all your money on the French *haute cuisine* here – like sea scallops with mint and cucumber, and guinea-hen with ratatouille and fennel – which is of the finest order. The seven-course dinner tasting menu will set you back $125.

Chinatown and Little Italy

If authentic Chinese, Thai, and Vietnamese food is what you're after, head for the busy streets of **Chinatown**. Mulberry Street is **Little Italy**'s main drag, and though often crowded with tourists, its lively carnival atmosphere can make dinner and coffee a worthwhile excursion.

Asian

Joe's Shanghai Map 4, G3. 9 Pell St, btw Bowery and Mott ☎212/233-8888. Probably Chinatown's most famous restaurant, this place is always packed, with good reason. Start with the soup dumplings and work through some seafood dishes for the main course. Communal tables.

New York Noodletown Map 4, G2. 28 Bowery, at Bayard ☎212/349-0923. Despite the name, noodles aren't the real draw at this down-to-earth eatery. The salty soft-shell crabs are delicious, and the soups and roast meats (try the baby pig) are good.

Thailand Restaurant Map 4, G2. 106 Bayard St, at Baxter ☎212/349-3132. The well-priced Thai food is eaten at long communal tables here. Crispy and spicy whole-fish dishes are standouts.

Italian

Lombardi's Map 5, H7. 32 Spring St, btw Mott and Mulberry ☎212/941-7994. Some of the best pizza in town, including an amazing clam pie; no slices, though. Ask for roasted garlic on the side.

Vincent's Clam Bar Map 5, H8. 119 Mott St, at Hester ☎212/226-8133. A Little Italy mainstay that serves fresh, cheap, and spicy seafood dishes – clams, mussels, and squid.

The Lower East Side

In spots, the **Lower East Side** seems like a throwback to early immigrant sweatshop days; at others it's a place where the city's hipsters hang out. Either way, it's still the best place to get a pickle.

American and Continental

Schiller's Liquor Bar Map 5, K6. 131 Rivington St, at Norfolk ☏212/260-4555. Fairly high-end restaurant made up to look like a prohibition-era speakeasy. The menu ranges from bistro staples like Cobb salad and steak *frites* to vintage Americana, such as mac-and-cheese and pork chops with sautéed onions.

WD-50 Map 5, L6. 50 Clinton St, btw Rivington and Stanton ☏212/477-2900. Experimental *haute-cuisine* spot crammed into a retrofitted corner *bodega*, with unconventional entrees like Mediterranean bass with artichokes, cocoa nibs, and brittle peanut. The nine-course tasting menu goes for $115.

Asian

Sticky Rice Map 5, K7. 85 Orchard St, at Broome ☏212/274-8208. Tasty, reasonably priced Thai food (entrees are $10–15) in a warm-but-hip space, with friendly service. The specialty is Thai barbecue, but there's plenty of veggie fare, including portobello and tofu satay, spicy curries, and noodle soups. As of this writing, it's BYOB, but the liquor license is pending.

Italian

'inoteca Map 5, K6. 98 Rivington St, at Ludlow ☏212/614-0473. Lower East Side mainstay whose bustling atmosphere can be exciting or annoying depending on your tolerance for noise and crowds. Still, there's a reason it's so popular: almost everything on the extensive wine list pairs well with the crisp panini, cheese, olives, and cured meats on the menu. For a quieter version of the same thing, try *'inoteca*'s little sister, *'ino*, 21 Bedford St, btw Downing and 6th Ave, West Village (☏212/989-5796).

Jewish

Katz's Deli Map 5, K5. 205 E Houston St, btw Essex and Ludlow ☏212/254-2246. Line up cafeteria-style or sit down and be served. The overstuffed pastrami or corned beef sandwiches, doused with mustard and with a side pile of pickles, should keep you going for about a week. Also famous for their egg creams. Don't lose your meal ticket or they'll charge you an arm and a leg. Open seven days a week.

The East Village

It seems a new Italian restaurant, noodle bar, or chic café opens every day in the **East Village**, and the prices here are typically lower than what you'll find for high-quality meals in the rest of the city. Even more inexpensive are the homely Indian restaurants on East 6th Street and the filling Ukrainian eateries a bit north.

American and Continental

Prune Map 5, I5. 54 E 1st St, btw 1st and 2nd ☎212/677-6221. Cramped yet adventurous, this East Village staple delivers one of the city's most exciting dining experiences, serving $23–29 entrees, such as grilled quail with merguez sausage and desserts like flourless chocolate cake topped with blood-orange caramel. Wonderful, reasonably priced brunch.

Asian

Dok Suni's Map 5, J3. 119 1st Ave, btw 7th and St Mark's ☎212/477-9506. This dimly lit, stylish, sometimes thumpingly loud restaurant is a favorite for Korean home cooking like *bibimbop* (stir-fried vegetables, rice, and beef in a spicy red-pepper sauce), seafood pancakes, and *kimchee* rice. Moderately priced.

Hasaki Map 5, H3. 210 E 9th St, at 3rd ☎212/473-3327. Some of the best sushi around is served at this subterranean Japanese cubbyhole that manages to be both popular and mellow. Sit at the sushi bar and the chefs will regale you with a variety of impromptu dishes you won't find on the menu.

Jewel Bako Map 5, I4. 239 E 5th St, btw 2nd and 3rd ☎212/979-1012. Expensive Japanese delicacies, including a lot of sushi/sashimi offerings you can't get elsewhere in New York and some exotic delicacies like live raw lobster (not for the faint of heart). A memorable dining experience, though very expensive.

🏃 **Momofuku Noodle Bar** Map 5, J2. 171 1st Ave at 11th St. ☎212/475-7899. The crowds outside sometimes outnumber the diners within at this wildly popular but minuscule noodle shop helmed by newly-minted celebrity chef David Chang. The specialty is ramen served in a variety of smoky, salty broths, but the soft-shell crabs, steamed buns, dumplings, and seasonal heritage pork fixed every which way are all worth trying. Chang's second restaurant, *Momofuku Ssäm Bar*, 207 2nd Ave, at 13th (☎212/254-3500), is more inventive, mixing Korean and New American cuisines, but less intimate.

Eastern European

Veselka Map 5, I3. 144 2nd Ave, at 9th ☎212/228-9682. East Village staple that offers fine homemade borscht (hot in winter, cold in summer), latkes, *pierogi*, and great burgers and fries 24 hours a day.

Indian

Gandhi Map 5, J3. 345 E 6th St, btw 1st and 2nd ☎212/614-9718. One of the best and least expensive of the East 6th Street Indian restaurants – and also one of the more spacious, with two open dining areas. Try the lamb *muglai* and the light, fluffy *poori* bread.

Italian

Frank Map 5, I4. 88 2nd Ave, btw 5th and 6th ☎212/420-0202. This tiny neighborhood mainstay – serving basic, traditional Italian dishes – is packed every night with hungry locals looking for the closest thing to a home-cooked meal at a very reasonable price.

Il Bagatto Map 5 K5. 192 E 2nd St, btw aves A and B ☎212/228-3703. Beloved Italian eatery that has long been a staple of the East Village dining scene. Offers rustic, authentic Italian fare – including melt-in-your-mouth homemade pasta ($12–16) – in an intimate, candlelit setting. The emphasis here is on traditional Roman cooking, so don't ask for cheese for your seafood dish – you just won't get it. If you're in the mood for a snack and glass of *vino*, go next door to *Posto Accanto*, run by the same owners.

Middle Eastern

Khyber Pass Map 5, I3. 34 St Mark's Place, btw 2nd and 3rd ☎212/473-0989. Afghan food, which, if you're unfamiliar with it, is filling and has plenty to offer vegetarians (pulses, rice, and eggplant are frequent ingredients). The lamb dishes are tasty. Excellent value for around $15 per person. Open until 1am daily.

Spanish

Xunta Map 5, J2. 174 1st Ave, btw 10th and 11th ☎212/614-0620. This electric East Village gem buzzes with hordes of young faces perched on rum barrels downing pitchers of sangría and choosing from the dizzying tapas menu; try the mussels in fresh tomato sauce, the shrimp with garlic, and the mushrooms in brandy. You can eat (and drink) very well for around $25, and see free live flamenco to boot.

Vegetarian

Angelica Kitchen Map 5, I2. 300 E 12th St, btw 1st and 2nd ☎212/228-2909. A popular vegetarian macrobiotic restaurant with a warm, lively atmosphere. Cooks up cheap, very basic dishes (brown rice and steamed vegetables) as well as more inventive daily specials with ethnic accents and quirky names like "Thai Mee Up"; entrees are in the $8–14 range. Bring your own booze or resign yourself to twig tea.

The West Village

The **West Village** offers a fine array of discreet, upscale, though increasingly trendy spots in its angled streets, and is probably the most popular neighborhood of all for langorous weekend brunches.

American and Continental

Blue Hill Map 5, D3. 75 Washington Place, btw MacDougal and 6th ☎212/539-1776. One of the better spots in the West Village, serving rustic American fare like parsnip soup and braised cod made from seasonal local ingredients. Don't miss the rich chocolate bread pudding. Crowded but with elbow room between tables; reserve well in advance.
Corner Bistro Map 5, A2. 331 W 4th St, at Jane ☎212/242-9502. Down-home pub with cavernous cubicles, a great jukebox, and maybe the best burger and fries ($6.50) in town. A mix of locals and die-hard fans line up nightly until 4am, but don't be discouraged – the line moves fast.
Mary's Fish Camp Map 5, B3. 64 Charles St, at 4th ☎646/486-2185. Lobster rolls, bouillabaisse, and seasonal veggies adorn the menu at this intimate West Village clam shack, where you can almost smell the briny air. Go early, as the reservation line lasts into the night – and bring a full wallet.
Perry Street 176 Perry St, at West St ☎212/352-1900. Jean-Georges Vongerichten's most appealing

restaurant: a surprisingly friendly, relaxing place whose sleek modernist decor is matched by impeccable service and flawless food. The French-inflected New American menu is focused yet inventive, particularly with seafood, and the desserts are divine. Come for the $24 three-course prix-fixe lunch; it's one of the best deals in town, and the afternoon light is lovely. Located on the ground floor of one of Richard Meier's celebrity-stuffed glass apartment towers on the Hudson River.

Spotted Pig Map 5, A3. 314 W 11th St, at Greenwich ☎212/620-0393. One of the trendiest new restaurants in town, this nonetheless looks like it's been here forever, with lots of weathered wooden pigs about and a loyal clientele of locals and celebrities. The ubiquitous Mario Batali is part owner, but young British-expat chef April Bloomfield presides over the kitchen, turning out lusty gastropub fare like fried calf livers and rabbit stew. Come early (before 6pm) to avoid the horrendous line; no reservations accepted.

Westville Map 5, B3. 210 W 10th St, btw Bleecker and W 4th ☎212/741-7971. Choice cubbyhole of a restaurant specializing in country cooking, with a loyal clientele willing to be wedged in like sardines to partake of the flame-broiled burger ($9), served on a Portuguese muffin, and the vegetable market plate, which you compose yourself from options like mashed sweet potatoes, garlic string beans and roasted fennel. An East Village location recently opened at 173 Ave A, at 11th (☎212/677-2933).

French and Belgian

Jarnac just west of Map 5, A2. 328 W 12th St, at Greenwich ☎212/924-3413. Cozy, West Village *boîte* whose hearty and authentic food makes a great low-key excuse for avoiding the trendy masses at nearby *Pastis*. The menu changes regularly, but *Jarnac* is principally a rustic French restaurant, with an occasional New York twist. Prices are moderate – the prix-fixe menu is a great deal at $34; most main courses run around $25–30.

Italian

Babbo Map 5, D3. 110 Waverly Place, btw 6th and MacDougal ☎212/777-0303. This Mario Batali eatery offers delicious, creative Italian dishes – beef-cheek ravioli and various takes on scrapple garner much of the praise – attentive service, and an interesting selection of wine; it's quite popular, so reserve well in advance. The tasting menu is $70; $120 with the wine pairing.

John's Pizzeria Map 5, C4. 278 Bleecker St, btw 6th and 7th ☎212/243-1680. A full-service restaurant that offers some of the city's best and most popular pizza, with a crust that is thin and coal-charred. Be prepared to wait in line. No slices, no take-aways. There's an Upper East Side branch at 408 E 64th St, btw 1st and York (☎212/935-2895), and a Midtown West branch at 260 W 44th St, btw Broadway and 8th (☎212/391-7560).

Lupa Map 5, E5. 170 Thompson St, btw Bleecker and Houston ☎212/982-5089. Another Mario Batali restaurant, this fine, moderately priced trattoria serves hearty, rustic Italian specialties such as *osso buco*, *saltimbocca*, and *gnocchi* with fennel sausage. Go before 6.30pm and you'll have no problem getting a table.

Mexican

Mi Cocina Map 5, A1. 57 Jane St, at 8th ☎212/627-8273. Authentic Mexican food, such as spiced, meat-stuffed *poblano* chillies, in an upscale setting. Often crowded, so be prepared to wait.

Spanish

Sevilla Map 5, B3. 62 Charles St, at 4th ☎212/929-3189. Wonderful Village old-timer that is still a favorite neighborhood haunt. Dark, fragrant (from garlic) spot with good, moderately priced food. Terrific paella and large pitchers of strong sangría.

Chelsea

Once filled with Cuban sandwich shops and cheap Central American joints, the art mecca of **Chelsea** is fast becoming a food mecca as well, with sleek and trendy restaurants – from tiny tapas bars to hangar-size dining halls – cropping up every week, especially in the district's western reaches. Alas, most are quite expensive. For bargain bites in the area, try one of the cafés listed on p.200.

American and Continental

Caféteria Map 6, F8. 119 7th Ave, at 17th ☎212/414-1717. Don't let the name fool you: while *Caféteria* is open 24hrs and has great chicken-fried steak, meatloaf, and macaroni and cheese ($8–15), this place is anything but a fluorescent-lit assembly line. Instead, it's minimalist-chic, with plastic chairs and a deep-bass groove, and always packed with beautiful young diners.

Cookshop Map 6, C7. 156 10th Ave, at 20th St ☎212/924-4440. Seasonal, local, sustainable, grass-fed – you'll see all the green watchwords put to use at this glass-walled corner outfit in the heart of Chelsea's gallery district. Rotisserie chicken and whole grilled fish ($21–26) are specialties, but there are good options for vegetarians, too. If you can't get a table, squeeze in at the bar for a glass of wine and a snack of smoked bluefish or anchovy deviled eggs.

Empire Diner Map 6, C7. 210 10th Ave, btw 22nd and 23rd ☎212/243-2736. One of Manhattan's original diners, with a gleaming chrome-ribbed Art-Deco interior. Serves up plates of simple (if not much better than average) American diner food 24hrs. A bit pricey for what you get.

Asian

Buddakan Map 6, D8. 75 9th Ave, at 16th St ☎212/989-6699. As famous for its setting as for its Asian tapas-style menu, newcomer *Buddakan* is housed in a show-stopping 16,000-square-foot space done up like a Rococo mansion. As with everything in or near the trendy Meatpacking District, some call this place pretentious, but the food holds its own, with delicious dim sum like *edamame* dumplings ($11) and larger entrees such as tender tea-smoked chicken with ginger chutney ($18).

Caribbean

Negril Map 6, D7. 362 W 23rd St, btw 8th and 9th ☎212/807-6411. An enormous aquarium and colorful decor add to the pleasure of eating at this Jamaican restaurant. Spicy jerk chicken or goat, stews, and other dishes keep 'em coming, as do the reasonable prices (around $10–25 for an entree). There's another location in Greenwich Village, at 70 W 3rd St, btw LaGuardia and Thompson (☎212/477-2804).

French

La Lunchonette Map 6, C8. 130 10th Ave, at 18th ☎212/675-0342. Tucked away in a remote corner

22

RESTAURANTS

of Chelsea but perpetually crowded with loyal patrons, this understated little restaurant features the best of French country cooking, including steak *au poivre*, rabbit stew, and lamb sausages with sautéed apples; entrees $15 to $24.

Italian

Bottino Map 6, C6. 246 10th Ave, btw 25th and 26th ☎ 212/206-6766. One of Chelsea's most popular restaurants, *Bottino* attracts the in-crowd looking for some honest Italian food served in a very downtown atmosphere. The homemade leek *tortelloni* (winter months only) is truly tantalizing.

Spanish

Sala One-Nine Map 6, H8. 35 W 19th St, btw 5th and 6th ☎ 212/229-2300. Behind an unassuming storefront on a rather dull block near Union Square is this buzzing bar and restaurant, which caters to a young, professional crowd with the usual range of Spanish tapas (croquettes, *chorizo*, tortilla) as well as an extraordinary made-to-order paella, enough to feed two for just $19.

Tia Pol Map 6, C7. 205 10th Ave, btw 22nd and 23rd ☎ 212/675-8805. Less than a quarter the size of *Sala One-Nine*, *Tia Pol* resembles a cozy, wood-paneled railroad flat and caters to an upscale, artsy crowd with inventive tapas at moderate prices ($3–14). The *chorizo* with chocolate and crisp-but-juicy suckling pig are perennial winners.

Union Square, Gramercy Park, and the Flatiron District

The area between **Union Square** and **Gramercy Park**, as well as the **Flatiron District**, which extends north to Madison Square Park, aren't especially trendy neighborhoods, but they hold an astonishing number of top-notch restaurants. Some of the most dramatic are housed in the soaring lobbies of old office buildings and department stores.

American and Continental

Blue Water Grill Map 6, I8. 31 Union Square West, at 16th ☏212/675-9500. High-quality seafood restaurant with commensurate high prices. Hard to go wrong here, though, whether it's grilled fish, caviar, or raw bar.

Chat 'n' Chew Map 6, I9. 10 E 16th St, btw 5th and Union Square West ☏212/243-1616. Cozy comfort food in a colorful diner setting, where you can get large portions of American classics like macaroni and cheese and fried chicken. Good budget option and great sweet-potato fries.

Craft Map 6, J8. 43 E 19th St, btw Broadway and Park ☏212/780-0880. Part of Tom Colicchio's growing empire, this sleek and stylish place serves up roast foie gras, dayboat scallops, and tasty sides of sautéed wild mushrooms. Not cheap – mains hover around $35 – or vegetarian friendly. A slightly more affordabe alternative is *Craftbar*, 900 Broadway, btw 19th and 20th (☏212/461-4300), though you lose some of the atmosphere.

Gotham Bar & Grill Map 5, F2. 12 E 12th St, btw 5th and University ☏212/620-4020. Hardly your standard bar and grill – entrees are in the $35–40 range – celebrity chef Alfred Portale's acclaimed eatery is considered one of the city's best, serving marvelous New American fare in an airy, elegant setting.

Gramercy Tavern Map 6, J7. 42 E 20th St, btw Park and Broadway ☏212/477-0777. Frequently ranked as New Yorkers' favorite restaurant, this place drips with old-school elegance, with none of the usual stuffiness. Among the many fine items that have been on the menu are rabbit sausage with spaetzle, asparagus and fiddlehead ferns, and baby lobster with artichoke and pearl onions. If your wallet allows, try the seasonal six-course tasting menu for around $100.

Shake Shack Map 6, I6. Madison Square Park, Madison Ave at 23rd ☏212/889-6600. Closed Dec–March. The meat for the burgers is ground daily, the fries are organic, the shakes made with truffle cookie dough and Valrhona chocolate – what do you expect from Danny Meyer, the force behind *Union Square Café* (below) and *Gramercy Tavern* (above)? Beautiful park setting and a great bargain, but be prepared to wait up to an hour in line unless you go at an off-hour on a cloudy day.

Union Square Café Map 6, H8. 21 E 16th St, btw 5th and Union Square West ☏212/243-4020. Choice California-style dining with a classy but comfortable downtown atmosphere. Not at all cheap – prices average $120 for two – but the creative menu is a real treat. No one does salmon like they do.

French

Les Halles Map 6, J5. 411 Park Ave South, btw 28th and 29th ☎212/679-4111. Bustling bistro, formerly helmed by *Kitchen Confidential* author Anthony Bourdain, with carcasses dangling in a butcher's shop in the front. Very pseudo–Rive Gauche, serving rabbit, steak *frites*, and other staples in the $15–25 range; good breakfasts, too. There's another location in the Financial District, at 15 John St, btw Broadway and Nassau (☎212/679-4111).

Indian

Curry in a Hurry Map 6, K5. 119 Lexington Ave, at 28th ☎212/683-0900. No-frills curry trough popular with local cab drivers. Excellent and filling Indian dishes for around $10.

Tabla Map 6, J6. 11 Madison Ave, at 25th ☎212/889-0667. Swank *nouveau* Indian fare in an elegant, glassed-in second-floor dining room; it's a bit overrun by young banker types but serves memorable food. Start off with the duck samosas and move on to the pan-seared skate with baby artichokes and chickpeas. Cheaper and more boisterous – but still quite elegant – is the first-floor *Bread Bar*, where you can get gourmet "street food" like a dense, spicy shepherd's-pie sandwich and crispy *sag paneer* pizza. Be sure to reserve ahead at both.

South American

Coffee Shop Map 6, J7. 29 Union Square West, at 16th ☎212/243-7969. Reasonably priced Brazilian-inspired food, plus great turkey burgers. A solid brunch and lunch spot and also a good late-night hangout; the kitchen's open until 5:30am from Wed to Sat and they serve great *caipirinha* drinks.

Midtown East

Catering mostly to lunchtime office-going crowds that swarm the sidewalks on weekdays, **Midtown East** has scores of salad-and-sandwich places and nondescript pub-like restaurants, most of them on the pricey side for underwhelming fare. While you probably won't want to make it the focal point of too many culinary excursions, there are a few timeworn favorites in the neighborhood.

American and Continental

Four Seasons Map 7, I7. 99 E 52nd St, btw Park and Lexington ☎212/754-9494. One of the city's most noted restaurants, not least for its decor: housed in Mies van der Rohe's Seagram Building, you'll find murals by Picasso, sculptures by Richard Lippold, and interior design by Philip Johnson. The menu is full of luxury foods like caviar and foie gras, making the pre-theater menu a bargain at $65.

Keens Steakhouse Map 6, H3. 72 W 36th St, btw 5th and 6th ☎212/947-3636. *Keens* has been around since 1885, and it feels like it as you walk into the inviting lobby and then the fusty yet comfortable restaurant, festooned with old clay pipes (now numbering 88,000) that they've been collecting here for more than one hundred years. You can drink and snack on the pub menu in the bar on the right, or have the full works in the restaurant. Steak and lamb chops are the specialties, and although they'll empty your wallet – reckon on $40 for a main course – they're mighty good.

Oyster Bar Map 7, I9. Lower level, Grand Central Terminal, 42nd St and Park Ave ☎212/490-6650. Atmospheric turn-of-the-nineteenth-century place located down in the vaulted dungeons of Grand Central Terminal, where midtown execs and others break for lunch. The oyster appetizers are particularly good, while seafood entrees go for a minimum of $25 per dish. If you're hard up, just saddle up to the bar for a bowl of excellent clam chowder or great creamy bowls of pan-roasted oysters or clams.

Asian

Hangawi Map 6, I4. 12 E 32nd St, btw 5th and Madison ☎212/213-0077. An elegant vegetarian and vegan-safe Korean restaurant. The autumn rolls are a great starter. A little pricey, but quite good.

Hatsuhana Map 7, H8. 17 E 48th St, btw 5th and Madison ☎212/355-3345. One of the best sushi restaurants in the city, with sushi lunch specials for as little as $19 (five pieces of sushi and a roll), $26 at dinner. Precise, consistent service and immaculately fresh fish. There's a second location nearby, at 237 Park Ave, at 46th (℡212/661-3400).

Vong Map 7, J7. 200 E 54th St, at 3rd ℡212/486-8664. Best French–Thai food in the city (as if there were any competition), courtesy of Jean-Georges Vongerichten (see p.230); housed in a trendy dining room in the bowels of the appropriately named Lipstick Building (it's shaped like a lipstick cylinder). Come before 6.30pm or after 10pm for the $35 three-course prix-fixe dinner, featuring dishes like coconut-milk soup, slow-cooked salmon, and Valrhona-chocolate cake – it's a bargain for a restaurant of this caliber.

Italian

Luna Piena Map 7, J7. 243 E 53rd St, btw 2nd and 3rd ℡212/308-8882. One of the better local Italian places in a neighborhood of many mediocre restaurants. The food is good and well priced at $10–20 an entree, the service is friendly, and there's a nice enclosed garden for warm summer evenings.

Scandinavian

Aquavit Map 7, H7. 65 E 55th St, btw Madison and Park ℡212/307-7311. Superb Scandinavian food – pickled herring, salmon, even reindeer – in a lovely atrium restaurant with a mock waterfall cascading down one of the walls. A real treat, and priced accordingly – the three-course fixed-price dinner is $82. If that sounds steep, try the Sunday-afternoon all-you-can-eat Swedish smorgasbord for $48.

Midtown West

While the majority of Manhattan's best dining occurs downtown, some good meals await you in **Midtown West**, a neighborhood whose restaurants encompass Greek, South American, Japanese, African, French, and everything in between. **Restaurant Row** (West 46th St between Eighth and Ninth aves) is a frequent stopover for theatergoers seeking a pre-show or late-night meal, though **Ninth Avenue** offers cheaper, more stylish, and generally better alternatives.

American and Continental

Burger Joint Map 7, F6. 119 W 56th St, btw 6th and 7th ☏212/245-5000. Part the red-velvet curtain behind the reception desk of the swank *Parker Meridien* hotel and you'll find this incongruously divey burger-shack that looks for all the world like it could be right on a beach somewhere. Thin, crisp fries are served in a paper bag, and juicy burgers are wrapped in paper, even if you eat them on site. Wash it all down with a pitcher of Sam Adams.

Eatery Map 7, D7. 798 9th Ave, at 53rd ☏212/765-7080. A trendy, moderately priced spot that's full of young, artsy locals day and night but also works well for pre- or post-theater grub. The menu is a mash-up of comfort food (burgers, mac-and-cheese), healthy bites (fresh-squeezed juice, *edamame*), and bistro fare (chicken *paillard*, hangar steak).

Joe Allen Map 7, E8. 326 W 46th St, btw 8th and 9th ☏212/581-6464. Restaurant Row mainstay with an old-fashioned feel and reliable American food at moderate prices. The calf's liver with spinach and potatoes has been on the menu for years. Popular pre-theater spot, so reserve well in advance unless you can arrive after 8pm.

Asian

Ollie's Noodle Shop Map 7, E9. 411 W 42nd St, btw 9th and 10th ☏212/921-5988. Good Chinese restaurant that serves noodle soups, barbecued meats, and spare ribs. Not, however, a place to linger. Very cheap, very crowded, and very noisy. There are three other branches on Broadway on the Upper West Side: one at no. 1991, at 68th (☏212/595-8181), a second at no. 2315, at 84th (☏212/362-3111), and a third at no. 2957, at 116th (☏212/932-3300).

Ruby Foo's Map 7, F8. 1628 Broadway, at 49th ☏212/489-5600. Best dining option in Times Square, with a wide-ranging Asian menu that runs from sushi platters to dim sum to Thai noodle dishes, all done surprisingly well despite the vast size of the place. There's another location at 2182 Broadway, at 77th (☏212/724-6700).

French

Le Bernardin Map 7, H7. 155 W 51st St, btw 6th and 7th ☏212/554-1515. The most storied seafood restaurant in the United States, serving chef Eric Ripert's masterful takes on traditional Brittany fish dishes in elegant surroundings. It's priced to match, too: the $59 prix-fixe lunch is a bargain next to the $107 prix-fixe dinner and $180 chef's tasting menu ($320 with wine pairing). But if you can swing it, this is one dinner you'll never forget.

Italian

Trattoria dell'Arte Map 7, F6. 900 7th Ave, btw 56th and 57th ⊤212/245-9800. Unusually nice restaurant for this rather tame stretch of Midtown, with a lovely, airy interior, exceptional service, and good food. Great, wafer-thin crispy pizzas and imaginative pasta dishes go for around $20–25, and there's a mouth-watering antipasto bar that's eagerly patronized by an elegant, out-to-be-seen crowd.

Jewish

Carnegie Deli Map 7, F6. 854 7th Ave, btw 54th and 55th ⊤212/757-2245. This place is known for the size of its sandwiches – by popular consent the most generously stuffed in the city, and a full meal in themselves. The chicken noodle soup is good, too. Not cheap, however, and the waiters are among New York's rudest.

Stage Deli Map 7, F7. 834 7th Ave, btw 53rd and 54th sts ⊤212/245-7850. Reliable all-night standby, and longtime rival to the *Carnegie Deli*. More genuine New York attitude – it's been here since 1937 – and big, overstuffed sandwiches, priced accordingly.

Mexican and South American

Churrascaria Plataforma Map 7, D8. 316 W 49th St, btw 8th and 9th ⊤212/245-0505. Housed in a vast, festive hall packed to the gills with beautiful people, this eminent Brazilian institution features a $51.95 prix-fixe dinner that includes all the various grilled meats you can manage to keep down – brought sizzling to the table. Don't miss the addictive *caipirinhas* (Brazil's national drink).

Hell's Kitchen Map 7, D8. 679 9th Ave, btw 46th and 47th ⊤212/977-1588. Lively party atmosphere – aided and abetted by six different kinds of frozen margarita – and sophisticated renderings of Mexican cuisine. Reserve first unless you're arriving early.

The Upper East Side

Upper East Side restaurants cater mostly to a discriminating mixture of Park Avenue matrons and the young upwardly mobile; many of the city's best Japanese and French restaurants are here. For a change of pace, try a wurst and some strudel at *Heidelberg*, the last remaining of Yorkville's old-world German luncheonettes.

American and Continental

Lenox Room Map 7, J2. 1278 3rd Ave, btw 73rd and 74th ☎212/772-0404. Fairly swank seafood spot centered on an expansive raw bar (over a dozen varieties of oyster), delicious tuna tartar, and other *fruits de mer*. Entrees $19–32.

Post House Map 7, H4. 26 E 63rd St, at Madison Ave ☎212/935-2888. Classic American food in an elegant, comfortable, typically Upper East Side setting. It's reasonably unpretentious for the area, and does very good steaks and chops, though not at all cheaply – steaks are around $40.

Rathbones Map 8, K7. 1702 2nd Ave, btw 88th and 89th ☎212/369-7361. Take a window seat to watch the stars arrive at over-priced celeb hotspot *Elaine's* (across the street) and eat here for a fraction of the price. Steaks, burgers, and fish for around $15 and a wide choice of beers.

Asian

Pig Heaven Map 8, K9. 1540 2nd Ave, btw 80th and 81st ☎212/744-4333. Good-value Chinese restaurant decorated with images of pigs, and serving lean and meaty spare ribs, among other things. In case you hadn't guessed, the accent is on pork; entrees go for $10–18.

Sushi of Gari Map 8, L9. 402 E 78th St, btw 1st and York ☎212/517-5340. Wondrous neighborhood sushi shop with an extensive list of top-quality fish. Try the tasting menu and you're in for a host of unusual sushi offerings – from *toro* and pickled radish to salmon and a droplet of cream cheese.

French

Café Boulud Map 7, H1. 20 E 76th St, btw Madison and 5th ☎212/772-2600. Part of celebrity chef Daniel Boulud's ballooning restaurant empire (he also runs *Daniel* and *DB Bistro Moderne*), this muted but elegant gem is an exceedingly pleasant (and pricey) place to savor classics like foie gras terrine and roasted duck, as well as fusion dishes like curried Thai lobster. Save room for the molten chocolate cake. Jackets recommended for men.

German

Heidelberg Map 8, K7. 1648 2nd Ave, btw 85th and 86th ☎212/628-2332. The atmosphere here is *mittel*-European kitsch, with gingerbread trim and waitresses in Alpine goatherd costumes. But the food is the real deal, featuring excellent liver-dumpling soup, *Bauernfrühstück* omelets, and pancakes (both sweet and potato). And they serve *weissbier* the right way, too – in giant, boot-shaped glasses. Entrees hover around $20.

Indian

Dawat Map 7, J6. 210 E 58th St, btw 2nd and 3rd ☎212/355-7555. One of the most elegant gourmet Indian restaurants in the city. Try the Cornish game hen with green chilli, or the leg of lamb. A bit pricey; entrees average about $18, a bit more for seafood.

Italian

Caffé Buon Gusto Map 7, J1. 243 E 77th St, btw 2nd and 3rd ☎212/535-6884. This stretch of the Upper East Side has plenty of cool Italian joints: what *Buon Gusto* lacks in style it makes up for in taste and low prices (mains are $9.95–13.95). The vodka sauce is exceptional.

Middle Eastern

Afghan Kebab House Map 7, K3. 1345 2nd Ave, btw 70th and 71st ☎212/517-2776. You can get a complete dinner of juicy lamb, chicken, and seafood kebabs, served with a variety of side dishes, for under $20 here, thanks in part to the fact that you have to bring your own booze. There's another branch at 764 9th Ave, btw 51st and 52nd (☎212/307-1612).

Rectangles Map 7, K2. 1431 1st Ave, btw 74th and 75th ☎212/744-7470. Newly relocated from the East Village, this Yemeni–Israeli restaurant features knockout standards like *baba ganoush*, couscous, and a spicy chicken soup that can instantly cure the common cold. Entrees are $14–18.

The Upper West Side

The **Upper West Side** encompasses a large chunk of real estate, and thus offers a wide array of dining choices. There are lots of generous burger joints, Chinese restaurants, friendly diners, and delectable, if a bit pricey, brunch spots, so you'll never be at a loss for a good meal.

American and Continental

Big Nick's Map 7, C1. 70 W 71st St, at Columbus ℡ 212/799-4444. If you want a hamburger or pizza on the Upper West Side, this fun, New York kind of place is a good choice: in his crowded, chaotic, little wooden-table restaurant, "Big Nick" has been serving them up all night long to locals for twenty-plus years.

Boat Basin Café Map 7, A1. W 79th St, at the Hudson River (access through Riverside Park) ℡ 212/496-5542. An outdoor restaurant, open May–Sept, with informal tables covered in red-and-white checked cloths, some under a sheltering overhang. The food is standard but inexpensive considering the prime location – they start at $3 for a hot dog with chips and go up to $25.95 for steak.

Docks Oyster Bar Map 8, B6. 2427 Broadway, btw 89th and 90th ℡ 212/724-5588. Popular uptown seafood emporium with a raw bar, great mussels, and a wide variety of high-quality fresh fish.

Reservations recommended on weekends. There's another branch at 633 3rd Ave, at 40th St (℡ 212/986-8080).

Tom's Restaurant Map 8, B1. 2880 Broadway, at 112th St ℡ 212/864-6137. Cheap, greasy-spoon fare. This is the *Tom's* diner of Suzanne Vega and *Seinfeld* fame (it was known as *Monk's* on the show), usually filled with students from Columbia. Great breakfast deals – you can get a large meal for under $6.

Asian

Hunan Park Map 7, D3. 235 Columbus Ave, btw 70th and 71st ℡ 212/724-4411. Some of the best Chinese food on the Upper West Side is served here, in a large, crowded room, with typically quick service and moderate prices ($7–12 per entree). Try the spicy noodles in sesame sauce and the dumplings. Just a few blocks from Lincoln Center.

Shun Lee Map 7, D4. 43 W 65th St, at Columbus ℡ 212/595-8895. This venerable local institution half a block from Lincoln Center has top-notch Chinese food; steer yourself toward the menu's many seafood delicacies. While the service and table settings here are strictly formal, you should feel free to dress casually.

Caribbean

Café con Leche Map 8, C9. 424 Amsterdam Ave, at 80th ☎212/595-7000. Great neighborhood Dominican joint that serves roast pork, rice and beans, and some of the hottest chilli sauce you've ever tasted. Cheap and very cheerful. There's another location further north on Amsterdam and 96th.

Calle Ocho Map 8, D8. 446 Columbus Ave, btw 81st and 82nd ☎212/873-5025. Very tasty Latino fare, such as *ceviche* and *chimchuri* steak with yucca fries, is served in an immaculately designed dining room and a hopping couch lounge, with tasty and potent *mojitos*.

La Caridad Map 7, C1. 2199 Broadway, at 78th ☎212/874-2780. Something of an Upper West Side institution, this tacky, no-frills eatery doles out plentiful and cheap Cuban–Chinese food to hungry diners (the Cuban-slanted dishes are better than the Chinese). Bring your own beer.

French and Belgian

Café Luxembourg Map 7, C3. 200 W 70th St, btw Amsterdam and West End ☎212/873-7411. Trendy Lincoln Center–area bistro that packs in (literally) a self-consciously hip crowd to enjoy its first-rate contemporary French food. The $44 three-course prix-fixe dinner is a good deal; not much here for vegetarians, though.

Jean Georges Map 7, E5. Trump International Hotel, 1 Central Park West, btw 60th and 61st sts ☎212/299-3900. Star chef Jean-Georges Vongerichten's eponymous restaurant – see also *Perry Street* (p.216) and *Vong* (p.224) – is a great place for a splurge, thanks to its perfectly rendered seafood and sublime desserts. The chef's tasting menu runs $148, but a three-course prix-fixe lunch with the same creativity and competence is just $24 (dinner is $68).

Indian

Mughlai Map 7, D3. 320 Columbus Ave, at 75th ☎212/724-6363. Uptown, upscale restaurant with entrees running $11–16. The food is surprisingly good.

Italian

Gennaro Map 8, C6. 665 Amsterdam Ave, btw 92nd and 93rd ☎212/665-5348. Truly great Italian food served in a tiny spot with room for only about fifty people (and thus perpetual lines to get in). Standouts include an incredible warm potato, mushroom, and goat cheese tart ($10.50), and braised lamb shank in red wine with Israeli couscous ($16.95). The desserts are also worth the wait.

Jewish

Barney Greengrass Map 8, C7. 541 Amsterdam Ave, btw 86th and 87th ☏212/724-4707. A crusty, bare-bones Upper West Side deli and restaurant that's been around since time began. The Nova Scotia salmon and sturgeon section is a particular treat – you'll do well getting either one scram-bled with eggs and onion and an H&H bagel. Cheese blintzes are tasty, too. Breakfast and lunch only; huge waits on weekends; closed Mon.

Mexican

Rosa Mexicano Map 7, D4. 61 Columbus Ave, btw 62nd and 63rd ☏212/977-7700. Right across from Lincoln Center, this festive spot does the trick for a pre- or post-opera meal. Don't miss the guacamole, which is mashed at your table in a stone bowl, or the pomegranate margaritas. Two other locations in New York, including 9 E 18th St, near Union Square (☏212/533-3350), and the original, 1063 First Ave, at 58th (☏212/753-7407).

Upper Manhattan: Morningside Heights, Harlem, and above

Though there are some sophisticated new restaurants moving into **Harlem**, soul food and barbecue still reign supreme, and if you're on a budget and eat meat, you'd be a fool not to try both during your visit. Many places in **Morningside Heights** cater to Columbia students and faculty, delivering solid bistro fare for good prices.

African

Sokhna Map 9, D9. 225 W 116th St, at Adam Clayton Powell Jr Blvd ☎212/864-0081. This comfortable place is a good bet for savory, inexpensive Senegalese food. Nine dollars at lunch will get you a filling peanut or seafood stew over rice; dinner is nearly as cheap, with whole grilled fish for $12, *shawarma* for $10, and vegetarian couscous for $6. Open until 2am.

Zoma Map 9, D9. 2084 Frederick Douglass Blvd, at 113th St ☎212/662-0620. One of the sleekest places around, delivering solid Ethiopian food in minimalist digs at low prices. As at other Ethiopian spots, the combination platters are your best bet: here the veggie combo goes for $17 and is big enough to share. Meat eaters should try the *doro wett*, or long-simmered chicken in spices.

American

Amy Ruth's Map 9, D9. 113 W 116th St, btw Lenox and 7th ☎212/280-8779. This bright, friendly soul-food diner draws Harlemites and visitors with its outstanding fried chicken and ribs – ones that most agree outshine those of the more famous *Sylvia's*. Try the "Al Sharpton" – fried or smothered chicken and waffles ($9.50). The desserts are excellent, too. Don't worry about the line; it moves pretty quickly.

New Leaf Café 1 Margaret Corbin Drive (190th St), Fort Tryon Park ☎212/568-5323. Bette Midler is one of the backers of this lovely café, a mandatory fueling station for any trip to The Cloisters (p.156). The restaurant is housed in a nifty 1930s park building, but the real treat is the year-round terrace cradled by trees, where you can get a reliably juicy burger ($13), various salads for lunch, and fancy New American fare like pancetta-wrapped monkfish ($26) for dinner. Proceeds go to the upkeep of the park. Live jazz on Thurs nights; closed Mon.

Sylvia's Restaurant Map 9, D8. 328 Lenox Ave, btw 126th and 127th ☎212/996-0660. The best-known Southern soul-food restaurant in Harlem – so famous that Sylvia now has her own package food and beauty-product line. While some feel the quality's fallen off in recent years, the fried chicken is still a deal at $10.95 and the candied yams are justly celebrated. Consider getting a music fix while you clog your arteries, either at the Saturday Jazz or Sunday Gospel brunch.

Italian

Max Soha Map 9, C8. 1274 Amsterdam Ave, at 123rd ☎212/531-2221. A welcome newcomer to the Morningside Heights food scene, this bustling corner trattoria with ample outdoor seating serves up cheap and tasty Italian food – try the beet, goat cheese, and avocado salad ($6.95) or the melt-in-your mouth *gnocchi* ($9.95) – to a bed-headed Columbia crowd. The same folks run a takeout panini joint down the block, at no. 1262.

Brooklyn

In **Brooklyn**, lower Atlantic Avenue offers some of the city's best Middle Eastern food; Brighton Beach features the most authentic Russian food in NYC; and Park Slope, Carroll Gardens, Cobble Hill, and Fort Greene all have stellar restaurant rows.

American and Continental

Junior's 386 Flatbush Ave, at DeKalb Ave, Downtown Brooklyn ☎718/852-5257. Open 24hrs and with enough lights to make it worthy of Vegas, *Junior's* offers everything from chopped-liver sandwiches and ribs to a full cocktail bar. Most of it is just so-so – the real draw is the cheesecake, for which the place is justly famous.

Peter Luger Steak House 178 Broadway, at Driggs, Williamsburg ☎718/387-7400. Catering to carnivores since 1887, *Peter Luger* just may be the city's finest steakhouse. The service is surly and the decor plain, but the porterhouse steak – the only cut served – is divine. Cash only; expect to pay at least $60 per person.

The Queen's Hideaway 222 Franklin St, at Green St, Greenpoint ☎718/383-2355. There's Led Zeppelin on the vintage turntable and plenty of cast-iron skillets in the closet-sized kitchen of this idiosyncratic restaurant with a big backyard. The menu changes nightly, but you can count on something pork-based. Closed Mon.

River Café 1 Water St, at Old Fulton, DUMBO ☎718/522-5200. There's no more romantic spot in all of New York than this riverfront eatery with spectacular glassed-in views of the East River and downtown Manhattan's skyline. The seafood is quite good, though perhaps an afterthought for most lovestruck patrons.

Italian

Al Di Là 248 5th Ave, at Carroll, Park Slope ☎718/783-4565. Husband-and-wife-run eatery serving Venetian country cooking at its finest. Standouts include beet ravioli, grilled sardines, *saltimbocca*, and salt-baked striped bass. Invariably crowded.

D.O.C. Wine Bar 83 N 7th St, at Wythe, Williamsburg ☎718/963-1925. Shaved artichoke salad, honey-drizzled sheep's-milk cheese, and cured meats are a few of the light but intensely savory treats at this rustic, wood-paneled spot. Friendly service from the Sardinian owners, too.

French

Loulou 222 Dekalb Ave, between Adelphi and Clermont, Fort Greene ☎718/246-0633. Reliably delicious, with a tendency toward seafood (half of the husband-and-wife ownership team hails from Brittany). Very good brunch – heavy on Nutella – and a tiny backyard for outdoor dining.

Middle Eastern

Waterfalls Café 144 Atlantic Ave, at Henry St ☎718/488-8886. Middle Eastern specialties with a Syrian touch, touted by many as the best in the city, and certainly the best on Atlantic Ave, a short walk south from Brooklyn Heights. Salads and other *meze* are the best option.

Russian

Primorski 282 Brighton Beach Ave, between 2nd and 3rd sts, Brighton Beach ☎718/891-3111. A huge menu of authentic Russian dishes, including blintzes and stuffed cabbage, as well as a few Georgian specialties such as *kachapuri* (cheese pie), at absurdly cheap prices. Live music at night, though less over-the-top than some of the bigger supper clubs.

Queens

The most ethnically diverse of all the boroughs, **Queens** holds the city's largest Greek, South American, Slavic, and Asian communities, and thus features some of the best examples of these cuisines. Notable in particular are **Astoria** – an old Greek neighborhood – and **Flushing**, which boasts the best Chinese restaurants in New York.

Chinese

Spicy and Tasty 39-07 Prince St, Flushing ☎718/359-1601. #7 to Flushing–Main Street. Tea-smoked duck is the signature dish at this Sichuan specialist; prepare yourself for plenty of spicy noodle dishes as well. Open till 3am.

Greek

Agnanti 19-06 Ditmars Blvd, Astoria ☎718/545-4554. Specialist in Greek *meze*, overlooking Astoria Park. In winter, the fireplace makes it cozy, and in summer, the sidewalk tables are packed. Don't miss the "specialties from Constantinople" section of the menu, with goodies like *bekri-meze*, wine-soaked cubes of tender meat.

Uncle George's 33-19 Broadway, at 34th, Astoria ☎718/626-0593. This well-known, incredibly cheap 24-hour joint caters to a huge cross-section of the neighborhood. Food can be uneven, but the grilled meats and oven-roasted potatoes don't fail.

Indian

Jackson Diner 37-47 74th St, between 37th and Roosevelt aves, Jackson Heights ☎718/672-1232. Come here hungry and stuff yourself silly with wonderfully light and reasonably priced Indian fare. The *samosas* and mango *lassis* are not to be missed.

Middle Eastern

Hemsin 39-17 Queens Blvd, Sunnyside ☎718/937-1715. #7 train to 40th Street–Lowery Street. Perfectly prepared Turkish food, from delicate salads to grilled kebabs. Don't forget the bread, exceptionally fluffy and chewy.

🏃 **Kabab Café 25-12 Steinway St, Astoria** ☎718/728-9858. The culinary highlight of Steinway Street's "Little Egypt," where Chef Ali lavishes regulars with traditional Middle Eastern goodies as well as his own creations, like honey-glazed duck. If it's too packed, head down the street to his brother's place, *Mombar* (no. 25-22). Cash only. BYOB. Closed Mon.

RESTAURANTS

Thai

 Sripraphai 64-13 39th Ave, Woodside ☎ 718/899-9599. #7 to 61st Street–Woodside Avenue. Truly authentic Thai food that puts anything in Manhattan to shame – and it's astoundingly cheap. Try "drunken" noodles with beef and basil, and staples like papaya salad and lemongrass soup, or flip through the photo menu for inspiration.

The Bronx

The Belmont area in **the Bronx** is one of the best places in the city to eat real Italian-American cuisine – much better than Little Italy in Manhattan. There's also quite a lot of cheap Latin food on offer.

Caribbean

The Feeding Tree 892 Gerard Ave, at 161st St, South Bronx ☎ 718/293-5025. At this friendly Jamaican takeout spot not far from Yankee Stadium, wash down the spicy jerk chicken with a cool sorrel drink. Plenty of vegetarian options, too.

Italian

Dominick's 2335 Arthur Ave, at 187th St, Belmont ☎ 718/733-2807. All you expect from a Belmont neighborhood Italian place: communal family-style seating, hearty food, and (usually) low prices – sometimes hard to gauge, as there's no printed menu or written check. Just listen closely to your waiter. Cash only.

Roberto's 603 Crescent Ave, between Arthur Ave and Hughes St, Belmont ☎ 718/733-9503. Renowned for its rich pastas, served on giant plates or baked in foil; chef's specials are always the best option. Not quite so stuck in a time warp as other Belmont favorites.

Mexican

Mister Taco 2255 White Plains Rd, at Astor, Central Bronx ☎ 718/882-3821. Makes for a great snack or meal after walking around the botanical garden or zoo (it's three blocks east of the parks). The tamales are the call here. Very little English spoken – just point and smile.

23

Drinking

The **bar scene** in New York City is a varied one, with a broader range of places to drink than in most American cities, and prices to suit most wallets. Some bars are open as early as 10am, though most kick off around 4pm unless they have a kitchen, in which case they may open for lunch; closing time is usually around 2am, but some places stay open till 4am, when they have to close by law. Bar kitchens usually stop serving around midnight or a little before.

The best bars are below 14th Street. The **West Village** takes in a wide range of tastes, budgets, and purposes. Equally good hunting grounds can be found in the **East Village**, **NoLita**, **SoHo**, and the **Lower East Side**. There's a decent choice of **Midtown** bars, though these tend to be geared to an after-work crowd and (with a few notable exceptions) can consequently be pricey and rather dull. The **Upper West Side** has a small array of bars, some interesting, although most cater to more of a clean-cut yuppie crowd. Across the park, **Upper East Side** bars are split between frat-boy- and sorority-girl-oriented pubs and old-school hotel bars. In northern Manhattan, the bars of **Harlem**, while not numerous, are some of the best places to see inexpensive live jazz.

Most visitors to New York may not have time or occasion to check out the bar scenes in the outer boroughs, but those who venture to Williamsburg, Park Slope, Brooklyn Heights, and Fort Greene in **Brooklyn** or to Astoria in **Queens** will find both some of the hippest and most neighborly spots around. Predominantly **gay and lesbian bars** in both Manhattan and the boroughs are grouped together and reviewed in Chapter 26.

Whether you wind up sipping a martini in a swank lounge or downing a pint in a seedy dive, you'll be expected to **tip**; figure a buck or more per drink. Remember also that smoking in bars is illegal, and that the legal drinking age is 21; if you look young, be prepared to show ID.

The Financial District

Bin 220 Map 4, G5. 220 Front St, btw Peck Slip and Beekman ☎212/374-9463. Handy new wine-bar that's proof-positive the South Street Seaport's becoming a cool place. *Bin 220* has a weathered-but-sleek feel with dim lights, atmospheric music, and two separate lists of Italian wine – one by each of the two co-owners – by the bottle, glass, and flight. Cheese, cured meats, olives, panini, and other Italian snacks are served, as is lunch.

The Full Shilling Map 4, F7. 160 Pearl St, btw Wall and Pine ☎212/422-3855. The wooden bar here was shipped in from Belfast and recently celebrated its centenary. Think excellent pub grub and copious pints of Guinness, with a clientele consisting of younger Wall Street types, and you get the general idea.

Jeremy's Alehouse Map 4, G5. 228 Front St, btw Peck Slip and Beekman ☎212/964-3537. An earthy sports bar near the Seaport, *Jeremy's* serves up cheap pints and machismo – as well as some of the city's best *calamari* and clams.

SoHo and NoLita

Ear Inn Map 5, B7. 326 Spring St, btw Washington and Greenwich ☎212/226-9060. This cozy pub, a stone's throw from the Hudson River, has a good mix of beers on tap, serves basic, reasonably priced American food, and claims to be the second-oldest bar in the city.

Fanelli Map 5, F7. 94 Prince St, at

23

DRINKING

Mercer ☎212/226-9412. Established in 1872, *Fanelli* is one of the city's oldest bars, relaxed and informal and a favorite of the not-too-hip after-work crowd. The food is simple American fare: burgers, salads, and such.

Pravda Map 5, G6. 281 Lafayette St, btw Houston and Prince ☎212/334-5015. Very tasteful, pseudo-exclusive bar with nothing Communist about the place but its name – instead, it's caviar and cocktails, all washed down with Champagne.

Sweet and Vicious Map 5, I7. 5 Spring St, btw Bowery and Elizabeth ☎212/334-7915. This neighborhood favorite is the epitome of rustic chic, with exposed brick and wood, replete with antique chandeliers. The atmosphere makes it seem quaint, as does the back garden.

Toad Hall Map 5, E8. 57 Grand St, btw Wooster and West Broadway ☎212/431-8145. Great, tiny, atmospheric bar with a pool table, a good jukebox, and none of the pretension or attitude of nearby establishments. There's no food, but you can order in or bring your own dinner.

TriBeCa

Grace Map 4, D2. 114 Franklin St, btw Church and West Broadway ☎212/343-4200. An excellent cocktail-and-olives spot teeming with old-school class – there's a 40-foot-long mahogany bar and a huge selection of malts. Top-notch drink selection for a thirtysomething clientele.

Knitting Factory Tap Bar Map 4, E3. 74 Leonard St, btw Church and Broadway ☎212/219-3006. You don't need a ticket to partake of the *Knitting Factory's* creative offerings: just grab a drink at the street-level bar, and music – usually indie rock or experimental jazz – will ooze through the walls from the three surrounding stages. Call ahead, though: for popular shows the bar's sometimes annexed to the main concert space (see p.254 for details).

The Lower East Side

Barrio Chino Map 5, K7. 253 Broome, btw Orchard and Ludlow ☎212/228-6710. Packed, popular bar in the quieter southern part of the Lower East Side; looks like a hip *taqueria*, but with Chinese accents such as paper lanterns. The exposed brick and cheek-by-jowl tables give it a warm, social feel, as do the fifty kinds of tequila and tasty *antojitos*, or bar snacks.

The Delancey Map 5, L7. 168 Delancey St, btw Clinton and Attorney ☎212/254-9920. A kind of twentysomething hipster superbar, this triple-level layer cake features a lounge, a basement bar, and a stage for up-and-coming acts, plus a nicotine-friendly rooftop bar with great views over the East River and the Williamsburg Bridge.

King Size Map 5, K9. 21 Essex St, btw Hester and Canal ☎212/995-5464. No sign and a shady doorway lead to this great late-night DJ bar that, despite its newness, speaks of cooler, shabbier times on the LES. Cheap drinks and friendly staff are added bonuses.

Kush Lounge Map 5, I6. 191 Chrystie St, btw Rivington and Stanton ☎212/677-7328. One of New York's more popular hookah bars brings a bit of Casablanca to the Lower East Side, with comfy ottomans, good, strong drinks and hookahs (the latter are $30 each), and great music. Wednesday is Brazilian night, with a live band and free food. On weekends, belly dancers show off their abs. A solid neighborhood choice. Indoor smoking allowed.

The East Village

Angel's Share Map 5, H3. 8 Stuyvesant St, at 3rd Ave ☎212/777-5415. Look for the pink awning and climb the dingy staircase to this elegant Japanese-run cocktail lounge, incongruously attached to the boisterous restaurant of the same name (the door to the bar is near the top of the stairs).

Here you'll find cocktails made to perfection by the crisply-bowtied bartenders, as well as a small menu of Japanese finger food.

Decibel Map 5, I3. 240 E 9th St, btw 2nd and 3rd ☎212/979-2733. Great, eclectically decorated underground sake bar with good tunes and a rocking atmosphere.

The inevitable wait for a table will be worth it, guaranteed.

Eleventh Street Bar Map 5, K2. 510 E 11th St, btw A and B ☏212/982-3929. Friendly pub (with a house cat) filled with locals and, occasionally, their beer-drinking pooches. Big round tables in the back make this place great for bigger groups, while subdued lighting lends itself to intimate tête-à-têtes.

Holiday Cocktail Lounge Map 5, J3. 75 St Mark's Place, btw 1st and 2nd ☏212/777-9637. An East Village classic, this Christmas-lights-bedecked dive has been around since the area was a haven for punk rockers and drug addicts. It's banged up and dilapidated, and you'll be drinking beer, whiskey, or the most basic cocktails. The real thing.

KGB Map 5, H4. 85 E 4th St, btw 2nd and Bowery ☏212/505-3360. This bordello-like bar tucked on the second floor is painted deep red for a reason: it claims to have been the HQ of the Ukrainian Communist Party. Today, it's best known as the site of A-list literary readings and other cultural fare, though you can drop in anytime for a drink. See ⓦwww.kgbbar.com for a schedule.

Lakeside Lounge Map 5, L2. 162 Ave B, btw 10th and 11th ☏212/529-8463. Owned by a local DJ and a record producer who have stocked the jukebox with old rock, country, and R&B. A down-home hangout, with live music four nights a week.

McSorley's Old Ale House Map 5, 3H. 15 E 7th St, btw 2nd and 3rd ☏212-473-9148. Storied dive founded in 1854 has wood-planked floors, lots of old photos, and two types of house-made ale – light and dark. It was made famous by New Yorker writer Joseph Mitchell, whose affectionate essay about the bar's early days, "McSorley's Wonderful Saloon," is still a great read. Crowd is a mix of Cooper Union students and literate tourists.

The West Village

Chumley's Map 5, B4. 86 Bedford St, btw Grove and Barrow ☏212/675-4449. It's not easy to find this former speakeasy and literary hangout, owing to its unmarked entrance (ask a local if you can't find it), but it's worth the effort, especially in winter when the good choice of beers and food lures in many a cold, hungry soul.

Most of the seats are reserved for restaurant patrons, so be prepared to stand if you're just drinking. Note: at the time of writing, *Chumley's* was closed due to a collapsed wall, but it was expected to reopen in October 2007. Call ahead just in case.

Employees Only Map 5, B4. 510 Hudson St, at Christopher ☎212/242-3021. Richly decorated cocktail lounge and dinner joint, featuring mixed drinks made with fresh ingredients (try the lavender-scented gin) and an in-house fortune-teller for a thirtysomething crowd.

the otherroom 143 Perry St, btw Greenwich and Washington ☎212/645-9758. A Far West Village favorite, this matchbook-sized bar has exposed brick walls and high candlelit tables, a good list of wines and beers (no liquor), and a clientele of well-heeled, artsy locals. It's heavenly in warm weather when the windows open up to the pretty street just a short distance from the river.

White Horse Tavern Map 5, A3. 567 Hudson St, at 11th ☎212/243-9260. Greenwich Village institution where Dylan Thomas drank his last drink before being carted off to hospital, where he died from alcohol poisoning. The beer and food are cheap and palatable, and outside seating is available in the summer – if you can battle your way past the crowds, that is. Come on a weekday afternoon, when it's practically deserted and you can linger.

Chelsea

Half King Map 6, B7. 505 W 23rd St, at 10th ☎212/462-4300. *Perfect Storm* author Sebastian Junger and some other literary types run this busy corner bar/bistro, the site of frequent readings. Day or night it's a pleasant, warm place, with decent if pricey pub fare, including a competent fish-and-chips. The large sidewalk seating area is popular in summertime.

The Park Map 6, C8. 118 10th Ave, btw 17th and 18th ☎ 212/352-3313. It's easy to get lost in this vast warren of rooms filled with fireplaces, geodes, and even a Canadian redwood in the middle of the floor. The garden is a treat, and the servers are some of the best-dressed in New York. The roof deck's open Fri and Sat after 11pm.

Passerby Map 6, C9. 436 W 15th St, btw 9th and 10th ☎212/206-7321.

This unmarked gem is popular with local artists (Björk, among others) for its quirky decor – it has a rainbow-checkered light-up floor – and expertly mixed cocktails. Late-night DJs give it a club feel without the Meatpacking District's velvet-rope hype.

Union Square and Gramercy Park

Cibar Map 6, K8. 56 Irving Place, btw 17th and 18th ☏ 212/460-5656. Innovative cocktails, elegant decor, and a sweet garden make this snug bar in the basement of the *Inn at Irving Place* (see p.185) a local hotspot for a slightly older crowd.

🏃 **Old Town Bar and Restaurant Map 6, J8. 45 E 18th St, btw Broadway and Park Ave South ☏ 212/529-6732.** One of the oldest and still one of the very best bars in the city, with a long, ornate bar, creaky wood floors, and lots of period detail. Come early or late, as it can get packed in prime hours with local suits

coming after work for reliable chili, burgers, and onion rings, and then staying for an extra pint or two.

Pete's Tavern Map 6, K8. 129 E 18th St, at Irving Place ☏ 212/473-7676. Opened in 1864, this former speakeasy claims to be the oldest bar in New York, but was in fact beaten by a decade by *McSorley's* (see p.241) on East 7th St. The place trades on its history these days, which has included such illustrious patrons as O. Henry, who allegedly wrote "The Gift of the Magi" here, in his regular booth.

Midtown East and Midtown West

Bar Room at the Modern Map 7, G5. 9 W 53rd St, btw 5th and 6th ☏ 212/333-1220. MoMA's bar is like the nicest airport lounge you've ever seen, with an appropriately mid-century-Modern feel: soft light, warm wood detailing,

and sprays of fresh flowers setting off sleek low banquettes and black granite floors. Food, should you want it, comes from the adjoining *Modern* restaurant and consists of things like seared diver scallops and steak tartare topped with a quail egg.

Jimmy's Corner Map 7, F9. 140 W 44th St, btw Broadway and 6th ☏212/221-9510. The walls of this long, narrow corridor of a bar, owned by ex-fighter/trainer Jimmy Glenn, are a virtual Boxing Hall of Fame. You'd be hard-pressed to find a more memorable dive anywhere in the city – or a better jazz/R&B jukebox.

Pen-Top Bar Map 7, H6. 700 5th Ave, at 55th ☏212/956-2888. Lofty views of Midtown are the main draw at this rooftop bar perched on the twenty-third floor of the *Peninsula Hotel*, which has both glassed-in and open-air seating areas. As with all Manhattan hotel bars, drinks are pricey, but here the setting makes it well worth the few extra bucks. Closed Sun.

P.J. Clarke's Map 7, J6. 915 3rd Ave, btw 55th and 56th ☏212/759-1650. One of the city's most famous watering holes, a spit-and-sawdust alehouse with a not-so-cheap restaurant out the back. You may recognize it as the setting of the film *The Lost Weekend*.

Rudy's Bar and Grill Map 7, D9. 627 9th Ave, btw 44th and 45th ☏212/974-9169. One of New York's cheapest, friendliest, and liveliest dive bars, a favorite with local actors and musicians. *Rudy's* offers free hot dogs and a backyard that's great in the summer.

Russian Vodka Room Map 7, F7. 265 W 52nd St, btw Broadway and 7th ☏212/307-5835. As you might expect, many different kinds of vodka, as well as excellent borscht and *pierogi*, plus a lot of Russian and Eastern European expats.

The Upper East Side

Bemelmans Bar Map 7, I1. 35 E 76th St, at Madison ☏212/953-0409. A New York institution known for its quirky murals by Ludwig Bemelmans, creator of the *Madeline* series of children's books, and its original, impeccably rendered cocktails, like the gin-gin mule (gin, ginger beer, fresh mint, and lime juice). Live piano music Tues–Sat nights.

Metropolitan Museum of Art Map 8, H8. 1000 5th Ave, at 82nd ☏212/535-7710. It's hard to imagine a more romantic spot to sip a glass of wine, whether it's enjoying one of the very best views in the city up on the Cantor

Roof Garden (open only in warm weather; see p.120) or on the Great Hall Balcony listening to live chamber music (Fri and Sat 5–8pm).
Phoenix Park Map 7, J3. 206 E 67th

St, btw 2nd and 3rd ☎212/717-8181. Nothing special about this Irish pub, but it's sociable, has decent food, a jukebox, TVs, and a pool table. Happy-hour beers are only $3.50.

The Upper West Side

Dead Poet Map 8, C9. 450 Amsterdam Ave, btw 81st and 82nd ☎212/595-5670. You'll be waxing poetic and then dropping dead – dead drunk, that is – if you imbibe through this sweet little bar's generous happy hour: from 4 to 8pm, draft beers, bottles, and shots are $3 a pop ($4 pints all night Mon and Tues). There's a back room with armchairs, books, and even a pool table.
Ding Dong Lounge Map 8, D2. 929 Columbus, btw 105th and 106th ☎212/663-2600. A bit of the East Village on the Upper West Side, with bed-headed Columbia hipsters and aging Gen Xers drawn like moths to the flame by its

happy-hour deals ($4 drafts from 4 to 7pm), vintage punk-rock posters, and nightly DJs.
Lobby Lounge Map 7, E5. 8 W 60th St, at Broadway ☎212/805-8876. This swank restaurant bar on the 35th floor of the Time Warner Center, just off the lobby of the *Mandarin Oriental Hotel* (p.192), has panoramic views of the city, with floor-to-ceiling windows overlooking Central Park, Columbus Circle, and beyond. It's quite dramatic, so don't let the host or hostess stick you in the back room. There's also an afternoon tea here for $38 per person.

23

DRINKING

Harlem

Lenox Lounge Map 9, D8. 288 Lenox Ave, btw 124th and 125th ☎212/427-0253. Elegant, Art-Deco Harlem landmark, formerly graced by Billie Holiday.

Celebrated for its swanky Zebra Room, whose ceiling is adorned with zebra skins. Jazz is played on weekends.
Moca Map 9, D8. 2210 Frederick

Douglass Blvd, at 119th ☏**212/665-8081.** This smooth new lounge at the west edge of Harlem attracts a stylish international crowd (it's over-25 only) with suggestive cocktails (try the sloe gin screw) and good soulful beats. Opens at 5pm nightly; happy hour Tues–Fri 5–8pm; $5 martinis every Mon.

Brooklyn

Barbès 376 9th St, at 6th Ave, Park Slope ☏**718/965-9177.** Hipster-style Parisian bistro not far from Prospect Park, with *pastis*, good wines, and an excellent array of live music.

Enid's 560 Manhattan Ave, at Driggs, Greenpoint ☏ **718/349-3859.** Good Guinness and a tolerable hipster quotient rule in this relaxed bar just north of Williamsburg. Great brunch on Sundays (be prepared for long lines).

Frank's Lounge 660 Fulton St, at South Elliott, Fort Greene ☏**718/625-9339.** This mellow bar with a classic-to-modern R&B jukebox comes alive at night when DJs spin hip-hop and the party spreads upstairs. A stone's throw from the Brooklyn Academy of Music.

Pete's Candy Store 709 Lorimer St, at Frost, Williamsburg ☏**718/302-3770.** A former Mafia joint fronting as a soda parlor, today *Pete's* is a haven of punk rock and cheap drinks. Hosts live music and the occasional spelling bee every night.

Union Pool 484 Union Ave, at Meeker, Williamsburg ☏**718/609-0484.** Great fun and a relaxed atmosphere at this longtime hipster hangout. Tasty drinks, good prices, and a lovely garden area out back.

Waterfront Ale House 155 Atlantic Ave, btw Clinton and Henry sts ☏**718/522-3794.** This inexpensive old-style pub has a huge range of beers, plus solid bar food (wings, burgers). Just south of Brooklyn Heights.

Queens

Bohemian Beer Garden 29–19 24th Ave, btw 29th and 31st, Astoria ☏718/728-9776. Old-world Czech Bohemians and twenty- and thirty-something bohemians mingle at New York's last remaining old-style beer garden, which features a variety of pilsners. Summer bands range in style from polka to rock to hip-hop. Well worth the train ride out to Queens.

Café-Bar 32–90 34th Ave, at 33rd, Astoria ☏718/204-5273. See review, p.205.

Lounge 47 47-10 Vernon Blvd, Long Island City, Queens ☏718/937-2044. LIC's unofficial living room, a few blocks east of P.S.1. This funky café/bar offers both mac-and-cheese and Indian *pakoras*, as well as tasty cocktails.

The Bronx

Yankee Tavern E 161st St at Gerard St, South Bronx ☏718/292-6130. If you can't get tickets to Yankee Stadium, the next best place to watch the ball game is with the fans at this bar right across the street. It's been serving – and rooting for the home team – since 1928.

24

Nightlife

New York is undeniably a **nightlife** city. This is a town where many bars don't get packed until 11pm, and clubs look like empty rooms until midnight or 1am. Even confirmed early birds should at least try on a few late nights to experience New York's legendary nocturnal energy.

Nightclubs run the gamut from dank, sweaty basements to sleek lounges (only some of which allow dancing) to labyrinthine showplaces with multiple dance floors, chill-out lounges, wet bars, and roof decks. The hippest (or at least biggest and most crowded) clubs these days are in West Chelsea (especially along West 27th Street) and in the Meatpacking District. Most play a mix of hip-hop, trance, electronica, world, house, R&B, and drum'n'bass; check local listings for specifics, as line-ups change nightly with the DJ. To get past the velvet rope, dress your best and arrive on the early side or on a weeknight; if a doorman gives you a hard time or keeps you waiting for ages, go elsewhere – there's no point spending your whole night on the sidewalk.

As for **live music**, New York has always been a town that's appreciated rock'n'roll. On any night of the week, you can hear decent indie rock at any number of small Lower East Side clubs (such as the *Mercury Lounge*), as well as more spacious joints in Brooklyn (*Southpaw*). The *Knitting Factory*, a TriBeCa institution, offers a hearty mix of jazz, electronica, and strange things created by laptops, while the perennially popular *SOB's* (Sounds of Brazil) hosts get-up-and-dance bands from all over the world.

Whatever you're planning to do after dark, remember to **carry ID** at all times – you'll likely be asked for proof that you're over 21 by every doorman; note that some venues do not even allow under-21s to enter, let alone drink, so call beforehand if you're concerned. For **tickets** to live music shows, visit Ⓦwww.ticketmaster.com or Ⓦwww.ticketweb.com; between them, the two cover most of the city's venues. They both charge hefty "convenience" fees, though, so you might consider picking your tickets up at the box office, rather than purchasing them online.

The sections that follow include the pick of the city's clubs and performance spaces. Since the music and club scenes are constantly changing, it's a good idea to get current what's-on info once you hit the ground. The listings magazine *Time Out New York* is pretty reliable; you can pick up the current week's issue for a few bucks at virtually any newsstand. The *New Yorker* and *New York* magazine have fewer listings (and no nightclubs), but their selections are solid. Otherwise, grab a free weekly like the *Village Voice* (Ⓦwww.villagevoice.com) or the *L Magazine* (Ⓦwww.thelmagazine.com). Both are found on street corners in self-serve newspaper boxes, as well as in many music stores and bars; they contain detailed listings for most scenes.

Rock music

New York's **rock music** scene is still built on white-boy guitar bands, with three-chord rock the default setting. That said, there's a lot more diversity than there used to be – more women on the scene, more foreign acts, more musical experimentation – especially in smaller clubs. In Manhattan, most of the energy is provided by bars and music clubs located in the East Village and on the Lower East Side; larger venues tend to be farther north, from Union Square to the Upper West Side. The listings below will point you to the primary spots where you should find something for your ears, no matter what you're looking for.

Large venues

Beacon Theatre Map 7, C2. 2124 Broadway, btw 74th and 75th ☏ 212/465-6500, ⓦ www.beacontheatrenyc.com. Gorgeous old 2800-seat theater with great acoustics, featuring well-established artists from Aimee Mann to Bob Dylan. Tickets $40–100.

Hammerstein Ballroom Map 6, E4. 311 W 34th St, btw 8th and 9th ☏ 212/777-6800 or 307-7171. Refurbished 2500-capacity ballroom with a hand-painted ceiling and three balconies. Hosts a few shows a month, mostly indie rock and electronic music by the likes of the Beastie Boys, Wilco, and the Chemical Brothers, as well as a number of theme nights. Tickets $20–60.

Madison Square Garden Map 6, E4. 7th Ave, at 32nd ☏ 212/465-6741, ⓦ www.thegarden.com. New York's largest concert venue, the Garden hosts not only hockey and basketball but also a good portion of the stadium rock acts that visit the city. Seating 20,000-plus, the arena is not the most soulful place to see a band – nor the cheapest, with tickets $40 and up – but it may be the only chance you get.

Radio City Music Hall Map 7, G7. 1260 6th Ave, at 50th ☏ 212/247-4777, ⓦ www.radiocity.com. Still one of the most spectacular places in the city to see a show, this legendary 5900-seat Art-Deco hall books an odd assortment of performers including, recently, Hillary Duff, Björk, and Tony Bennett, as well as reunion tours for aging rock bands like the Moody Blues. Tickets $40–130.

Roseland Ballroom Map 7, E7. 239 W 52nd St, btw Broadway and 8th ☏ 212/247-0200, ⓦ www.roselandballroom.com. Opened in 1919, this historic ballroom was once frequented by Adele and Fred Astaire, among others. Now a ballroom-dancing school, it turns into a 3500-capacity concert venue a couple of times a month, hosting rock and pop acts, like Lily Allen and Silverchair. Take a gander at the shoes and photographs displayed in the entry hall. Tickets $10–50.

Small to mid-sized venues

Arlene's Grocery Map 5, K6. 95 Stanton St, btw Ludlow and Orchard ☏ 212/995-1652, ⓦ www.arlenesgrocery.net. This intimate former *bodega* hosts nightly gigs by local, reliably good indie bands. Go on Monday nights for the free rock'n'roll karaoke – it's great fun, and the crowd really gets into it. Cover $7–10.

Bowery Ballroom Map 5, I7. 6 Delancey St, at Bowery ☎212/533-2111, ⊛www.boweryballroom.com. A minimum of attitude among staff and clientele, great sound, and even better views have earned this 550-capacity venue praise from fans and bands alike. Great bar and solid line-up. Shows $10–40.

Fillmore New York at Irving Plaza Map 6, K8. 17 Irving Place, btw 15th and 16th ☎212/777-6800, ⊛www.irvingplaza.com. Host to an impressive array of rock and pop acts, with an occasional foray into country, though the acoustics are muddled since the balcony juts way out toward the stage. Stand on the ground floor in front of the balcony for the best sound. Capacity is around 1000. Tickets $15–35.

Highline Ballroom Map 6, C8. 431 W 16th St, btw 9th and 10th ☎212/414-5994, ⊛www.thehighlineballroom.com. Performance artist Diamanda Galas, indie rockers the Squirrel Nut Zippers, folk-rock queen Suzanne Vega, and vegan DJ Moby have all played this handy new music venue on the border of Chelsea and the Meatpacking District. Simple and well appointed, with good sightlines (no annoying columns), it fits 400–700 depending on the event and has good cocktails and bar food like mini-Kobe beef burgers. Tickets $15–35.

Living Room Map 5, K6. 154 Ludlow, at Stanton ☎212/533-7237, ⊛www.livingroomny.com. Warm and welcoming folk-rock club on a street that can be anything but. The front room has a bar, couches (naturally), and windows that open to the street. Head to the back, behind the curtain, where singer-songwriters grace the stage seven nights a week. The piano comes courtesy of Norah Jones, who got her start here. No cover; one-drink minimum.

Mercury Lounge Map 5, K5. 217 E Houston St, at Essex ☎212/260-4700, ⊛www.mercuryloungenyc.com. Small, dark Lower East Side mainstay, with a moody back room hosting a mix of local, national, and international rock acts. It's owned by the same crew as the *Bowery Ballroom*. Tickets generally $8–20, usually around $10.

Southpaw 125 Fifth Ave, btw Sterling and St John's, Brooklyn ☎718-230-0236, ⊛www.spsounds.com. Cavernous, old-school indie-rock club on a strip of Park Slope that's becoming more and more like Williamsburg, with boutiques and bars. Inside it's pleasantly unfussy, with a big bar and a stripped-down stage that keeps the focus on the music. Tickets $7–20.

24

NIGHTLIFE

Jazz

Jazz has been a mainstay of New York's cultural scene since the 1920s and 1930s, when the form was honed and perfected by Chick Webb, Duke Ellington, Ella Fitzgerald, Billie Holiday, and many others in the clubs of Greenwich Village and Harlem. These are still the most popular neighborhoods for jazz, though some of the outlying clubs (the *Jazz Standard*, *Smoke*, the *Jazz Gallery*) are excellent, too, and feel a bit less touristy. Midtown jazz clubs tend to be slick dinner-dance joints – expensive and overrun by businesspeople looking for culture. Call ahead to reserve a seat, as many places will fill up by show time; most venues will hold your spot without a credit card number, so you won't be penalized if you change your mind.

Venues

55 Map 5, C3. 55 Christopher St, btw 6th and 7th ☎212/929-9883, Ⓦwww.55bar.com. Relaxing, unpretentious, underground jazz bar; the best of the old guard, with traditional and modern tunes to soothe the soul. Early set, starting at 6 or 7pm, is free; late set at 9.30 or 10pm is $5–15. Two-drink minimum for both.
Birdland Map 7, E9. 315 W 44th St, btw 8th and 9th ☎212/581-3080, Ⓦwww.birdlandjazz.com. Not the original place where Charlie Parker played, but an established supper club nonetheless. Hosts some big names, with sets nightly at 9 and 11pm. Music charge $20–50, with a $10 food/drink minimum and a free drink if you sit at the bar.

The Blue Note Map 5, D4. 131 W 3rd St, at 6th ☎212/475-8592, Ⓦwww.bluenote.net. The famous names here aren't really worth the attendant high prices, cattle-herd atmosphere, and minimal legroom. Cover charges vary wildly, from $7 to $65, plus a $5 minimum per person at the tables or a one-drink minimum at the bar. Sets are at 9 and 11.30pm. On Fri and Sat, the jam sessions after 1am are free if you've seen the previous set, or $8 if you haven't.
Iridium Jazz Club Map 7, F7. 1650 Broadway, btw 51st and 52nd ☎212/582-2121, Ⓦwww.iridi-umjazzclub.com. Contemporary jazz performed seven nights a week amid Surrealist decor. The godfather of electric guitar Les

Paul plays every Monday. Tickets $30–40, with $10 food and drink minimum. Sunday jazz brunch $22 includes free drink.

Jazz Gallery Map 5, C7. 290 Hudson, btw Dominick and Spring ℡212/242-1063, ⓦjazzgallery .org. This excellent little second-floor club in the no-man's-land south of the West Village and above TriBeCa is one of the city's great jazz secrets, with none of the commercialism of the larger venues. Seats are folding chairs and benches and there's no bar, but you can get a glass of wine in a plastic cup. Trumpotor Roy Hargrove got his start here and sometimes comes back with his big band, a real treat. Tickets $12–15.

Jazz Standard Map 6, J5. 116 E 27th St, btw Park Ave South and Lexington ℡212/576-2232, ⓦwww.jazzstandard.com. Tucked beneath the acclaimed barbecue restaurant *Blue Smoke*, this spacious underground club has a loyal clientele of its own thanks to its great sound and strong bookings. Fans of barbecue really should consider doing the dinner-theater thing; the food is justly famous. Try "Rhapsody in Cue" – ribs, pulled pork, chicken, and sausage. Tickets $15–30.

Smoke Map 8, B2. 2751 Broadway, btw 105th and 106th ℡212/864-6662, ⓦwww.smokejazz.com. This Upper West Side joint brightens up a neighborhood that's stuffed with creative people but conspic-uously lacking in music clubs. Very intimate setting means every seat in the house – even the bar stools – is a good one. Sets start at 9pm, 11pm, and 12.30am. There's a retro happy hour with $3 cocktails Mon–Sun 5–8pm. Cover from nothing to $25.

Village Vanguard Map 5, C2. 178 7th Ave, at 11th ℡212/255-4037, ⓦwww.villagevanguard.com. A NYC jazz landmark that cele-brated its seventieth anniversary a few years back, the *Vanguard* supplies a regular diet of big names in a wedge-shaped room that oozes jazz history. Photos of Bill Evans, Miles Davis, and other jazz greats who've played here line the walls. Admission is usu-ally $20, with a $10 drink mini-mum. Sets are at 9 and 11pm; if you go to the early one on an off night, they'll sometimes let you stay for the later one free.

Zinc Bar Map 5, E5. 90 W Houston, at LaGuardia ℡212/477-8337, ⓦwww.zincbar.com. This base-ment jazz/world music venue on the border of SoHo and the Village is a handy place to go for a cheap set or two and a couple of drinks, with tons of neigh-borhood character and a loyal bunch of regulars who typically cram in shoulder to shoulder for top-shelf music at bargain prices. Hosts new talent and established greats such as Astrud Gilberto. Three sets every night; cover is $7, with a two-drink minimum at tables (if you're lucky enough to snag one).

Other types of music

The best of the rest, in world music, avant-garde, country, and hybrid musical forms you never knew existed.

Venues

Barbès 376 9th St, at 6th, Brooklyn ☎718/965-9177, ⓦ www.barbes-brooklyn.com. #F to 7th Ave/9th St. Tickets free–$10. A cool addition to the New York (not just Brooklyn) music scene, this amiable neighborhood bar fills its backroom with an eclectic line-up of gypsy jazz and world-music performers. Show up early to get a seat.

The Knitting Factory Map 4, E3. 74 Leonard St, btw Church and Broadway ☎212/219-3055, ⓦ www.knittingfactory.com. This famous three-story club has three stages and two bars with a great beer selection. It used to be known for its avant-garde jazz but lately the bookings have been tending toward big-name indie rock bands – great to see in such an intimate setting – local acts, and DJs. Be warned that the Old Office, one of the performance spaces, is minuscule and painfully loud; bring earplugs. Tickets $10–20.

Rodeo Bar Map 6, K5. 375 3rd Ave, at 27th ☎212/683-6500, ⓦ www.rodeobar.com. Dust off your spurs, grab your partner, and head down to the *Rodeo* for live country tunes seven days a week. This is a down-home, unpretentious place that would seem to belong pretty much anywhere but New York, but here it is. No cover.

SOB's (Sounds of Brazil) Map 5, C6. 204 Varick St, at Houston St ☎212/243-4940, ⓦ www.sobs.com. Premier place to hear hip-hop, Brazilian, West Indian, Caribbean, and other world-music acts within the confines of Manhattan. Vibrant, with high-quality music and a sexy vibe. Two shows nightly, times vary. Admission $7–25 with $10–15 minimum cover at tables.

Clubs

New York's – especially Manhattan's – **club life** is a rapidly evolving creature. While many of the name DJs remain the same, venues shift around, opening and closing according to finances and fashion. To ensure that the party is still there, check the listings in *Time Out New York* (on sale at newsstands), the *Village Voice* or *The L Magazine* (free in newspaper boxes and at bookstores). Fliers placed in record and clothing stores in the East Village and Lower East Side are a good way to find out about the latest clubs and one-off nights; many also offer substantial discounts.

Cielo 18 Little West 12th St, btw 9th and Washington ☎212/645-5700, ⓦwww.cieloclub.com. Arguably the best of the Meatpacking District clubs, with a terrific sound system, a sunken dance floor surrounded by cushy banquettes, and top DJs, most from Europe. There's a smoking patio out back. Very tight door, but once you get inside you're golden. Monday night's "Deep Space" party has become a fixture on the scene and isn't too hard to get into. Cover $5–20.

Lotus Map 6, C9. 409 W 14th St, btw 9th and 10th ☎212/243-4420, ⓦwww.lotusnewyork.com. A pioneer when it opened in this neighborhood a few years ago, *Lotus* remains the quintessential Meatpacking District club, a three-tiered glamour palace with a fancy restaurant (sidewalk seating in summer), multiple lounges, and a disco. It has a bit of a Vegas feel, drawing slick businessmen, models, and hard-partying celebrities, but it's enticing in a decadent way. There's a strict door policy, so be sure to look smart. $20 cover. Closed Mon.

Marquee Map 6, C5. 289 10th Ave, at 27th ☎646/473-0202, ⓦwww.marqueeny.com. Self-aware and stylish, *Marquee* has a notoriously strict door policy; once inside you'll be treated to lots of attitude, lavish furnishings, and a glassed-in upper lounge, all topped off with one hell of a chandelier. The music's nothing special… but nobody's here to listen to it anyway. Cover $20.

Mehanata Map 5, K7. 113 Ludlow St ☎212/625-0981. More commonly known as just "the Bulgarian Bar" and formerly located in TriBeCa, this is one strange and crazy joint. Open Thurs–Sat only, it starts to heat up around 10 or 11pm and turns into an international electro-punk-pop dance party in the wee hours. Homemade mixed drinks and the "Get Naked, Get a Free Shot" sign help patrons lose their inhibitions. **Movida Map 5, C5. 28 7th Ave, btw Bedford and Leroy ☎ 212/206-0900, ⓦ www.movidanyc.com.** A dream come true for East Village rockers looking for something a little more salubrious than the tattered bars of their home turf, this tri-level West Village club offers dance, rock, cage dancers, mirrors, and excellent drinks. All is brought together with an incongruous luxury-yacht theme. No cover.

Sapphire Map 5, J5. 249 Eldridge St, at Houston ☎ 212/777-5153, ⓦ www.sapphirenyc.com. Pleasantly sleazy lounge, with a black-lit interior and an art gallery out back, frequented by thirtysomething hipsters. Music of all kinds, from old-school and classic rock on Thurs to deep house Tues, and Latin-tinged tunes on Mon. Open nightly; free–$5.

(24)

NIGHTLIFE

25

The performing arts and film

From Metropolitan Opera glitter to Lower East Side grunge, the range and variety of the **performing arts** in New York is as endless as you might expect. Not only are there hundreds of resident arts companies, but nearly every touring company worth its salt makes a stop in New York City. So there's always plenty to see; the only difficulty is seeing all you want to and still having money left over for your hotel and food. On Broadway, and even Off-Broadway, theater is notoriously expensive, but if you know where to look, there are a variety of ways to get cheaper tickets, and on the Off-Off-Broadway fringe you can see a stellar play for little more than the price of a movie ticket. As for dance, music, and opera, the big mainstream events are extremely expensive, but smaller ones are often equally as interesting and quite economical; you can catch a smokin' jazz set for as little as $7. New York (along with LA) gets the premieres of most American films (and many foreign ones before they reach Europe) and has a very healthy art-house and revival scene.

Listings for the arts can be found in a number of places. The most useful sources are the clear and comprehensive listings in

Time Out New York, the free *Village Voice* (especially the pull-out "Voice Choices" section), or the also-free *New York Press*, all especially useful for things downtown and vaguely "alternative." For more selective listings, see "The Week" section in the weekly *New York* magazine, the "Goings On About Town" section of the *New Yorker*, or Friday's "Weekend" or Sunday's "Arts and Leisure" sections of the *New York Times*. Specific Broadway listings can be found in the free *Official Broadway Theater Guide*, available at theater and hotel lobbies or at NYC & Company visitor centers (see p.20).

Theater

Theater venues are referred to as Broadway, Off-Broadway, or Off-Off-Broadway depending on the number of seats in the house: Broadway theaters have five hundred or more, Off-Broadway 101 to 499, and Off-Off Broadway one hundred or fewer. The designations do not correspond to location, but most Broadway houses are indeed in the theater district; Off-Broadway and Off-Off-Broadway theaters are scattered all around town. In the past few years on **Broadway**, serious dramas like Tom Stoppard's *Coast of Utopia* trilogy, Alan Bennett's *History Boys*, and John Patrick Stanley's *Doubt* have taken the city by storm, while lively, imaginative musicals like *Spring Awakening*, *Avenue Q*, *Hairspray*, *The 25th Annual Putnam County Spelling Bee*, and *Grey Gardens* have drawn crowds and acclaim.

Off-Broadway, while less glitzy, is the best place to discover new talent and adventurous American theater, even if the ticket prices have crept up to Broadway levels in recent years. Here you'll find social and political drama, satire, ethnic plays, and repertory. Lower operating costs also mean that Off-Broadway often serves as a forum to try out what sometimes ends up as a big Broadway production. Lastly, **Off-Off-Broadway** is New York's fringe: shows range from shoestring productions

25

THE PERFORMING ARTS AND FILM

of the classics to outrageous performance art; likewise, prices and quality can vary, from $10 to $20 and from electrifying to execrable.

Tickets

Tickets for Broadway shows can cost as much as $125 for orchestra seats (sometimes even $200 for the hottest show in town) and as little as $25 for day-of-performance rush tickets for some of the longer-running shows. Off-Broadway's best seats are cheaper than those on Broadway, averaging $40–60. Off-Off-Broadway tickets should rarely set you back more than $15.

Line up at the one of the **TKTS booths** (☎212/768-1818, ⓦ www.tdf.org), where you can obtain cut-rate tickets on the day of performance (up to half off plus a $3 service charge) for many Broadway and Off-Broadway shows (though seldom for the recently opened and very popular shows). The main booth, located at Duffy Square, where Broadway and Seventh Avenue meet between 45th and 47th streets, is open Monday through Saturday 3–8pm, 10am–2pm for Wednesday and Saturday matinees, and Sunday from 3pm until one half-hour before the latest curtain time being sold. (Note: A major renovation of the Times Square booth was supposed to wrap up by early 2008; if it's not finished when you visit, go to the temporary booth in the *Marriott Marquis Hotel*, on 46th St between Broadway and 8th Ave.) The South Street Seaport booth is at the corner of Front and John streets. It's open Monday through Saturday 11am–6pm and Sunday 11am–4pm; you can get Saturday and Sunday matinee tickets all day Friday and Saturday. The lines at this branch tend to be much shorter than those at Times Square, and the selection larger because tickets go on sale earlier.

Look for twofer **discount coupons** in the NYC & Co. visitor centers and many shops, banks, restaurants, and hotel lobbies. These entitle two people to a hefty discount and, unlike TKTS, it's possible to book ahead – though again, don't expect to find coupons for the latest shows. The Hit Show Club (☎212/581-4211, ⓦwww.hitshowclub.com) also provides discount vouchers for up to fifty percent off, which you present at the box office. Same-day standing-room and student-rush tickets are also available for select sold-out shows for $20–25; check the website of the show you're interested in seeing or ask at the box office, as the details vary considerably: some have cash-only policies, others hold a daily lottery for a limited number of front-row tickets, still others sell tickets to students (with ID) only.

If you're prepared to pay full price you can, of course, go directly to the theater, or contact one of the following **ticket sales agencies**. Tele-Charge (☎212/239-6200 or 1-800/432-7250, ⓦwww.telecharge.com) and Ticketmaster (☎212/307-4100 or 1-800/755-4000, ⓦwww.ticketmaster.com) sell tickets over the phone to Broadway shows, but note that no show is represented by both these agencies. Ticket Central (☎212/279-4200, ⓦwww.ticketcentral.com) sells tickets to Off-Broadway and Off-Off-Broadway productions 24hrs through its website or noon to 8pm daily over the phone or at its box office at Playwrights Horizons, 416 W 42nd St, btw 9th and 10th avenues (there's no service charge if you buy in person).

On- and Off-Broadway theaters

Astor Place Theater Map 5, H3. 434 Lafayette St, between Astor and 4th ☎212/254-4370. Since 1992, the theater has been the home of the comically absurd but very popular performance artists The Blue Man Group (ⓦwww.blueman.com).

Atlantic Theater Map 6, D7. 336 W 20th St, btw 8th and 9th ☎212/645-1242. An old church on a lovely block in Chelsea, now housing the Atlantic Theater Company, founded in 1985 by playwright David Mamet and actor William H. Macy. It presents work by Mamet – of course – as well as Chekhov and others.

Brooklyn Academy of Music (BAM) 30 Lafayette Ave, between Ashland and St Felix, Brooklyn ☎718/636-4100, ⓦwww.bam.org. BAM presents theater and modern dance performances on its three stages. The academy has imported a number of historic productions over the years, including several by Ingmar Bergman, as well as the best of cutting-edge performing arts. The annual Next Wave festival, held every autumn, is the city's most exciting showcase for large-scale performances by the likes of Philip Glass and Laurie Anderson, among others.

New Amsterdam Theatre Map 6, F1. 214 W 42nd St, between 7th and 8th ⓣ**212/307-4100.** Disney's over-the-top, refurbished Times Square palace – rescued from neglect and overhauled in 1997 – was home to Julie Taymor's Tony Award–winning extravaganza *The Lion King* from 1998 until 2006, when *Mary Poppins* took its place. (*The Lion King* reopened in the Minskoff Theatre, 200 W 45th St.)

New York City Center Map 7, F6. 131 W 55th St, between 6th and 7th ⓣ**212/581-1212,** ⓦ**www .mtc-nyc.org.** The highly regarded Manhattan Theatre Club mounts Off-Broadway productions at two stages at City Center, and Broadway productions at the 650-seat Biltmore Theatre (261 W 47th, btw Broadway and 8th ⓣ212/239-6200). Past productions include John Patrick Stanley's *Doubt* and Donald Margulies' *Sight Unseen*.

New York Theatre Workshop Map 5, H4. 79 E 4th St, between Bowery and 2nd ⓣ**212/460-5475,** ⓦ**www.nytw.org.** Innovative and respected space that seems to choose cult hit shows – it was the original host of the hugely successful *Rent*.

The Public Theater Map 5, H3. 425 Lafayette St, between Astor and 4th ⓣ**212/239-6200,** ⓦ**www.publictheater.org.** This major Off-Broadway venue produces serious and challenging theater from new, mostly American playwrights, including Pulitzer Prize-winner Suzan-Lori Parks. In the summer, the Public puts on the free Shakespeare in the Park festival at the open-air Delacorte Theater in Central Park (ⓣ212/539-8500).

Shubert Theater Map 7, F9. 225 W 44th St, between 7th and 8th ⓣ**212/239-6200.** Fred Astaire and Katharine Hepburn are just two of the stars to have graced the Shubert's stage. These days, it's home to the Monty Python musical send-up *Spamalot*.

Studio 54 Map 7, E7. 524 W 54th St, between Broadway and 8th ⓣ**212/239-6200.** The legendary 1970s disco has seen new life as home to a series of acclaimed Broadway revivals, starting with *Cabaret* in the 1990s and, more recently, the 1963 musical *110 in the Shade*.

THE PERFORMING ARTS AND FILM

Off-Off-Broadway and performance-art spaces

The Flea Map 4, E2. 41 White St, btw Broadway and Church ☎212/352-3101, ⊛www.theflea .org. "Raising a joyful hell in a small space" is the apt motto of the rowdy team behind this 75-seater in TriBeCa. They put on a medley of music, performance, and dance – usually all three of the experimental variety. The Flea gets some big names, though; its production of *The Guys*, about firefighters who died on 9/11, had a rotating cast that included Susan Sarandon, Sigourney Weaver, and Tim Robbins.

The Kitchen Map 6 C8. 512 W 19th St, at 10th ☎212/255-5793, ⊛www.thekitchen.org. This may well be the best small performance space in the city, with an impressive history of supporting edge-pushing multimedia artists, including Kiki Smith, Laurie Anderson, Meredith Monk, and Philip Glass.

La MaMa E.T.C. Map 5, H4. 74A E 4th St, btw Bowery and 2nd ☎212/475-7710, ⊛www.lamama .org. The mother of all Off-Off theaters, this "Experimental Theater Club" has been staging theater, performance, and dance for more than thirty years.

Ontological-Hysteric Theatre Map 5, I2. 131 E 10th St, at 2nd ☎212/533-4650, ⊛www.ontological.com. Produces some of the best and strangest radical theater in the city; especially famous for the work of indie theater legend Richard Foreman.

Performing Garage Map 5, E8. 33 Wooster St, btw Broome and Grand ☎212/966-3651, ⊛www .thewoostergroup.org. The well-respected experimental Wooster Group (whose most famous member is Willem Dafoe) performs in this SoHo space. Tickets are gold dust but worth every effort.

P.S.122 Map 5, J3. 150 1st Ave, at 9th ☎212/477-5288, ⊛www.ps122.org. This converted school in the East Village is a perennially popular venue for a jam-packed schedule of performance art, dance, theater, and one-person shows.

Theater for the New City Map 5, J2. 155 1st Ave, at 10th ☎212/254-1109. Known for encouraging the development of new playwrights and integrating dance, music, and poetry with drama. In summer, TNC hosts free outdoor performances at a variety of venues, and in late May sponsors the Lower East Side Festival of the Arts.

Literary events and readings

92nd Street Y Map 8, J6. 1395 Lexington Ave, at 92nd ☎212/415-5500,

THE PERFORMING ARTS AND FILM

ⓦ www.92y.org. Quite simply, the definitive place to hear all your Booker, Pulitzer, and Nobel Prize-winning favorites, as well as many other exciting new talents. **KGB Map 5, H4. 85 E 4th St, 2nd floor, btw 2nd and Bowery** ⓣ212/505-3360, ⓦ www.kgbbar .com. This richly atmospheric old bar, housed in the former headquarters of the Ukrainian Communist Party, hosts some of the city's best readings, usually by young and edgy writers, with cheap beers fueling the comradely environment. **Symphony Space Map 8, B5. 2537 Broadway, at 95th** ⓣ212/864-5400, ⓦ www.symphonyspace.org. The highly acclaimed "Selected Shorts" series, in which actors read the short fiction of a variety of authors, packs the Symphony Space theater and can be heard across the country on the radio.

Dance

As with theater, the range of **dance performances** offered in the city is vast. New York has five major ballet companies, dozens of modern troupes, and untold thousands of soloists – you would have to be very particular indeed in your tastes not to find something of interest. Events are listed in broadly the same periodicals and websites as music and theater – though you might also want to pick up *Dance Magazine* (ⓦ www.dancemagazine.com). The following is a list of some of the major **dance venues and companies** in the city, though a lot of the smaller, more esoteric companies and solo artists also perform at spaces like the Kitchen, the Flea, and P.S.122, which are listed under "Off-Off-Broadway and performance-art spaces."

American Ballet Theatre Map 7, D4. At the Metropolitan Opera House, Lincoln Center, 65th and Columbus ⓣ212/362-6000, ⓦ www.abt.org. The renowned American Ballet Theatre performs at the Opera House from early May into July, and at New York City Center in the fall. Prices for ballet at the Met range from $275 for the best seats at special performances to $20 for standing-room tickets, which go on sale the morning of the performance.

Brooklyn Academy of Music 30 Lafayette St, btw Ashland and St Felix, Brooklyn ☎718/636-4100, Ⓦwww.bam.org. One of the busiest and most daring dance producers in New York. In the autumn, BAM's Next Wave Festival showcases the hottest international attractions in avant-garde dance and music; in winter visiting artists appear, and each spring BAM hosts the annual DanceAfrica Festival, America's largest showcase for African and African-American dance and culture.

City Center Map 7, F6. 131 W 55th St, btw 6th and 7th ☎212/581-1212, Ⓦwww.citycenter.org. This large Midtown venue hosts some of the most important troupes in modern dance, such as the Paul Taylor Dance Company, the Alvin Ailey American Dance Theater, and the American Ballet Theatre; it also hosts the Fall for Dance Festival each fall, with tickets priced at $10.

Dance Theater Workshop Map 5, F8. 219 W 19th St, btw 7th and 8th ☎212/924-0077, Ⓦwww.dtw .org. DTW boasts more than 175 performances from nearly 70 artists and companies each season. The theater has an unintimidating, relaxed atmosphere, and ticket prices are very reasonable.

Danspace Project Map 5, I2. St Mark's Church, 131 E 10th St, at 2nd ☎212/674-8194, Ⓦwww .danspaceproject.org. Experimental contemporary dance, with a season running from September to June in one of the more beautiful performance spaces.

The Joyce Theater Map 6, E8. 175 8th Ave, at 19th ☎212/242-0800, Ⓦwww.joyce.org. The Joyce hosts short seasons by a wide variety of acclaimed dance troupes such as Pilobolus, the Parsons Dance Company, and Donald Byrd/The Group. In a separate space, Joyce SoHo, at 155 Mercer St, btw Prince and Houston (☎212/431-9233), the Joyce puts on a three-weekend concert series featuring collaborating choreographers every spring.

Juilliard Dance Workshop Map 7, D4. Juilliard Theater, 155 W 65th St, at Broadway ☎212/799-5000. Juilliard School's dance division often gives free workshop performances, and each winter six students work with six composers to present a "Composers and Choreographers" concert at Lincoln Center's Alice Tully Hall.

Midsummer Night Swing Map 7, D4. At Lincoln Center, 65th and Columbus ☎212/875-5766, Ⓦwww .lincolncenter.org. Open-air summer dance night on Lincoln Center's plaza where you can learn a different dance en masse each evening (everything from

THE PERFORMING ARTS AND FILM

polka to rockabilly) and watch a performance, all for $15.
New York City Ballet Map 7, D4. At Lincoln Center, 65th and Columbus ☎212/870-5570, ⓦwww.nycballet .com. Lincoln Center's major bal-

let venue, the New York State Theater, is home to the revered New York City Ballet, which performs for a nine-week season each spring.

Classical music and opera

New Yorkers take serious **music** seriously. Long lines form for anything popular, many concerts sell out, and summer evenings can see a quarter of a million people turning up in Central Park for free performances by the New York Philharmonic. The range of what's available is wide – but it's big names at big venues that pull in the crowds.

Opera venues

Amato Opera Theater Map 5, H5. 319 Bowery, at 2nd ☎212/228-8200, ⓦwww.amato.org. This Bowery venue presents an ambitious and varied repertory of classics performed by up-and-coming young singers and conductors. Performances at weekends only. Closed in the summer.
Juilliard School Map 7, D4. 60 Lincoln Center Plaza, at 65th and Broadway ☎212/799-5000, ⓦwww .juilliard.edu. Right next door to the Met (see below), Juilliard students often perform under the direction of a famous conductor, usually for low ticket prices.
Metropolitan Opera House Map 7, D4. At Lincoln Center, 64th and Columbus ☎212/362-6000, ⓦwww

.metopera.org. New York's premier opera venue is home to the Metropolitan Opera Company from September to late April. The sets are unbelievably lavish and the performances are of the first order. Tickets are expensive and can be quite difficult to obtain, but thanks to a new program, 200 orchestra-level seats for Mon–Thurs performances (worth $100 each) are reserved and sold for $20 apiece two hours before curtain. Standing-room tickets ($15–20) go on sale at 10am and can be purchased on the phone, online, or at the box office. Student discount tickets ($25 weekdays, $35 weekends) must be purchased at the box office (so you can flash your ID).

The New York State Theater Map 7, D4. At Lincoln Center, 64th and Columbus ☎ 212/870-5570, ⓦ www .lincolncenter.org. Playing David to the Met's Goliath, the New York City Opera's wide and adventurous program varies wildly in quality – sometimes it's startlingly innovative, occasionally it's mediocre – but seats go for less than half the Met's prices.

Concert halls

Alice Tully Hall Map 7, D4. At Lincoln Center, 64th and Columbus ☎ 212/721-6500, ⓦ www .lincolncenter.org. A smallish venue for chamber orchestras, string quartets, and instrumentalists. Prices similar to those at Avery Fisher, below.

Avery Fisher Hall Map 7, D4. At Lincoln Center, 64th and Columbus ☎ 212/875-5030, ⓦ www.lincolncenter.org. Home of the New York Philharmonic, as well as visiting orchestras and soloists. Ticket prices for the Philharmonic are in the range of $23–94 – an often fascinating alternative is attending the NYP open rehearsals at 9.45am on concert days, which cost just $15. Avery Fisher also hosts the very popular Mostly Mozart Festival every Aug.

Bargemusic Map 4, J5. Fulton Ferry Landing, Brooklyn ☎ 718/624-4061,

Free summer concerts

In light of high concert ticket prices, it's welcoming that so many events in the city, especially during summer, are free. The **SummerStage Festival** (☎ 212/360-2777, ⓦ www.summerstage.org) in **Central Park** puts on an impressive range of free concerts of all kinds of music throughout the summer (see box, p.118). On occasional Wednesday nights the **New York Grand Opera** performs operas at SummerStage. Central Park is also one of the many open-air venues for the **New York Philharmonic**'s Concerts in the Park series (☎ 212/875-5709, ⓦ www.nyphilharmonic .org), which are held all over Manhattan and the outer boroughs in July, and the similar **Met in the Parks** series (☎ 212/362-6000, ⓦ www.metopera.org) in June. In August, the **Lincoln Center Out of Doors Festival** (☎ 212/875-5766, ⓦ www.lincolncenter .org) puts on a packed and varied slate of free music and dance performances in **Damrosch Park**, at 62nd Street and Amsterdam Avenue.

Ⓦ www.bargemusic.org. Chamber music in a wonderful river setting below the Brooklyn Bridge on Wed, Fri, and Sat at 8pm, and Sun at 4pm. Tickets are $35, or $30 for senior citizens, and $20 for students.

Brooklyn Academy of Music 30 Lafayette St, between Ashland and St Felix, Brooklyn ☎ **718/636-4100,** Ⓦ www.bam.org. The BAM Opera House is the perennial home of Philip Glass operatic premieres and also hosts a number of contemporary imports from international companies, often with a large modern-dance component.

Carnegie Hall Map 7, F6. 154 W 57th St, at 7th ☎ **212/247-7800,** Ⓦ www.carnegiehall.org. The greatest names from all schools of music have performed here, from Tchaikovsky and Toscanini to Gershwin and Billie Holiday. Labeled "one of the finest orchestral showplaces on the planet" by Alex Ross in *The New Yorker*.

Merkin Concert Hall Map 7, D3. 129 W 67th St, between Broadway and Amsterdam ☎ **212/501-3330,** Ⓦ www.merkinconcerthall.org. In the Elaine Kaufman Cultural Center, this intimate and adventurous venue is a great place to hear music of any kind.

Cabaret and comedy

Comedy clubs are rife in New York, though the **cabaret** scene – after a brief uptick in the late 1990s – is less than omnipresent at the moment; the list below represents the best-known venues in town, but as ever, check *Time Out New York*, *New York* magazine, and the *Village Voice* for the fullest and most up-to-date listings.

Café Carlyle Map 7, I1. 35 E 76th St, at Madison ☎ **212/744-1600,** Ⓦ www.thecarlyle.com. Legendary crooner Bobby Short may be gone, but the *Carlyle* still has a full line-up of name performers like Eartha Kitt and Elaine Stritch. The Woody Allen–fronted Eddy Davis New Orleans Jazz Band

plays Monday nights from Sept to Dec. Cover $85–100, more if you want to be seated close to the stage, with a two-drink minimum. Jackets required for men.

Caroline's Map 7, F8. 1626 Broadway, at 49th ☎ **212/757-4100,** Ⓦ www.carolines.com. This Times Square spot books some of the best stand-up acts in town. Cover $15–45; two-drink minimum.

Chicago City Limits Theater Map 7, K5. 318 W 53rd St, btw 8th and 9th ☏212/888-5233, ⓦwww.chicagocitylimits.com. New York's oldest improv theater, playing one show Wed–Fri, two on Sat. Closed Sun–Tues. Admission is $15 with a two-drink minimum.

Comix Map 6, D9. 353 W 14th St, btw 8th and 9th ☏212/524-2500, ⓦwww.comixny.com. Opened in fall 2006, this is one of the bigger comedy ventures in town, with tiered seating around a stage large enough for sketch troupes but not too big for a single comic. Cover varies; two-item minimum (food or drink).

Joe's Pub Map 5, H3. 425 Lafayette St, btw Astor and 4th ☏212/239-6200, ⓦwww.publictheater.org. The hipper, late-night arm of the Public Theater (see p.261), this is one of the nicest and most popular music venues in town, with a wide range of cabaret acts nightly, from the premier Kurt Weill interpreter Uta Lemper to indie rock icons like Elvis Costello and Liz Phair.

Stand Up New York Map 7, C1. 236 W 78th St, at Broadway ☏212/595-0850, ⓦwww.standupny.com. Upper West Side all-ages forum for established comics, many of whom have appeared on *Leno*, *Letterman*, and the like. Nightly shows, three on weekends. Weekdays $10 cover, Fri and Sat $16. Two-drink minimum.

Film

New York is a movie-lover's dream, sporting a slew of Hollywood **megaplexes** with all the charm of airport terminals but great seating and sound systems, plus a good number of downtown art venues featuring a range of **foreign and local independent flicks**. Simply put, there's something here for everyone. For listings your best bets are the weekly *Village Voice*, the weekly *Time Out New York*, or the Friday *New York Times*. Beware that listings in papers are not always entirely accurate; the Movie Clock at ⓦwww.villagevoice.com is a handy corrective, with locations and showtimes for everything playing in the city. Ticket prices have risen to as high as $11, and there are no reduced matinee prices in Manhattan, nor cheap evening tickets.

The city also boasts a number of major **film festivals** (see Chapter 30), the two biggest ones being the New York Film Festival, which runs for two weeks from the end of September at Lincoln Center's Alice Tully Hall (☎212/496-3809, Ⓦwww.filmlinc.com), and the fast-rising Tribeca Film Festival (☎212/941-2400, Ⓦwww.tribecafilmfestival.org), which takes place in late April and early May in various downtown venues. Lastly, if you don't mind the heat and would rather watch your movies outside, **Bryant Park**, at Sixth Avenue and 42nd Street (☎212/512-5700, Ⓦwww.bryantpark.org), hosts free, outdoor screenings of old Hollywood favorites on Monday nights at sunset throughout the summer — be sure to get there early, as space on the grass fills up very quickly.

Art house and revivals

Anthology Film Archives Map 5, I5. 32 2nd Ave, at 2nd ☎212/505-5181, Ⓦwww.anthologyfilmarchives.org. Bastion of experimental filmmaking where programs of mind-bending abstraction, East Village indie flicks, auteur retrospectives, and the year-round Essential Cinema series rub shoulders.
Film Forum Map 5, C6. 209 W Houston St, btw 6th and 7th ☎212/727-8112, Ⓦwww.filmforum.org. The cozy three-screen Film Forum has an eccentric but famously popular program of new independent movies, documentaries, and foreign films, plus the occasional revival.
IFC Center Map 5, D4. 323 6th Ave, at 3rd ☎212/924-7771, Ⓦwww .ifccenter.com. Multiple revivals daily and a good number of very small indie films from the newest entrant into the art-house scene, affiliated with the US's popular cable-TV Independent Film Channel. Features a much larger screen and a better sound system than you'll find at its competitors.
Museum of the Moving Image 35th Ave, at 36th St, Astoria, Queens ☎718/784-0077, Ⓦwww.movingimage.us. The Museum of the Moving Image (see p.172) is well worth a trip out to Queens either for the films — serious director retrospectives, silent films, and a good emphasis on cinematographers — or for the cinema museum itself. Films are shown only on weekends.

Walter Reade Theater Map 7, D4. 165 W 65th St, btw Broadway and Amsterdam ☎212/496-3809, ⓦwww.filmlinc.com. Simply the best place in town to see great films. Opened in 1991, this beautiful modern theater, with perfect sightlines, a huge screen, and impeccable sound, elevates the art of cinema to the position it deserves within Lincoln Center. The emphasis is on foreign cinema and the great auteurs.

26

Gay and lesbian New York

There are few places in America – indeed in the world – where **gay culture** thrives as it does in New York. Difference is quite simply accepted as a fact of life here, and when it hasn't been, all hell has broken loose, as with the Stonewall Riots of 1969, the genesis of the gay rights movement. Today, same-sex couples can be found holding hands all over town, and several neighborhoods have particularly thriving gay social scenes. **Chelsea** remains the most visible gay enclave, especially for men. Bars, clubs, and coffee shops abound on and around Eighth Avenue, as do see-and-be-seen gyms. As rents have risen there, some Chelsea boys have drifted northward to **Hell's Kitchen**, which now has a solid clutch of gay bars and clubs. A strong gay presence also lingers in the vicinity of **Christopher Street** in the **West Village**, home to a number of rollicking piano bars and old-school gay pubs, including the **Stonewall**. Younger, edgier gay bars and clubs are sprinkled around the **East Village** and in Brooklyn's **Williamsburg** neighborhood, while for lesbians the West Village and **Park Slope** in Brooklyn have the most active communities. Of course, the best time for gay travelers to visit New York is the last Sunday in June, when the annual

Gay media

The following are a selection of outlets with up-to-date listings and insider information on the gay and lesbian scene.

Go Magazine ⓦ www.gomag.com. Well-edited, up-to-date listings of events all over town, from trivia nights at local lesbian bars to art openings and performances.

HX Magazine ⓦ www.hx.com. Vital homosexual listings mag.

Metrosource Magazine ⓦ www.metrosource.com. National gay-and-lesbian lifestyle magazine with a local directory of gay-friendly professionals and businesses.

Gay Pride March draws half a million revelers into the streets, capping off a week of celebrations at bars and clubs all over town. (See ⓦ www.nycpride.org for more information.)

Accommodation

The vast majority of **hotels** in New York – especially those downtown – warmly welcome same-sex couples. If in doubt, though, try one of the following places, which specifically cater to gay men and lesbians and are convenient for the Chelsea/West Village scene.

Chelsea Mews Guest House Map 6, D9. 344 W 15th St, btw 8th and 9th ☎ 212/255-9174. A large Victorian home converted into an all-male guesthouse with eight rooms available, two with private bath. No kitchens, but there are hot plates in the rooms, which are very well appointed. The best feature, though, is the large backyard garden. Local calls, continental breakfast, and laundry are included in the price. Rooms $150–200 (includes tax). No credit cards.

Chelsea Pines Inn Map 6, D9. 317 W 14th St, btw 8th and 9th ☎ 212/929-1023, ⓦ www.chelseapinesinn. com. Well-priced hotel, whose guests are mostly gay. Offers clean, comfortable, attractively furnished rooms in an old brownstone on the Greenwich Village/ Chelsea border. Best to book in advance; three-night minimum stay on weekends. Rooms from $200 with private bath, $175 shared.

Chelsea Savoy Hotel Map 6, F6. 204 W 23th St, at 7th T 212/929-9353, W www.chelseasavoynyc.com. This relative newcomer, housed in a new, rather nondescript building on busy 23rd Street, makes up for a lack of charm with modern amenities in every room. Rooms from $145.

Colonial House Inn Map 6, D7. 318 W 22nd St, btw 8th and 9th T 212/243-9669, W www.colonialhouseinn.com. Economical twenty-room bed-

and-breakfast in a brownstone in the heart of Chelsea. Also welcomes straight guests. Boasts a clothing-optional roof deck. Rooms from $115 (shared bath); $145 en suite.

Incentra Village House Map 5, A1. 32 8th Ave, btw 12th and Jane T 212/206-0007, W www.incentravillage.com. This twelve-room townhouse, dating from 1841, is well positioned for exploring both the Village and Chelsea. Some rooms have kitchenettes and fireplaces, all have private baths. Three-night minimum stay on weekends. Also welcomes straight guests. Rooms from $199.

Bars

Gay men's **bars** cover the spectrum: from relaxed, mainstream cafés to hard-hitting clubs full of glamour and attitude. Most of the more established places are in Greenwich Village and Chelsea, with a few hangers-on along Avenue A in the East Village. For women, Park Slope in Brooklyn edges out the East Village and Hudson Street in the West as the center of happenings.

Mainly for men

Barracuda Map 6, F7. 275 W 22nd St, btw 7th and 8th T 212/645-8613. A favorite spot in New York's gay scene and as laid-back as you'll find in Chelsea.

Two-for-one happy hour from 4 to 9pm during the week, crazy drag shows and pick-up lines, and a hideaway lounge out back. **Barrage Map 7, D8.** 401 W 47th St, at 9th T 212/586-9390. Newish gay bar in Hell's Kitchen, with a cafe-lounge feel – airy in front when the glass-paned garage door is rolled up, intimate in back – and an amiable local crowd. Happy hour goes from 5 to 8pm and from 11 to midnight and gets you $2 off every drink.

Brandy's Piano Bar Map 8, K8. 235 E 84th St, btw 2nd and 3rd ☏212/744-4949. Handsome uptown cabaret/piano bar with a mixed, and generally graying, clientele and a boisterous singing staff. Music from 9.30pm to close.

The Dugout Map 5, A5. 185 Christopher St, at Weehawken ☏212/242-9113. This friendly West Village hangout with TV, pool table, and video games might be the closest you'll find to a gay sports-bar. Right by the river.

Easternbloc Map 5, K3. 505 E 6th St, at Ave A ☏212/777-2555. Happening new gay bar with a young, hip Chelsea–East Village crowd, Soviet-era kitsch, and groovy DJs. Two-for-one drinks 7–10pm nightly.

g Lounge Map 6, E8. 225 W 19th St, btw 7th and 8th ☏212/929-1085. Nearly as stylish as its "guppie" clientele, this large, sleek, and deservedly popular lounge also features a DJ nightly.

Marie's Crisis Map 5, C4. 59 Grove St, btw 7th and Bleecker ☏212/243-9323. Often packed and always fun, this well-known cabaret/piano bar is popular with tourists and locals alike. Features old-time singing sessions nightly from 5.30pm.

Metropolitan 559 Lorimer St, Brooklyn ☏718/599-4444. Williamsburg's best (and, so far, only) gay bar with a mixed gay-and-lesbian twentysomething art-school crowd and rotating DJs. Wednesday is girls' night. Two fireplaces make it a snug spot in the winter, while the multilevel patio is great for alfresco drinking in summer.

The Monster Map 5, C3. 80 Grove St, at Waverly ☏212/924-3558. Large, campy bar with drag cabaret, piano, and downstairs dance floor. Very popular, especially with tourists, yet still has a strong neighborhood feel.

Phoenix Map 5, J1. 447 E 13th St, between 1st and A ☏212/477-9979. This relaxed East Village favorite is much loved by the so-not-scene-they're-scene boys and guys who really just want a drink and to play Ms Pacman. Open till 4am.

Pyramid Club Map 5, K3. 101 Ave A, btw 6th and 7th ☏212/228-4888. East Village gay-Goth-punk mainstay, with a DJ spinning hits from the 1980s on Friday nights for a packed dance floor of college-age and twentysomething hipsters. Occasional theater and live music, too.

Rawhide Map 6, E7. 212 8th Ave, at 21st ☏212/242-9332. Hell-bent for leather, *Rawhide* opens at 10am for those who have beer for breakfast and closes at 4am. Dancers daily starting at 8pm Mon–Sat and at 6pm on Sun.
Stonewall Map 5, C3. 53 Christopher St, between Waverly and 7th ☏212/463-0950. Yes, that *Stonewall*, site of the seminal 1969 riot, mostly refurbished and flying the pride flag like they own it – which, one supposes, they do.

Mainly for women

An Beal Bocht 445 W 238th St, between Greystone and Waldo, The Bronx ☏718/884-7127, ⓦwww .anbealbochtcafe.com. Equal parts students, lesbians, and Irish expats, this Riverdale favorite pulls in women from across the city and serves up Guinness, oatmeal, and frequent live music until all hours.

Cattyshack 249 4th Ave, Brooklyn ☏212/230-5740, ⓦcattyshackbklyn.com. One of the newest and coolest lesbian bars in New York. On the borderlands of Park Slope, the happening dance floor (go-go girls on week-ends), sleek lounge areas, roof deck, and great jukebox justify the trip out to Brooklyn (take the #R to Union Street). Daily happy hour and Wednesday karaoke; hetero-friendly.
Cubby Hole Map 5, A2. 281 W 12th St, btw Greenwich and 4th ☏212/243-9041. Welcoming, kitschy West Village dyke bar. Small but generally crowded and something of a required stopover, as it's been here forever.
Ginger's 363 5th Ave, Brooklyn ☏718/788-0924. Great Park Slope lesbian bar with a bustling scene centered on the pool table, the likes of Bob Marley and John Coltrane on the jukebox, and an outdoor patio. Super-comfortable space and friendly people.
Henrietta Hudson Map 5, B5. 438 Hudson St, at Morton ☏212/924-3347, ⓦwww.henriettahudson.com. Laid-back bar by day, dance club by night (see p.276). Happy hour 5–7pm.
Rubyfruit Bar & Grill Map 5, A4. 531 Hudson St, at 10th ☏212/929-3343. A cozy, friendly place for grown-up dykes, *Rubyfruit* is all about couches, cheap drinks, and good company.

Clubs

The gay and lesbian **club scene** in New York runs the gamut from outrageous, campy affairs with go-go dancers and drag shows to mellow gatherings that feel like college parties. See the media sources in the box on p.272 for listings, or check out the Gay & Lesbian pages in *Time Out New York*, available at any newsstand or bookstore.

Don Hill's Map 5, B7. 511 Greenwich St, at Spring ⊤212/219-2850, ⓦwww.donhills.com. An open-to-all, up-for-anything place where you'll find Brit-pop drag queens, mod-rock dominatrixes, and the occasional submissive metal fan. Pole dancers and porn complete the vibe.

The Eagle Map 6, B5. 554 W 28th St, between 10th and 11th ⊤646/473-1866, ⓦwww.eagle-ny.com. Bilevel leather club with regular and special fetish events that are by far the most storied and popular in New York. Dress code some nights; check the website.

Henrietta Hudson Map 5, B5. 438 Hudson St, between Morton and Barrow ⊤212/924-3347, ⓦwww.henriettahudson.com. On Wed–Sun nights this bar heats up with DJs and dancing. Weekly theme nights include salsa- and merengue-filled "Provacame" (Wednesday), disco (Friday), and a mix of hip-hop, R&B, and reggae the rest of the time.

La Nueva Escuelita Map 6, E2. 301 W 39th St, at 8th ⊤212/631-0588, ⓦwww.escuelita.com. Exclusive and elusive, this is also one of the city's very best gay clubs. It's all about kitsch, dress-up, salsa, drag, and (wo)men. Expect to wait in line for a while.

Lovergirl Map 4, E3. At the Millionaires Club, 283 Worth St, btw Broadway and Church ⊤212/252-3397, ⓦwww.lovergirlnyc.com. The Saturday-night hip-hop party in this TriBeCa bar is considered one of the best in the city.

Mr. Black Map 5, G4. 643 Broadway, at Bleecker ⊤212/253-2560, ⓦwww.basementnyc.com. Newish dance club packs a sexy young crowd into its basement lair, which plays up its dungeon-like atmosphere to decadent effect. Saturday night is "Boys Gone Wild."

27

Shopping

New York's **shops** are reason alone to visit the city. Even if the invasion of chains, like Barnes & Noble and even the world's largest K-Mart, have caused some worry, many of the oldest and oddest stores remain, and nothing beats discovering a quirky, independent shop that may specialize in vintage cufflinks or rubber stamps.

Remember that an 8.375 percent **sales tax** will be added to your bill unless you're buying clothes or footwear items costing less than $110, in which case the sales tax is waived; vendors in open-air markets may not charge sales tax if you pay in cash. Finally, wherever you're shopping, be careful: Manhattan's crowded, frenzied stores are ripe territory for pickpockets and bag-snatchers.

Antiques

New York is the premier **antiques** source in the country, with museum-quality pieces available (typically costing a fortune) as well as lots of interesting, fairly priced stuff at the junkier end of the market. Prime locations for browsing or buying are the East and West villages, SoHo, Chelsea, and the Upper East Side.

Chameleon Map 7, J5. 223 E 59th St, btw 2nd and 3rd ☎212/343-9197, ⓦwww.chameleon59.com. Interesting collection of antique lighting fixtures dating from the nineteenth century to the 1960s, many from NYC residences.

Las Venus Map 5, K6. 163 Ludlow St, at Stanton ☎212/982-0608, ⓦwww.lasvenus.com. Fun basement shop packed with Eames chairs, Verner Panton lamps, and more. Two more locations, one right around the corner at 113 Stanton St and the other inside ABC Carpet and Home, at 888 Broadway, btw 18th and 19th.

The Showplace Map 6, H6. 40 W 25th St, btw 5th and 6th ☎212/741-8520, ⓦwww.nyshowplace.com. Four-floor indoor market of more than 200 dealers of antiques and collectibles. plus an espresso bar.

Books

Book lovers bemoan the steady disappearance of New York's independent **bookstores**, and attribute their loss to the phenomenon of Barnes & Noble superstores, but there's still no shortage of places to find books, no matter how esoteric your tastes may be.

Independent bookstores

McNally Robinson Map 5, H6. 50 Prince St, at Mulberry ☎212/274-1160; ⓦwww.mcnallyrobinsonnyc.com. Owner Sarah McNally comes from the Canadian McNally Robinson publishing clan but runs this large, pleasant bookstore in NoLita as an independent. Great service – the staff here are friendly and very knowledgeable about books. Readings are held in the small tearoom.

St Mark's Bookshop Map 5, H3. 31 3rd Ave, at 9th ☎212/260-7853, ⓦwww.stmarksbookshop.com. One of the best bookstores in the city if you're artsy or an academic; stocks a good array of titles on politics, feminism, the environment, and literary criticism, as well as more obscure subjects. Also the best place to buy art and radical political magazines. Open till midnight daily.

Shakespeare & Co. 939 Lexington Ave, at 69th ☎212/570-0201 (Map 7, J3); 716 Broadway, at Washington

Place ☎ 212/529-1330 (Map 5, G4); 137 E 23rd St, at Lexington ☎ 212/570-0201 (Map 6, K7); and 1 Whitehall St, at Stone ☎ 212/742-7025 (Map 4, E8); ⓦ www.shake-andco.com. Classic independent seller of new books with great fiction and psychology selections. There's also a branch in Brooklyn at the Brooklyn Academy of Music (see p.163).

Three Lives & Co. Map 5, C3. 154 W 10th St, at Waverly ☎ 212/741-2069, ⓦ www.threelives.com. Exceptional, much-loved literary bookstore that has an especially good array of books by and for women, as well as general titles. A-list readings take place in the spring and fall.

Secondhand books

Argosy Book Store Map 7, I5. 16 E 59th St, between Lexington and Park ☎ 212/753-4455, ⓦ www .argosybooks.com. Unbeatable for antiquarian, rare, and out-of-print books. Also sells pamphlets, maps, autographs, and prints, as well as more mainstream titles (though you can usually find them cheaper elsewhere). Closed Sat & Sun in summer, and Sun year-round.

The Strand Map 5, G2. 828 Broadway, at 12th ☎ 212/473-1452, ⓦ www.strand-books.com. With about eight miles of books and a stock of 2.5 mil-lion-plus titles, this is the largest book operation in the city, and it recently got bigger with the addition of a second floor, where readings by top authors are held. In addition to used books, The Strand carries thousands of remaindered paperbacks and reviewers' copies of new hard-covers at half-price. Amazingly, all these books are catalogued online, so you can check ahead for availability. There's an annex location in the Financial District at 95 Fulton St (☎ 212/732-6070).

Travel and other specialty bookstores

The Complete Traveler Map 6, I3. 199 Madison Ave, at 35th ☎ 212/685-9007, ⓦ www.ctrarebooks.com. Antiquarian bookshop carrying old guidebooks, including a huge collection of vintage Baedekers, as well as collectible editions of exploration and discovery books, children's titles, and more.

Oscar Wilde Memorial Bookshop Map 5, C3. 15 Christopher St, btw Gay and Greenwich ☎ 212/255-8097, ⓦ www.oscarwildebooks.com. Aptly situated gay and lesbian bookstore – the first one in the world, according to its owners – with a rare book collection, signed and first editions, and signed, framed letters from famous authors.

Clothes, fashion, and accessories

If you're prepared to search the city with sufficient dedication, you can find just about anything in New York. Every international designer of note has a boutique here, and, though the sales clerks can be haughty if you don't look sufficiently rich, browsing the high-end collections can be a great way to get in touch with the fashion world. All the same, it's bargain shopping that animates most visitors, as you'll see if you enter any of the discount emporia, where sharp elbows and sloppy displays are par for the course, but everyone seems to leave with a huge bag and a smile.

Chain stores

American Apparel Map 5, J5. 183 E Houston St, at Orchard ☎212/598-4600. LA-based T-shirt company that's made a full-court press on New York in recent years, hawking American-made T-shirts and retro (usually Eighties) fashions, all in bright, high-quality cotton. Ten other Manhattan locations.
Diesel Map 7, J5. 770 Lexington Ave, at 60th ☎212/308-0055. Italian-designed clubwear and lots of denim. Also at 1 Union Square, at 14th St.
Forever 21 Map 5, F1. 40 E 14th St, at Broadway ☎212/228-0598. The newest (so far) of the cheap-but-chic chains, where plenty of thirtysomethings scour the racks alongside preteens for babydoll dresses, tube tops, and kitschy sunglasses. Come early, before half the clothes end up on the floor. Another store at 50 W 34th St, near Macy's.
H&M Map 6, I8. 111 5th Ave, at 18th ☎212/539-1741. Swedish-based mass-market chain that churns out trendy fashions – the hard-to-resist prices make up for the sometimes shoddy quality. Look for special collections by guest designers like Roberto Cavalli and Madonna. Seven other locations in NYC, though this is one of the newest, biggest, and least hectic.

Designer stores

Anna Sui Map 5, F6. 113 Greene St, btw Prince and Spring ☎212/941-8406.
Diane Von Furstenberg Map 6, C9. 874 Washington St, at 14th St ☎646/486-4800.
DKNY Map 7, I5. 655 Madison Ave, btwn 68th and 69th ☎212/223-3569; **Map 7, I3. 420 W Broadway, at Spring** ☎646/613-1100.

Dolce & Gabbana Map 8, I8. 1055 Madison Ave, at 80th ☎212/249-4100.

Gianni Versace Map 7, H7. 647 5th Ave, btw 51st and 52nd ☎212/317-0224.

Giorgio Armani Map 7, I4. 760 Madison Ave, at 65th St ☎212/988-9191.

Gucci Map 7, H7. 685 5th Ave, at 54th St ☎212/826-2600.

Hermès Map 7, I5. 691 Madison, at 62nd ☎212/759-7585.

Marc Jacobs Map 5, F6. 163 Mercer St, btw Houston and Prince ☎212/343-1490.

Stella McCartney Map 6, D9. 429 W 14th St, at 9th Ave ☎212/255-1556.

Funky, trendy, hip

Canal Jean Co Map 5, F7. 718 Broadway, at 7th ☎212/226-3663. Enormous warehousey store sporting a prodigious array of jeans, jackets, T-shirts, dresses, hats, and more, new and secondhand. Young, fun, and reasonably cheap.

Intermix Map 5, B3. 365 Bleecker St, at Charles ☎212/929-7180. Very popular mini-boutique chain known for its pieces from top and up-and-coming designers like La Rok and Michael Kors. Also carries shoes and accessories. Four other Manhattan locations.

Marc by Marc Jacobs Map 5, B3. 403 Bleecker St, at Perry ☎212/924-0026. The only Marc by Marc Jacobs store in New York feels right at home on this pleasant corner of the West Village, with geeky-chic clerks and grunge-inspired clothes that aren't cheap but are far more affordable than anything in the Marc Jacobs store in SoHo.

Uniqlo Map 5, F7. 546 Broadway, at Spring ☎212/237-8800. A three-level, 36,000-square-foot shop, with plenty of room between the racks, helpful and numerous sales assistants, and fashion-forward clothes rarely topping $100.

Vintage and secondhand

Allan & Suzi Map 8, C9. 416 Amsterdam Ave, at 80th St ☎212/724-7445. Beautiful, way-over-the-top fashion from the 1960s and 70s. Claims to have single-handedly restarted the platform-shoe craze back in the late 90s, and continues to offer a wide range of outlandish vintage threads.

Edith & Daha Map 5, K6. 104 Rivington, at Ludlow ☎212/979-9992. Extremely popular with the trendy vintage set, this used-clothing emporium has some amazing finds (particularly shoes) for those willing to sift through the massive stock.

INA Map 5, H6. 21 Prince St, at Elizabeth ☎212/334-9048. Designer resale shop usually crammed with end-of-season, barely worn pieces by the hot designers *du jour* at fair prices. The men's store is at 262 Mott St, between Houston and Prince (☎212/334-2210).

Love Saves the Day Map 5, I3. 119 2nd Ave, at 7th ☎212/228-3802. Cheap vintage as well as classic lunchboxes and other kitschy nostalgia items, including valuable Kiss and *Star Wars* dolls.

Screaming Mimi's Map 5, G4. 382 Lafayette St, btw 4th and Great Jones ☎212/677-6464. One of the most established vintage stores in Manhattan, with vintage threads (including lingerie), bags, shoes, and housewares at reasonable prices.

Tokio 7 Map 5, J3. 64 E 7th St, btw 1st and 2nd ☎212/353-8443. Attractive secondhand and vintage designer consignment items – a little pricier than elsewhere, but a good selection.

Discount department stores

Century 21 Map 4, E6. 22 Cortlandt St, at Church ☎212/227-9092. The mother ship of discount department stores, where you can find some terrific bargains on top labels (though

Sample sales

At the beginning of each season, designers' and manufacturers' showrooms are full of leftover merchandise that is removed via informal **sample sales**. You'll always save at least fifty percent off the retail price, though you may not be able to try on the clothes and you can never return them. The best times for sample sales are spring and fall. Short of waiting for advertisement fliers to be stuffed into your hands while walking through the Garment District, the below sources are helpful. *Time Out New York*, available at any newsstand, also lists sales happening that week.

Clothingline Map 6, D3. 261 W 36th St, 2nd floor, btw 7th and 8th ☎212/362-1020, ⓦwww.clothingline.com. Large Garment District space that holds sample sales for rafts of hot designers; check online for schedule or call their sample-sale hotline on ☎212/947-8748.

Daily Candy ⓦwww.dailycandy.com. *The* website to find out about coveted designs at bargain rates before the city's fashionistas commence their stampede.

not the most recent line) if you can deal with the crammed and disorganized displays.

Loehmann's Map 6, F8. 101 7th Ave, btw 16th and 17th ☎212/352-0856. Designer clothes at knockdown prices at this five-story chain store, which is better organized than Century 21 but has fewer real finds. There's a new location at Broadway and 73rd St on the Upper West Side (☎212/882-9990).

Shoes and accessories

Kenneth Cole Map 7, H8. 610 5th Ave, at 49th ☎212/373-5800. Classic and contemporary shoes, beautiful bags, excellent full-grain leather. Call for more locations.

Manolo Blahnik Map 7, H7. 31 W 54th St, at 5th ☎212/582-3007. World-famous strappy stilettos, good for height (of fashion), hell for feet. More popular than ever thanks to their prominence in *Sex and the City*.

Otto Tootsi Plohound Map 6, I7. 137 5th Ave, at 20th St ☎212/460-8650; **and Map 5, G6. 273 Lafayette, btw Prince and Houston** ☎212/431-7299. If you want to run with a trendy crowd, these shoes will help. Very current designs.

Robert Marc Map 7, I6. 575 Madison Ave, btw 56th and 57th ☎212/319-2000. Exclusive New York distributor of designer glasses frames like Lunor, Freudenhaus, and Beausoleil; also sells Retrospecs, restored antique eyewear from the 1890s to the 1940s. Very expensive and very hot. Call for seven other locations.

Sigerson Morrison Map 5, H6. 28 Prince St, at Mott ☎212/219-3893. Kari Sigerson and Miranda Morrison make timeless, simple, and elegant shoes for women, and have just expanded into a large new shop. A required pilgrimage for shoe-worshippers.

Department stores

Barneys Map 7, I5. 660 Madison Ave, at 61st ☎212/826-8900. The *ne plus ultra* of designer shopping, this nine-story flagship appeals to both young fashionistas and ladies who lunch, with chic, up-to-the-minute designer garments from top labels (Chloe, Miu Miu, etc). Excellent menswear and cosmetics departments, too.

Bergdorf Goodman Map 7, H6. 754 5th Ave, at 57th ☎212/753-7300. One of New York City's ritziest department stores; drop by if only to check out the window displays, which approach high art. Top-notch service and all the best brands. The men's store is across 5th Ave.

Bloomingdale's Map 7, J5. 1000 3rd Ave, at 59th ☎212/705-2000. "Bloomie's", as it's referred to affectionately by regulars, has the atmosphere of a large, bustling bazaar, packed with concessionaires offering perfumes and designer clothes, housewares, and just about everything else. In 2004, a smaller outpost opened in SoHo at 504 Broadway (btw Broome and Spring).

Henri Bendel Map 7, H6. 712 5th Ave, btw 55th and 56th ☎212/247-1100. This store, housed in the former Coty perfume building, with windows by René Lalique, is more genteel in its approach than the biggies. Has a reputation for exclusivity and showcasing top modern designers.

Jeffrey Map 6, C9. 449 W 14th St, at 10th ☎212/206-3928. Generally regarded as the most cutting-edge department store in the city, this Meatpacking District magnet has a well-edited selection of top labels arrayed around a plashing fountain, with plenty of surprisingly amiable sales-people lurking about to "start a dressing room for you," should you find yourself with an arm-load of clothes.

Macy's Map 6, G3. 151 W 34th St, on Broadway at Herald Square ☎212/695-4400 or 1-800/289-6229. The largest department store in the world, with two buildings, two million square feet of floor space, and ten floors (four for women's garments alone).

Saks Fifth Avenue Map 7, H8. 611 5th Ave, at 50th ☎212/753-4000. This 10-story flagship, first opened in 1924, helped make the Saks name synonymous with style worldwide. It continues to cater to an international clientele with top brands and gracious service. The ground floor, a maze of cosmetics counters, is lovely when decorated with sparkling white branches at Christmastime.

Takashimaya Map 7, H6. 693 5th Ave, btw 54th and 55th ☎212/350-0100. This beautiful Japanese department store offers a scaled-down assortment of expensive merchandise simply displayed, and exquisitely wrapped purchases. The *Tea Box* café on the lower level has an assortment of teapots and loose teas.

The Diamond District

The strip of 47th Street between Fifth and Sixth avenues is known as the **Diamond District**. Crammed into this one block are more than 100 shops: combined they sell more jewelry than any other block in the world. The industry has traditionally been run by Hasidic Jews, and you'll run into plenty of black-garbed men with *payess* (sidelocks) here.

Some good starting points are Andrew Cohen, Inc, for **diamonds** (579 5th Ave, 15th floor); Myron Toback, a trusted dealer of **silver** findings (25 W 47th St); and Bracie Company, Inc, a friendly business specializing in **antique and estate jewelry** (608 5th Ave, Suite 806). Once you buy, there's AA Pearls & Gems, the industry's choice for **pearl- and gem-stringing** (10 W 47th St), and, if you want to get your gems graded, the **Gemological Institute of America** (580 5th Ave, 2nd floor).

Food and drink

Food – the buying as much as the consuming of it – is a New York obsession. Though you can find a deli on pretty much any corner, it's in the gourmet markets and specialty shops – cheese, bread, smoked fish, what have you – that the city really shines.

Agata & Valentina Map 8, L9. 1505 1st Ave, at 79th ☏212/452-0690. Considered by many to be the top gourmet grocer in town, with fresh pasta made on the premises, an enviable gourmet deli and cheese counter, a variety of pricey delicacies, and the best butcher in town.

Barney Greengrass Map 8, C7. 541 Amsterdam Ave, btw 86th and 87th ☏212/724-4707. "The Sturgeon King" – an Upper West Side smoked-fish brunch institution since 1908 that also sells brunch-makings to go.

Chelsea Market Map 6, D9. 75 9th Ave, btw 15th and 16th ☏212/243-6005. A complex of eighteen former industrial buildings, among them the late nineteenth-century Nabisco Cookie Factory. Houses a number of small grocers, including a butcher, two bakers, and a dairy – all of which are of high quality.

Dean & Deluca Map 5, G6. 560 Broadway, at Prince ☎212/226-6800. One of the original big neighborhood food emporia. Very chic, very SoHo, and not at all cheap.

Murray's Cheese Shop Map 5, C4. 254 Bleecker St, btw 6th and 7th ☎212/243-3289. A variety of more than three hundred fresh cheeses and excellent fresh panini sandwiches, all served by knowledgeable staff. Free tastings on Sat afternoons.

Russ & Daughters Map 5, J5. 179 E Houston St, btw Allen and Orchard ☎212/475-4880. The original Manhattan gourmet shop, set up around 1900 to sate the appetites of homesick immigrant Jews. Sells smoked fish, caviar, pickled vegetables, cheese, and bagels.

Zabar's Map 8, B9. 2245 Broadway, btw 80th and 81st ☎212/787-2000. The apotheosis of New York food-fever, Zabar's is still the city's pre-eminent food-store. Choose from an astonishing variety of cheeses, cooked meats, salads, fresh-baked bread and croissants, excellent bagels, and cooked dishes to go. Not to be missed.

Greenmarkets

Several days each week, long before sunrise, hundreds of farmers from Long Island, the Hudson Valley, and parts of Pennsylvania and New Jersey set out in trucks transporting their fresh-picked bounty to New York City, where they are joined by bakers, cheesemakers, and others at 44 citywide **greenmarkets**. Usually you'll find apple cider, jams and preserves, flowers and plants, maple syrup, fresh meat and fish, pretzels, cakes and breads, herbs, honey – just about anything and everything produced in the rural regions around the city – not to mention occasional live-worm composts and baby dairy goats.

Call ☎212/788-7476 for the greenmarket nearest you; the largest and most popular is held in Union Square at East 17th St and Broadway, year-round on Mon, Wed, Fri & Sat from 8am to 6pm.

Music

While the Virgin Megastore has muscled out many home-grown enterprises (and smaller chains, like Tower Records), there's still a handful of local shops that cater to music buffs, many carrying both new and used merchandise, vinyl, and special imports.

Chains

Virgin Megastore Map 7, F9. 1540 Broadway, at 45th ☏212/921-1020; and Map 6, J9. 52 E 14th St, at Union Square ☏212/598-4666. A colossal selection of every imaginable genre with great sales, like the one hundred top CDs of all time for $10 each.

Independent and secondhand

Fat Beats Map 5, D3. 406 6th Ave, btw 8th and 9th, 2nd floor ☏212/673-3883. The name says it all. It's the source for hip-hop on vinyl in New York City.
J&R Music World Map 4, E5. 23 Park Row, btw Beekman and Anne ☏212/238-9000. A large downtown store – they own most of the block – with a decent selec-

tion of CDs and good prices. All sorts of electronic gadgets to play them on, too.
Mondo Kim's Map 5, H3. 6 St Mark's Place, at 3rd ☏212/505-0311. Old-school East Village movie and music shop, with three stories of punk-rock attitude; the ground floor has racks of new and used CDs and vinyl, with a heavy emphasis on rock-and-roll.
Other Music Map 5, G4. 15 E 4th St, at Lafayette ☏212/598-9985. This sweet spot has a dedicated following among NYU students and other lovers of indie rock in its many guises: post-punk, neo-disco, garage rock, emo, lo-fi, and the like. Mostly small labels, lots of imports, both new and used.

Art galleries

There are roughly five hundred **art galleries** in New York, and even if you have no intention of buying anything, many of them are well worth seeing. **Chelsea** is the biggest and most densely packed gallery district in the city – indeed, in all of America – with more than three hundred spaces showing all manner of contemporary art. The **Upper East Side** – particularly Madison Avenue from 64th Street to about 83rd Street – has around fifty galleries, most geared for wealthy collectors, with antiques and the occasional (minor) Old Master. **Midtown**'s galleries are tucked above the shops along 57th Street between Sixth and Third avenues; several of these are first-rate, showing well-known modern and contemporary artists, particularly painters. While not the artistic hotbed it was in the 1980s, **SoHo** still has a smattering of decent, well-established galleries, as does TriBeCa, which is home to a couple of the city's best nonprofit art spaces. Galleries on the **Lower East Side**, and in **DUMBO** and **Williamsburg** in Brooklyn, thrive on cutting-edge art, especially mixed media and installation art.

Opening hours for most galleries are roughly Tuesday to Saturday from 10am to 6pm. Note that many galleries are closed on weekends in the summer and for the whole month of August. The best day to gallery-hop is Thursday, the most popular day for openings, especially in Chelsea. We suggest you take in the best shows before the galleries close at 6pm, then make the rounds of the **openings** – free wine-and-beer affairs that run from 6 to 8 or 9pm at galleries with new shows. Pick up a copy of the *Gallery Guide* – available upon request in the larger galleries – for listings of current shows and each gallery's specialty. The website Ⓦ www.artcal.net has a very handy list of all the week's openings, with full descriptions, including pictures and recommendations. The weekly *Time Out New York* magazine also offers broad listings of the major commercial galleries.

SoHo and TriBeCa

apexart Map 4, E2. 291 Church St, btw Walker and White ☎ 212/431-5270, Ⓦ www.apexart .org. TriBeCa gallery showcasing eight thought-provoking group shows per year; recent subjects have included "temporality."

Artists Space Map 4, E1. 38 Greene St, btw Canal and Grand, 3rd floor ☎ 212/226-3970, Ⓦ www.art-istsspace.com. One of the most respected alternative spaces; founded in 1972. Features frequently changing theme-based exhibits, film screenings, and the like.

Louis Meisel Map 5, E6. 141 Prince St, at West Broadway ☎ 212/677-1340, Ⓦ www.meiselgallery.com. Specializes in Photorealism as well as Abstract Illusionism. Past shows have included Richard Estes, Jock Sturges, and Chuck Close.

Chelsea

Barbara Gladstone Map 6, B6. 515 W 24th St, between 10th and 11th ☎ 212/206-9300, Ⓦ www.gladstone-gallery.com. Paintings, sculpture, and photography by hot con temporary artists like Matthew Barney, Sarah Lucas, and Rose-marie Trockel.

Cheim & Read Map 6, B6. 547 W 25th, btw 10th and 11th ☎ 212/242-7227, Ⓦ www.cheimread.com. Established gallery featuring works by highly regarded American and European artists such as Andy Warhol, Robert Mapplethorpe, and Louise Bourgeois, as well as younger types.

Gagosian Map 6, B6. 555 W 24th St, btw 10th and 11th ☎ 212/741-1111, Ⓦ www .gagosian.com. This stalwart of the New York scene, owned by an ex–LA poster salesman, features modern and contemporary art by the likes of De Kooning, Lichtenstein, and Schnabel, as well as British stars Damien Hirst and Jenny Saville. Uptown location at 980 Madison Ave, at 76th (☎212/772-7962).

Lehmann Maupin Map 6, B6. 540 W 26th St, btw 10th and 11th ☎212/255-2923, Ⓦwww.lehmannmaupin.com. Shows a range of top-tier international and American contemporary artists (Tony Oursler, Tracey Emin) in Rem Koolhaas–designed quarters.

Matthew Marks Map 6, B7. 523 W 24th St, btw 10th and 11th ☎212/243-0200, Ⓦwww.matthewmarks.com. The driving force behind Chelsea's emergence as the art capital of the US, this 9000-square-foot gallery represents such well-known minimalist and abstract artists as Ellsworth Kelly, Nan Goldin, and Lucian Freud. See also the branches at 522 and 526 W 22nd St.

Paula Cooper Map 6, B7. 534 W 21st St, btw 10th and 11th, 2nd floor ☎212/255-1105, Ⓦwww.paulacoopergallery.com. Another influential gallery that shows a wide range of contemporary painting, sculpture, drawings, prints, and photographs, particularly minimalist and abstract works by the likes of Sophie Calle and Sol LeWitt.

Robert Miller Map 6, B6. 524 W 26th St, btw 10th and 11th ☎212/366-4774, Ⓦwww.robertmillergallery.com. Exceptional shows of twentieth-century art, including sculpture, paintings by David Hockney and Lee Krasner, and photographs by artists such as Diane Arbus and Robert Mapplethorpe.

Sonnabend Map 6, B7. 536 W 22nd St, btw 10th and 11th ☎212/627-1018, Ⓦwww.artnet.com/sonnabend. A top gallery featuring painting, photography, and video from contemporary American and European artists, including Jeff Koons, Candida Höfer, and Gilbert and George.

Midtown and the Upper East Side

Castelli Gallery Map 7, H1. 18 E 77th St, btw 5th and Madison ☎212/249-4470, Ⓦwww.castelligallery.com. One of the original dealer-collectors, Leo Castelli was instrumental in aiding the careers of Rauschenberg and Warhol. The gallery offers big contemporary names at big prices.

Knoedler & Co. Map 7, H3. 19 E 70th St, btw 5th and Madison ☎212/794-0550, Ⓦwww.knoedlergallery.com. Highly renowned gallery – the oldest in NYC – specializing in abstract, Pop Art, postwar, and contemporary, with a focus on the New York School. Shows some of the best-known names in twentieth-century art, including Stella, Rauschenberg, and Frankenthaler.

Mary Boone Map 7, H6. 745 5th Ave, btw 57th and 58th, 4th floor ☎ 212/752-2929, ⓦ www .maryboonegallery.com. This top gallery specializes in installations, paintings, and works by up-and-coming European and American artists. Check out the Chelsea branch at 541 W 24th St, between 10th and 11th.

PaceWildenstein Map 7, I6. 32 E 57th St, at Madison ☎ 212/421-3292, ⓦ www.pacewildenstein.com. Celebrated gallery that has carried works by most of the great modern American and European artists, from Picasso to Rothko. Its two Chelsea satellites, at 534 W 25th St and 545 W 22nd St, specialize in edgier works, mixed media, and large installations.

Lower East Side

Gallery Onetwentyeight Map 5, K6. 128 Rivington, btw Essex and Norfolk ☎ 212/674-0244, ⓦ www .galleryonetwentyeight.com. Diminutive gallery featuring solo and group shows of contemporary art – painting, sculpture, mixed media, you name it. Wed–Sat 1–7pm.

DUMBO and Williamsburg

d.u.m.b.o. arts center 30 Washington St, btw Plymouth and Water, Brooklyn ☎ 718/694-0831, ⓦ www .dumboartscenter.org. Founded in 1997, this nonprofit arts group has helped turn DUMBO (see p.162) into an art mecca of sorts. They show artists' work in their large gallery. Thurs–Mon 10am–6pm.

Pierogi 2000 177 N 9th St, btw Bedford and Driggs, Brooklyn ☎ 718/599-2144, ⓦ www .pierogi2000.com. Galleries come and go in Williamsburg, but this one has stayed. It was founded

Open studios

Several neighborhoods better known for housing artists than galleries sponsor **open studio tours**, when the artists leave their doors open and let you admire their works in progress (and buy completed work). The Harlem Open Artist Studio Tour takes place over one weekend each fall; see ⓦ www.hoast.org for the lowdown. In June the Brooklyn Waterfront Artists Coalition has an open-studios tour of its own, featuring the studios and galleries of the Red Hook and Carroll Gardens sections of Brooklyn; see ⓦ www.bwac.org.

by artist and sign painter Joe Amrhein in 1994, well before the neighborhood swelled into the hipster haven it is today. Check out the famous "flat files" – hundreds of works on paper that you can peruse provided you don white gloves. Thurs–Sun 11am–6pm.

Smack Mellon Studios 92 Plymouth St, at Washington, Brooklyn ☎718/834-8761, ⓦwww .smackmellon.org. DUMBO gallery for mid-career and female artists; it's part of an organization that provides studios, metalwork shops, and computers for under-recognized creative types. Wed–Sun noon–6pm.

29

Sports and outdoor activities

New York is one of the most avid **sports** cities in America. TV stations cover most regular-season games and all postseason games in the big four American team sports: **baseball**, **football**, **basketball**, and **ice hockey**. Some tickets can be hard to find, some impossible, and most don't come that cheap. **Tickets** for most events can be booked through Ticketmaster (T 212/307-7171, W www.ticketmaster.com), but the company levies an outrageous service charge on every ticket; sports franchises have followed suit, tacking on $8 or more per ticket if you buy online or over the phone. If you can get there, buy advance tickets direct from the stadium box office. You can try to pick up tickets on the day of the event, of course, but you risk not getting a seat. Be very careful if you decide to buy an "extra" ticket off someone standing outside (or online); though some sellers are honest, others make a living selling fakes that look almost identical to real tickets; their bar codes won't scan at the gate, however, at which point the perpetrator will be long gone.

Many **participatory activities** in the city are free or affordable. You can swim either at the local pools or the borough beaches, usually for a small fee; jogging is still one of the city's main obsessions, and there are an ever-increasing number of spaces to bike or rollerblade.

Baseball

From April to October, the **New York Yankees** and the **New York Mets** play 162 games (81 home games each; playoffs run through Oct), giving you plenty of excuses to head out for a sunny day at the ballpark, not to mention the fact that baseball games, of all spectator sports, are by far the least expensive.

The Yankees are the most successful sports franchise in history, with the most World Series titles (26 to date). If you get to the game early, you can visit Monument Park, where all their greats are memorialized (see p.174 for more on Yankee Stadium). The Mets have been on a rollercoaster ride ever since the lovably inept team of 1962 matured into the 1969 World Series champions, and then took a nose dive from their second World Series win in 1986 to the "worst team money can buy" in the early 1990s, and back up to making the finals – only to be beaten by the Yankees – in 2000. Both teams are building new stadiums next door to the ones currently in use and plan to inaugurate them in 2009.

Shea Stadium 126th St, at Roosevelt Ave, Queens; box office Mon–Fri 9am–6pm, Sat, Sun & holidays 9am–5pm; tickets $5–82; ☏718/507-8499, ⓦwww.mets.com. #7 to Willets Point/Shea Stadium.

Yankee Stadium 161st St, at River Ave, The Bronx; box office Mon–Sat 9am–5pm, Sun 10am–4pm; tickets $12–63; ☏718/293-6000, ⓦwww.yankees.com. #D or #4 to 161st Street/Yankee Stadium.

Basketball

The National Basketball Association's (NBA) regular season begins in November and runs through the end of April. The two professional teams in the New York area are the **New York Knicks** (Ⓦwww.nba.com/knicks, ☎212/465-5867), who play at Madison Square Garden, and the **New Jersey Nets** (Ⓦwww.nba.com/nets), whose venue is the Continental Airlines Arena at the Meadowlands Sports Complex in New Jersey, though plans are afoot to move them to Brooklyn. The **New York Liberty** (Ⓦwww.wnba.com/liberty), of the Women's NBA, play their games at Madison Square Garden during the summer.

The Knicks have a loyal following that includes such celebrities as Spike Lee, Woody Allen, and Sarah Jessica Parker. It can be difficult to get tickets to see them play, though less so than in the past. Long playing in the shadow of the Knicks, the Nets have emerged as one of the more exciting teams in the NBA, and tickets can now also prove difficult to obtain.

Madison Square Garden Map 6, E4. 7th Ave, between 31st and 33rd; Knicks tickets $34.50–330; Liberty tickets $10–$54.50; box office Mon–Fri 9am–6pm, Sat 10am–6pm, closed Sun; ☎212/307-7171, Ⓦwww.thegarden.com. #A, #C, #E, #1, #2, or #3 to Penn Station.

Continental Airlines Arena Meadowlands Sports Complex, off routes 3, 17, and Turnpike exit 16W, East Rutherford, New Jersey; box office 9am–6pm, Sat 10am–6pm, Sun noon–5pm; tickets $10–215; ☎1-800/7NJ-NETS, Ⓦwww.meadowlands.com.

Football

The National Football League (NFL) season stretches from September until the Super Bowl, typically played on the fourth Sunday in January. Although tickets for both local teams, the **Giants** (Ⓦwww.giants.com) and the **Jets** (Ⓦwww.newyorkjets.com), sell out well in advance, if you're willing to pay the price you can buy tickets outside the stadium before the game (from scalpers). Both teams play at Giants Stadium in East Rutherford, New Jersey.

With a twenty-year waiting list for season tickets, the Giants, who have won two Super Bowls (in 1987 and 1991), have a devoted following. Since 1984, the Jets have been subtenants at Giants Stadium. While the Jets have not had the historical success of the Giants, they are generally as competitive.

Giants Stadium Meadowlands Sports Complex, off routes 3, 17, and Turnpike exit 16W, East Rutherford, New Jersey; box office Mon–Fri 9am–6pm, Sat 10am–6pm, Sun noon–5pm; tickets $75 and $85; ☏ 201/935-8222. Regular buses are available to Giants Stadium from Port Authority Bus Terminal on 42nd St and 8th Ave.

Ice hockey

After a players' strike that scrapped the entire 2004–05 season, the two New York National Hockey League (NHL) teams, the **Rangers** and the **Islanders**, are back up and skating. The Rangers (ⓦwww.newyorkrangers.com) play at Madison Square Garden (see "Basketball," for location and ticket info), while the Islanders (ⓦwww.newyorkislanders.com) take the ice at Nassau Coliseum on Long Island. The exceptional **New Jersey Devils** (ⓦwww.newjerseydevils.com), who've won the Stanley Cup (hockey's biggest prize) three times – in 1995, 2000, and 2003 – play at the new Prudential Center in Newark. The regular hockey season lasts throughout the winter and into early spring, when the playoffs take place. Prices for games range from $15 to $100.

As for team quality, the Rangers ended a 54-year drought in 1994, when they won the Stanley Cup; they haven't won it since, but they've made it to the playoffs the past couple of seasons. The Islanders, New York's "other" hockey team, won four consecutive Stanley Cups in the early 1980s and have recently undergone something of a resurgence after years of mediocrity, reaching the playoffs in 2007.

SPORTS AND ACTIVITIES

Bicycling

There are over one hundred miles of **bike paths** in New York; those in Central Park and along the Hudson River are among the nicest, and with a little street maneuvering you can now bike the full 32-mile periphery of Manhattan. Transportation Alternatives, at 127 W 26th St, Suite 1002 (☎212/629-8080, ⓦwww.transalt.org), concentrates on the environmental aspects and physical benefits of bicycling while lobbying for funding for bike-related projects, like ramps for bridge access, free bike racks, bike lanes, and additional car-free hours in Central Park. They also sponsor the New York Century Bike Tour in September (a 15-, 35-, 55-, 75-, or 100-mile ride through the boroughs), and have some good maps and links to other routes in areas close to the city.

Bicycle Habitat Map 5, G3. 244 Lafayette St, btw Prince and Spring ☎212/431-3315, ⓦwww.bicyclehabitat.com. Known for its excellent repair service, this punk-rock bike shop offers tune-ups and free estimates. The very knowledgeable staff helps cyclists of all levels of expertise, and they have a great gear selection, too.

Five Borough Bike Club ☎212/932-2300 ext 115, ⓦwww.5bbc.org. This club organizes day and weekend rides throughout the year, including the Montauk Century, a one-hundred-mile ride from New York to Montauk, Long Island, each May.

Gotham Bikes Map 4, D3. 112 W Broadway btw Duane and Reade ☎212/732-2453, ⓦwww.togabikes.com. Friendly staff and top-shelf bikes and bike repair in the heart of TriBeCa, with easy access to the Hudson River Greenway. Also rents bikes for $10/hr or $30/day, but you have to get here early on a sunny day if you want to snag one. The store is owned by Toga Bikes, which has locations on the Upper West and Upper East sides; see website or call for locations.

New York Cycling Club ☎212/828-5711, ⓦwww.nycc.org. Very friendly cycling club offering day rides, evening whizzes around Central Park, weekends away, and lots of social activities in between.

SPORTS AND ACTIVITIES

Chelsea Piers

The **Chelsea Piers** complex, entered at West 23rd St at the Hudson River (☎212/336-6666, ⓦwww.chelseapiers.com), covers six blocks spread over four completely renovated piers, on which all manner of activity takes place.

At Pier 60, the **Sports Center** (☎212/336-6000) features a quarter-mile running track, the largest rock-climbing wall in the Northeast, three basketball courts, a boxing ring, a 24-yard swimming pool, whirlpool, indoor sand-volleyball courts, exercise studios offering more than one hundred classes weekly, a cardi-ovascular weight-training room, a sundeck right on the Hudson River, and spa services. Day-passes are available for $50. Open Mon–Thurs 5am–11pm, Fri 5am–10pm, Sat & Sun 8am–9pm. Pier 60 also has a sleek bowling alley, 300 New York (see below).

On Pier 61, the **Sky Rink** (☎212/336-6100) offers year-round ice-skating on an indoor rink. Sessions start at 12.30pm and cost $11.50, or $9 for children under 12 and seniors; free in summer. Ice-skate rentals cost $6.50.

Bowling

300 New York Map 6, A7. Pier 60, W 23rd St at the West Side Highway ☎212/835-2695, ⓦwww.3hundred. com. Sleek, dark bowling alley with forty lanes, hip-hop videos on rotation, a restaurant, and cocktail waitresses to take your drink orders while you play. Lessons available. Sun–Thurs 9am–11pm, Fri–Sat 9am–2am. Before 5pm $8 per person, per game; after 5pm $8.75; shoe rental $5.

Bowlmor Lanes Map 5, F2. 110 University Pl, between 12th and 13th ☎212/255-8188, ⓦwww.bowlmor. com. Fun, very popular bowling alley that caters to the NYU crowd with a packed bar and thumping tunes. Monday night features glow-in-the-dark bowling with live DJ music (10pm–2am, $22 includes unlimited bowling and shoe rental). Open Sun 11am to midnight, Mon & Thurs until 2am, Tues & Wed until 1am, Fri & Sat until 3:30am. Before 5pm $8.95 per person, per game ($9.45 Fri–Sat); after 5pm $9.45 ($9.95 Fri–Sat), shoe rental $5.50.

Leisure Time Bowling Map 6, E1.
Port Authority Bus Terminal, 8th Ave
near 40th St, 2nd floor ☎ 212/268-
6909, ⓦ www.leisuretimebowl.com.
This is the best place to bowl in
the city. Recently spiffed up with
a new cocktail lounge and restaurant, but still pleasantly seedy,
as befits a bowling alley in a
bus station. Open Sun 1–11pm,
Mon–Thurs 10am–midnight,
Fri 10am–1am, Sat 1pm–1am.
Mon–Fri before 5pm $6.50 per
game per person, all other times
and holidays $9.50. Shoe rental
is $5.

Pools and baths

John Jay Pool Map 7, M1. 77th St,
at Cherokee Place ☎ 212/794-6566.
The city's parks department runs
52 outdoor swimming pools
that are free and open to the
public from late June until early
September. Above the FDR
Drive, this six-lane, fifty-yard pool
surrounded by playgrounds and
park benches is one of the best.
Although it opened in 1940, it
is in remarkably great condition.
For a complete list of city pools,
including hours and locations, go
to ⓦ www.nycgovparks.org.

Russian & Turkish Baths Map 5, I2.
268 E 10th Street. ☎ 212/473-8806
or 674-9250. An ancient place,
something of a neighborhood
landmark and still going strong,
with steam baths, a sauna, and
an ice-cold pool, as well as
massage facilities and a restaurant. Towels, robe, and slippers
included with $25 admission
(extra for massages, treat-
ments, etc). Open Mon, Tues,
Thurs & Fri 11am–10pm, Wed
9am–2pm (women only 2–10pm),
Sat 7.30am–10pm, and Sun
7.30am–2pm (men only 2–10pm).

Horse racing

Aqueduct Racetrack, in Howard Beach, Queens, has **thoroughbred racing** from October to May. To get there by subway, take
the #A train to the Aqueduct station. Belmont Park, in Elmont,
Long Island, is home to the **Belmont Stakes** in June, one of the
three races in which 3-year-olds compete for the Triple Crown,

horse racing's highest honor. Belmont thoroughbred racing is open May to July and September to October. Take the #F train to 169th Street and then the N6 bus to the track, or take the Long Island Railroad to the Belmont Race Track stop. For both Belmont and Aqueduct, call ☏718/641-4700, or visit ⓦwww.nyra.com. Admission at both tracks ranges from $1–5 depending on when you go and where you sit. Wagering, on the other hand, runs from $2 on up into the stratosphere.

Ice-skating

The Pond at Bryant Park Map 6, H1. 5th Ave, between 40th and 42nd ☏1-866/221-5157, ⓦwww.thepondatbryantpark.com. New York City's newest place to skate is Bryant Park, where a medium-sized rink awaits those brave enough to face the winter cold. Skating is free and skate rental is $7.50. Open late Oct through mid-Jan daily 8am–10.30pm.
Rockefeller Center Ice Rink Map 7, H8. 5th Ave, between 49th and 50th ☏212/332-7654, ⓦwww.therinkatrockcenter.com. Without a doubt the slickest place to skate; the sunken rink is surrounded by skyscrapers and, in holiday season, the city's towering Christmas tree. Due to its popularity, the rink is often crowded, however. Go at off times, or at lunch, when skating is only $5; at other times it's $10–14 for adults and $7.50–8.50 for seniors and under-11s; skate rental is $7.50.

Open early Oct to mid-April daily from around 8:30am to 10pm (midnight on weekends), with half hour breaks throughout the day to clean the ice. Call or see website for exact hours.
Sky Rink Map 6, A8. At Chelsea Piers, W 23rd St, at the Hudson River ☏212/336-6100. See the box on p.298.
Wollman Rink Map 7, G5. In Central Park at 62nd St ☏212/439-6900. The city's best skating experience, where you can skate to the marvelous, inspiring backdrop of the lower Central Park skyline – incredibly impressive at night. Adults $9.50, $12 at weekends; children $4.75, $5.00 at weekends; skate rental $5. Bring a lock or rent one onsite for $3.75. Open Mon & Tues 10am–2.30pm, Wed & Thurs 10am–10pm, Fri & Sat 10am–11pm, Sun 10am–9pm.

Central Park

Central Park is an obvious focus for recreation, from croquet and chess to soccer and swimming. Joggers, in-line skaters, walkers, and cyclists have the roads to themselves on weekdays 10am–3pm & 7–10pm and all day on weekends. In addition, boaters can head to the **Loeb Boathouse** (℡212/517-2233) to hire out rowboats and kayaks in warm-weather months ($10/hr); you can also rent bikes here (from $9/hr). To find out what is going on where and when, including walking tours and family events, consult the park's official website, ⌖www.centralparknyc.org, which has a full list of the week's activities, or drop by one of the visitor centers for a schedule. For much more on Central Park, see Chapter 14.

In-line skating

You'll see commuters to freestylists on **in-line skates** – also known as Rollerblades – in New York. The best place to skate is the skate circle near **Naumberg Bandshell** in Central Park at 72nd Street. World-class bladers also maneuver between cones with all kinds of fancy footwork just inside Central Park's Tavern on the Green entrance, near West 68th Street. Outside of Central Park, the best place to skate is along the greenways by the Hudson and East rivers.

Blades Map 7, D2. 156 W 72nd St, between Amsterdam and Columbus ℡212/787-3911, ⌖www.blades. com. Skate rental $20 for 24 hours. The two other Blades stores in Manhattan sell but do not rent skates; call for locations.

Jogging

Jogging is still very much the number-one fitness pursuit in the city. A favorite circuit in Central Park is the flat and sandy

1.57-mile loop around the **Jacqueline Kennedy Onassis Reservoir**; just make sure you jog in a counterclockwise direction or you'll get glares (and possibly some comments). The asphalt **loop** road around the park is six miles. Contact **New York Road Runners**, 9 E 89th St (☏ 212/860-2280, ⓦ www.nyrr. org), to find a running partner or get their schedule of races, including half-marathons in all five boroughs, lots of 10Ks in Central Park, and the ING New York City Marathon, held each November. The Hudson River Parkway, East River Promenade, Riverside Park, Prospect Park, and almost any other stretch of open space large enough to get up speed are also well-used jogging haunts.

Paragon Sports Map 6, I8. 867 Broadway, at 18th St ☏ 212/255-8036, ⓦ www.paragonsports.com. New York City's largest sporting-goods store is a dizzying emporium of gear and clothing for every activity (or just for show) spread over three floors. There's a vast selection of running shoes in the basement and the staff can be knowledgeable, but it's best to come in knowing what you want, as not all of them are runners.

Super Runners Shop Map 7, I9. Grand Central Terminal Main Concourse, ☏ 646/487-1120, ⓦ www. superrunnersshop.com. Friendly shop, with helpful salespeople who really know their stuff. There's the full complement of running shoes, plus clothes, sporty sandals, and other gear for the serious runner, like ampules of high-calorie goo to slurp during long runs. Three other locations: two on the Upper East Side and one on the Upper West Side. Call or see website for details.

Soccer

Formerly the New York–New Jersey Metrostars, the **New York Red Bulls** (☏ 201/583-7000, ⓦ www.redbull.newyork. mlsnet.com) are the area's Major League Soccer team; they play at Giants Stadium, and tickets ($20–38) are often available. The season runs from April to mid-November.

Tennis

The **US Open Championships** (Ⓦwww.usopen.org), held in late August and early September at the USTA Billie Jean King National Tennis Center in Flushing, Queens, is the top US tennis event of the year. **Tickets** go on sale the first week or two of June at the Tennis Center's box office (Ⓣ718/760-6200), which is open Monday to Friday 9am–5pm and Saturday 10am–4pm. To book by phone, call Ticketmaster on Ⓣ866/673-6849. Promenade-level seats at the stadium cost $22–99 (better seats can cost several hundred dollars), and become more expensive at night and closer to the finals – for which they are incredibly hard to obtain.

If you'd like to play tennis, there are both **public and private courts** all round the city, but getting on can be difficult; the former are all controlled through the City Parks department and require a $100 permit (Ⓣ212/360-8133). The nicest such courts are at Central Park, but they are also the most crowded; try Riverside Park (see p.147) instead. You can also try a private club: rates at places like the Midtown Tennis Club, at 341 8th Ave, btw 26th and 27th (Ⓣ212/989-8572, Ⓦwww. midtowntennis.com), can run anywhere from $45–50 per hour for outdoor courts and $65–80 for indoor courts, depending on the season and the time of day.

Parades and festivals

N ew York City doesn't skimp on celebrations, staging numerous **parades and festivals** throughout the year. The events, though often political or religious in origin, are just as much an excuse for music, food, and dance as anything else. Almost every large ethnic group in the city holds an annual get-together, often using Fifth Avenue as the main drag.

Chances are, your stay will coincide with at least one such celebration. For more details and exact dates, phone ☏1-800/NYC-VISIT or go to ⒲www.nycvisit.com. Also, look at listings in the *Village Voice*'s "Voice Choices" or *Time Out New York*'s "Around Town" sections.

January

Chinese New Year and Parade First full moon between Jan 21 and Feb 19; ☏212/431-9740, ⒲www. explorechinatown.com. A noisy, joyful occasion celebrated for two weeks along and around Mott Street in Lower Manhat-

tan, as well as in Sunset Park, Brooklyn and Flushing, Queens. Restaurants go all out, but you must reserve in advance.
Winter Antiques Show Mid-Jan; ☏718/292-7392, ⒲www.winterantiquesshow.com. The foremost American antiques show in the country. Held at the Seventh

Regiment Armory, Park Ave and 67th St.

Restaurant Week Late Jan–early Feb ☎212/484-1200, ⓦwww.restaurantweek.com). For about ten weekdays, you can get a prix-fixe three-course lunch at some of the city's finest establishments for $24.07, or a three-course dinner for $35. This can be quite a savings at restaurants like Nobu; you must make reservations months in advance for the most desirable spots. Also held in July.

February

Empire State Building Run-Up Early Feb; ☎212/860-4445, ⓦwww.nyrr.org. Sponsored by the New York Road Runners, contenders race up the 1576 steps of this New York City landmark.

Westminster Kennel Club Dog Show Mid-Feb; ☎212/213-3165, ⓦwww.westminsterkennelclub.org. Second only to the Kentucky Derby as the oldest continuous sporting event in the country, this show at Madison Square Garden welcomes 2500 canines competing for best in breed, along with legions of fanatic dog-lovers.

March

St Patrick's Day Parade March 17; ☎212/484-1222. Based on an impromptu march through the Manhattan streets by Irish militiamen on St Patrick's Day in 1762, this parade is a draw for every Irish band and organization in the US and Ireland. Starting around 11am at St Patrick's Cathedral on Fifth Ave, it heads uptown to 86th Street.

Greek Independence Day Parade Late March; ☎718/204-6500. A patriotic nod to the old country, with floats of pseudo-classically dressed Hellenes. When Independence Day (March 25) falls in Orthodox Lent, the parade is shifted to April or May. It usually kicks off from 60th St and runs up Fifth Ave to 79th St.

The Circus Animal Walk Late March to early April; call ☎212/465-6741 for tickets, visit ⓦwww.ny1.com for the exact date. At midnight the elephants, camels, llamas, and other creatures from Ringling Brothers' Barnum & Bailey Circus march from their point of arrival to Madison Square Garden prior to opening night. A unique city sight.

April

Easter Parade Easter Sun. Decked out in outrageous Easter bonnets, New Yorkers stroll along Fifth Ave, from around 49th St up to 55th St, in what's more a collective fashion appreciation than a structured march. There's also

PARADES AND FESTIVALS

"Eggstravaganza," a children's festival that includes an egg-rolling contest, on the Lower Forty Acres in Central Park.

New Directors, New Films Early April; ☎212/875-5638, ⓦwww.filmlinc.com. Lincoln Center and MoMA co-present this two-week series, one of the city's best, though rarely surrounded by hype. Films range from the next indie hits to never-to-be-seen-again works of genius, with many foreign films.

Sakura Matsuri: Cherry Blossom Festival Late April; free with $5 garden admission; ☎718/623-7200, ⓦwww.bbg.org. Music, art, dance, traditional fashion, and sword-fighting demonstrations celebrate Japanese culture and the brief, sublime blossoming of the Brooklyn Botanic Garden's (see p.166) two hundred cherry trees.

May

Five Boro Bike Tour Early May; ☎212/932-2453, ⓦwww.bikenewyork.org. Cars are banished from the 42-mile route that touches every borough, and some 30,000 cyclists take to the streets.

Tribeca Film Festival Early May; ☎212/941-2400, ⓦwww.tribecafilmfestival.org. Begun in 2002, this glitzy fest grows exponentially each year. Programming,

at various theaters downtown, is a mix of blockbusters and indie work.

Ukrainian Festival Mid-May; ☎212/674-1615. This extravaganza fills a weekend on East 7th St between 2nd and 3rd aves with marvelous Ukrainian costumes, folk music and dance, and authentic foods. At the Ukrainian Museum (222 E 6th St) there's a special exhibition of *pysanky* – traditional hand-painted eggs.

Fleet Week End of May; ⓦwww.fleetweek.navy.mil. The boisterous annual welcome of sailors from the US, Canada, Mexico, and the UK, among others, is held at the Intrepid Sea, Air & Space Museum (see p.107).

June

Museum Mile Festival First Tues evening; ☎212/606-2296, ⓦwww.museummilefestival.org. Museums along the Mile (see p.129), including the Museum of the City of New York, the Guggenheim, and the Met, are open, free of admission, 6–9pm, and streets are closed to cars and filled with performers.

National Puerto Rican Day Parade Second Sun; ☎718/401-0404, ⓦwww.nationalpuertoricandayparade.org. Seven hours of bands, flag-waving, and baton-twirling from 44th to 86th streets on Fifth

Ave, with an estimated two million people in attendance.

Mermaid Parade First Sat after June 21; ☎718/372-5159, ⓦ www.coneyislandusa.com. At this hilarious event, participants dress like mermaids and King Neptune and saunter down the Coney Island boardwalk, after which everyone throws fruit into the sea. Not to be missed.

JVC Jazz Festival Late June; ☎212/501-1390, ⓦ www.festival-productions.net. The jazz world's top names appear at Carnegie Hall, the Beacon, and other venues around the city.

Pride Week Late June; ☎212/807-7433, ⓦ www.nycpride.org. The world's biggest lesbian, gay, bisexual, and transgender Pride event kicks off with a rally and ends with a march down Fifth Ave, a street fair in Greenwich Village, and a huge closing-night dance.

July

Independence Day July 4, at around 9pm ☎212/494-4495. The fireworks above the East River are visible from all over Manhattan, but the best places to view them are the South Street Seaport, the Esplanade in Brooklyn Heights, or the waterfront in Williamsburg, starting at about 9pm. FDR Drive below 42nd Street is closed to cars to make way for the crowds.

New York City Tap Festival Mid-July; ☎646/230-9564, ⓦ www.atdf.org. A week-long festival featuring hundreds of tap dancers who perform and give workshops.

Restaurant Week Mid-July. See p.305.

August

Harlem Week All month; ☎212/862-8477, ⓦ www.har-lemdiscover.com. What began as a week-long festival around Harlem Day on Aug 20 has stretched into a month of celebrating African, Caribbean, and Latin heritage with live performances, lectures, and parties.

Hong Kong Dragon Boat Festival First weekend in Aug; ☎718/767-1776, ⓦ www.hkdbf-ny.org. Flushing Meadows is the site of this highly competitive race of 38-foot-long sculls, for which huge crowds turn out.

New York International Fringe Festival Mid-Aug; ☎212-279-4488, ⓦ www.fringenyc.org. With more than two hundred theater and dance companies performing at various downtown venues, this series is the biggest of its kind. It's a chance to see the next hit show before it moves to a bigger stage.

30

PARADES AND FESTIVALS

September

West Indian-American Day Parade and Carnival Labor Day (first Mon in Sept); ☎718/467-1797, ⓦwww.wiadca.com. Brooklyn's largest parade, modeled after the carnivals of Trinidad and Tobago, features music, food, floats with enormous sound systems, and scores of steel-drum bands – not to mention more than a million attendees.

Broadway on Broadway Early Sept; ☎212/768-1560, ⓦwww.broadwayonbroadway.com. Free performances in Times Square of songs by casts of the major Broadway musicals, culminating in a shower of confetti.

Feast of San Gennaro Ten days in mid-Sept; ☎212/226-6427, ⓦwww.sangennaro.org. Boisterous event in honor of the patron saint of Naples, held along Mulberry Street in Little Italy (see p.57). On the final Sunday, the saint's statue is carried through the streets with donations of dollar bills pinned to its cloak; the rest of the time it's basically a giant food fest.

African-American Day Parade Late Sept; ☎212/862-7200. Features loudspeakered hip-hop floats, drum-and-bugle corps, and plenty of local politicians. Runs from 111th St and Adam Clayton Powell Blvd to 142nd St, then east toward 5th Ave in Harlem.

New York Film Festival Late Sept to mid-Oct; ☎212/875-5600, ⓦwww.filmlinc.com. One of the world's leading film festivals unreels at Lincoln Center (see p.142); tickets can be hard to come by, as anticipated arthouse hits get their debut here.

October

Columbus Day Parade Second Mon in Oct; ☎212/249-9923, ⓦwww.columbuscitizensfd.org. One of the city's largest binges pays tribute to New York's Italian heritage and the day Columbus "disovered" America. Runs along Fifth Ave from 44th to 79th streets.

DUMBO Art Under the Bridge Festival Mid-Oct; ☎718/694-0831, ⓦwww.dumboartscenter.org/festival. More than 700 emerging and professional artists show their work in open studios, bands perform, and bizarre installations fill the streets in the stylish neighborhood of DUMBO, in Brooklyn.

Village Halloween Parade Oct 31; ☎845/758-5519, ⓦwww.halloween-nyc.com. In the 7pm procession on 6th Ave from Spring to 23rd streets you'll see spectacular costumes, floats, and more. The music is great and the spirit is wild and gay. Get there early for a good viewing spot; the parade is very popular.

November

New York City Marathon First Sun in Nov; ☎212/423-2249, Ⓦwww.ingnycmarathon.org. Some 30,000 runners from all over the world – from the Kenyan champs to regular folks in goofy costumes – assemble for this 26.2-mile run through the five boroughs. One of the best places to watch is Central Park South, near the finish line.

Veterans Day Parade Nov 11; ☎212/693-1476. The United War Veterans sponsor this annual event on Fifth Ave from 39th to 23rd streets, in which uniformed veterans from World War II onward march by military unit along flag-lined boulevards, with confetti descending like snow from above.

Macy's Thanksgiving Day Parade Thanksgiving Day (fourth Thurs in Nov); ☎212/494-4495, Ⓦwww.macysparade.com. A made-for-TV extravaganza, with big corporate floats, a handful of celebrities, dozens of marching bands from around the country, and Santa Claus's first appearance of the season. Some two million spectators watch it along Central Park West from 77th St to Columbus Circle and along Broadway down to Herald Square, 9am–noon.

Rockefeller Center Christmas Tree Lighting Late Nov; ☎212/632-3975, Ⓦwww.rockefellercenter.com. Switching on the lights on the enormous tree in front of the ice rink marks the official start to the holiday season. A memorable and heart-warming experience, but the crowds can be oppressive.

December

Holiday Windows Beginning around Dec 1. The windows on Fifth Ave, especially those of Lord & Taylor and Saks Fifth Avenue, are displays of fantasy and flair; Barneys, on Madison Ave, always does a tongue-in-cheek take on the tradition. Prepare for crowds, or go immediately after Christmas.

Hanukkah Celebrations Usually in mid-Dec. During the eight nights of this Jewish holiday, a menorah-lighting ceremony takes place at Brooklyn's Grand Army Plaza (☎718/778-6000), and the world's largest menorah is lit on Fifth Ave near Central Park (☎212/736-8400).

New Year's Eve in Times Square Dec 31; ☎212/768-1560, Ⓦwww.timessquarebid.org. Several hundred thousand revelers party in the cold streets. There are also fireworks at the South Street Seaport, Central Park, and Brooklyn's Prospect Park. Elsewhere in the city, more family-oriented, alcohol-free First Nights take place, with dancing, music, and food.

Kids' New York

N ew York can be a wonderful city to visit with **children**. Obvious attractions like skyscrapers, ferry rides, kid-focused museums and theaters, and all the adventures provided by Central Park will certainly entertain, but a visit with kids may also give you opportunity to appreciate the simpler pleasures of the city, from watching street entertainers to introducing your children to new and diverse foods and neighborhoods. Free events, especially common in the summer, range from puppet shows and nature programs in the city's parks to storytelling hours at local libraries and bookstores.

For further listings, see Friday's *Daily News* or *New York Times*, the weekly *New York* and *Time Out New York* magazine, sas well as the monthly *Time Out New York Kids*. The New York CVB maintains a thorough directory of kid-friendly activities, available online or from its information kiosk, 810 Seventh Ave, between 52nd and 53rd streets (Mon–Fri 8.30am–6pm, Sat & Sun 8.30am–5pm; ☎212/484-1222, ⓦwww.nycvisit.com).

Museums

You could spend an entire holiday just checking out the city's many **museums**, which almost always contain something of interest for kids. The following is a brief overview of the ones that should evoke an enthusiastic response. See the appropriate chapters for more details on these and other museums.

American Museum of Natural History and the Rose Center for Earth and Space Map 8, E9. Central Park West, at 79th. Daily 10am–5.45pm; $14, seniors/students $10.50, children $8; IMAX films, the Hayden Planetarium, and certain special exhibits cost extra; ☎212/769-5100, ⓦwww.amnh.org. The planetarium is sure to sate most kids' intergalactic interest, and the dinosaurs are also a sure-fire hit. In the winter, the Butterfly Conservatory is popular with younger ones.

Children's Museum of the Arts Map 5, G8. 182 Lafayette St, btw Broome and Grand. Wed, Fri, Sat & Sun noon–5pm, Thurs noon–6pm; $8, by donation Thurs 4–6pm; ☎212/941-9198, ⓦwww.cmany.org. Art gallery of works by or for children. Kids are encouraged to look at different types of art and then create their own, with paints, clay, plaster of Paris, and other simple media.

Children's Museum of Manhattan Map 8, C8. 212 W 83rd St, btw Broadway and Amsterdam. Tues–Sun 10am–5pm; $9, children $6; ☎212/721-1234, ⓦwww.cmom.org. A terrific participatory museum, with exhibit space over five floors and lots of quirky activities (a temporary Dr. Seuss show

involved cooking green eggs and ham). For ages 1–12; highly recommended.

FDNY Fire Zone Map 7, G7. 34 W 51st St, btw 5th and 6th aves. Mon–Sat 9am–7pm, Sun 11am–5pm; $4, seniors $1; ☎212/698-4520, ⓦwww.fdnyfirezone.org. A multimedia bonanza where kids don fire-fighter gear and learn about safety, then practice their skills in simulated conflagration (not recommended for kids under 4).

Intrepid Sea, Air & Space Museum Map 7, A8. Pier 86, W 46th St at 12th Ave. April–Sept Mon–Fri 10am–5pm, Sat–Sun 10am–6pm; Oct–March Tues–Sun 10am–5pm, last admission 1 hour prior to closing; $16.50, students/seniors $12.50, children ages 12–17 $11.50, children 6–11 $6, children 2–5 $4.50, under-2s free; ☎212/245-0072, ⓦwww.intrepidmuseum.org. Closed for restoration until fall 2008, but highly worthwhile when it's open for the world's fastest spy plane, a guided missile submarine, and other modern and vintage air- and sea-craft. Not recommended for kids under 5.

Museum of the City of New York Map 8, H3. 1220 5th Ave, at 103rd St. Tues–Sun 10am–5pm (Tues 10am–2pm for pre-registered tour groups only); suggested donation $9, students $5, families $20, children free; ☎ 212/534-1672, ⓦ www.mcny.org. The permanent exhibit "New York Toy Stories" is a super way to bring young ones back to simpler times, when wooden toys, rubber balls, and board games were just about the only options. The museum is undergoing renovation through 2011; check the website for exhibit status.

National Museum of the American Indian (Smithsonian Institution) Map 4, E8. 1 Bowling Green, at Battery Park. Daily 10am–5pm, Thurs until 8pm; free; ☎ 212/514-3700, ⓦ www.si.edu/nmai. Kids will enjoy the ancient dolls, feathered headdresses, and replica reservation home and schoolroom. Programs often include theater troupes, performance artists, dancers, and films.

New York City Fire Museum Map 5, C7. 278 Spring St, between Hudson and Varick. Tues–Sat 10am–5pm, Sun 10am–4pm; $5, seniors/students $2, under-12s $1; ☎ 212/691-1303, ⓦ www.nycfiremuseum.org. An unspectacular but pleasing homage to New York City's firefighters, with fire engines from yesteryear, helmets, and dog-eared photos.

South Street Seaport Museum Map 4, 6H. 207 Front St, at the east end of Fulton St at the East River ☎ 212/748-8758, ⓦ www.southstseaport.org. Nov–Mar daily 10am–5pm, Apr–Oct Tues–Sun 10am–6pm; $8, students & seniors $6, ages 5–12 $4. While the Intrepid is being restored, this is another option for getting close to the water. The small fleet of historic ships includes an 1893 fishing schooner and a hard-working harbor tugboat. Crafts run harbor tours (summers only).

Sights and entertainment

The Bronx Zoo Bronx River Parkway at Fordham Rd. Hours vary by season; $14, seniors $12, children $10, suggested donation on Wed, rides and some exhibits additional; ☎ 718/367-1010, ⓦ www.bronxzoo.org. #2 or #5 to West Farms Square–East Tremont Avenue. The children's section of the country's largest urban zoo offers a giant spider web to climb on and some of the tamer animals to pet. Kids will appreciate spring, when baby animals are born.

New York Aquarium W 8th St and Surf Ave, Coney Island, Brooklyn. Hours vary by season; $12, seniors and children 2–12 $8; ☎ 718/265-

Central Park

Year-round, **Central Park** provides sure-fire entertainment for children. In the summer, it becomes one giant playground. The following are merely a few of the highlights; for detailed information on these and other sights, see Chapter 14.

The Carousel Mid-park at 64th St. For just $1.25, children can take a (surprisingly fast) spin on the country's largest hand-carved horses.

Central Park Wildlife Conservation Center Fifth Ave at 64th. A small but enjoyable zoo, with sea lions, penguins, monkeys, and the Tisch Children's Zoo.

Hans Christian Andersen statue 72nd St, on the east side next to the boat pond. A fifty-year tradition of hosting storytelling sessions; June–Sept Sat 11am–noon.

Loeb Boathouse East side at 72nd St. Rent a rowboat on the Central Park lake and enjoy the views, or take a gondola ride in the evening. Bike rentals available too.

Wollman Rink East side at 62nd St. ☎212/396-1010. Ice-skating during the winter; in the summer it's Victorian Gardens, an old-fashioned amusement park.

FISH, ⓦ www.nyaquarium.com. Walruses, sea otters, sea lions, penguins, and seals abound, and open-air whale and dolphin shows are held several times daily, as are animal feedings. Call for show info.

Shopping: toys, books, and clothes

Books of Wonder Map 6, H8. 18 W 18th St, btw 5th and 6th ☎212/989-3270. Excellent kids' bookstore, with a great Oz section, a story hour on Sun at noon, and author appearances in the spring and fall on Sat.

Dylan's Candy Bar Map 7, J5. 1011 Third Ave, at 60th St ☎646/735-0078. Kids will catch a sugar high just walking in the door of this hip shop with a paralyzing selection, from sour-bright-gummy everything to retro candies for the parentals.

F.A.O. Schwarz Map 7, H6. 767 5th Ave, at 58th ☎212/644-9400. This multi-story toy emporium features an onsite ice-cream parlor and a giant danceable floor piano. Very popular (and very expensive), but a slightly less frenzied experience than the Toys 'R' Us in Times Square.

Penny Whistle Toys Map 8, D8. 448 Columbus Ave, at 81st St ☎212/873-9090. Wonderful shop selling a fun, imaginative range of toys that deliberately eschews guns and war accessories; includes replicas of rare old-fashioned toys. Highly recommended.

The Red Caboose Map 7, H9. 23 W 45th St, between 5th and 6th, on the lower level – follow the flashing railroad sign in back of lobby ☎212/575-0155. A unique shop specializing in models, particularly train sets.

Tannen's Magic Studio Map 6, G3. 45 W 34th St, 6th floor, between 5th and 6th aves ☎212/929-4500. Kids will never forget a visit to the largest magic shop in the world, with nearly 8000 props. The staff is made up of magicians who perform throughout the day.

Toys 'R' Us Map 7, F9. 1514 Broadway, between 44th and 45 sts ☎646-366-8800. This Times Square megastore contains, among a million other things, a full-size Ferris wheel, a giant, roaring Tyrannosaurus rex, and bulk bins full of Legos.

Theater, circuses, and more

The following is a highly selective roundup of miscellaneous **activities**, particularly cultural ones that might be of interest to young children.

Barnum & Bailey Circus Map 6, E4. Madison Square Garden ☎212/465-6741, Ⓦwww.ringling.com. This large touring circus is usually in New York between the end of March and the beginning of May. The real highlight is before the circus starts, when the elephants are escorted from the railyards into Manhattan – worth staying up for.

Big Apple Circus Map 7, D4. Lincoln Center ☎212/721-6500, Ⓦwww.bigapplecircus.org. Small circus that performs in a tent in Damrosch Park next to the Met, from late Oct to early Jan. Tickets $20–30 for matinees.

New Victory Theater Map 6, F1. 209 W 42nd St, at 7th ☎ 646/223-3020, ⓦ www.newvictory.org. Everything about this theater is kid-oriented, including the duration of performances (60–90 minutes), which can be music, dance, storytelling, and more, often with workshops before or after the show. Closed during the summer.

Trapeze School New York Map 5, A6. Hudson River Park, Pier 40, W Houston St at 12th Ave ☎ 917/797-1872, ⓦ www.trapezeschool. com. Two-hour classes on the flying trapeze, for ages 6 and up, start at $65 and include an amazing view over the Hudson River from high atop the rig. Parents must accompany children, but if this seems too daunting you can just go sit in the park and watch the high-flyers practice.

32

Directory

Consulates Australia, 150 E 42nd St, btw Lexington and 3rd (☎212/351-6500); Canada, 1251 6th Ave, at 50th (☎212/596-1628); Ireland, 345 Park Ave, at 51st, 17th floor (☎212/319-2555); New Zealand, 780 3rd Ave, btw 48th and 49th (☎212/832-4038); UK, 845 3rd Ave, btw 51st and 52nd (☎212/745-0200).

Electric current 110V AC with two-pronged plugs. Unless they're dual voltage, all British appliances will need a voltage converter as well as a plug adapter. Note that some converters may not be able to handle certain high-wattage items, especially those with heated elements. Most laptops these days come with alternate-voltage AC adapters, and therefore only need a plug adapter.

Emergencies For police, fire, or ambulance dial ☎911. Identification Carry some at all times, as there are any number of occasions on which you may be asked to show it. Two pieces of ID are preferable and one should have a photo – passport and credit card or driving license are the best bets.

Laundry Hotels do it but charge a lot. You're much better off going to an ordinary Laundromat or a dry cleaner. Some Laundromats and dry cleaners will wash, dry, and fold your clothes for you for around sixty cents to $1 per pound. See the Yellow Pages phone book or its website, ⓦwww.citidex.com, for locations near you.

Left luggage Since 9/11, left-luggage storage has been suspended in New York train and bus stations. Your best bet is to ask your hotel to keep your luggage for you until you are ready to leave – most are happy to do this, although there may be a fee.

Lost property For items lost on buses or on the subway, check with the NYC Transit Authority, at the 34th Street/8th Avenue subway station at the north end on the lower level mezzanine (Mon–Wed & Fri 8am–noon, Thurs 11am–6.30pm; ☎212/712-4500). For things lost in a cab, visit the Taxi & Limousine Commission (TLC) at 167 E 51st St, between Lexington and 3rd (☎212/826-3246).

Public holidays You'll find all banks, most offices, some stores, and certain museums closed on the following days: Jan 1, Martin Luther King's Birthday (third Mon in Jan), Presidents' Day (third Mon in Feb), Memorial Day (last Mon in May), Independence Day (July 4 or, if it falls on a weekend, the following Mon), Labor Day (first Mon in Sept), Columbus Day (second Mon in Oct), Veterans' Day (Nov 11), Thanksgiving (the fourth Thurs in Nov), and Christmas Day (Dec 25). Also, New York's numerous parades mean that on certain days – St Patrick's Day, Gay Pride Day, Easter Sunday, and Columbus Day, to name a few

– much of 5th Ave is closed to traffic altogether.

Tax Within New York City you'll pay an 8.375-percent sales tax on top of marked prices on just about everything but the essentials (food in supermarkets) and clothes and shoes under $110.

Time New York City is three hours ahead of West Coast North America, five hours behind Britain and Ireland, fourteen to sixteen hours behind East Coast Australia (variations for Daylight Savings Time), and sixteen to eighteen hours behind New Zealand (variations for Daylight Savings Time).

Tipping Expected everywhere a service is performed and preferred in cash; in restaurants, it's easiest just to double the tax (equaling around sixteen percent), but if the service was high quality, consider upping that amount to twenty percent. A dollar per bag for the bellhop is standard, as is fifteen percent or so for taxi drivers on top of the fare. In bars, standard New York practice is a dollar a drink.

Contexts

Contexts

History

To Europe she was America, to America she was the gateway of the earth. But to tell the story of New York would be to write a social history of the world.

H.G. Wells

Early days and colonial rule

Before the arrival of European explorers, Native Americans populated the area now encompassing New York City. In 1524, 32 years after Christopher Columbus had sailed to the New World, **Giovanni da Verrazano**, an Italian in the service of the French king Francis I, arrived in New York Harbor. Less than a century later, in 1609, **Henry Hudson**, an Englishman employed by the Dutch East India Company, landed at Manhattan and sailed his ship upriver as far as Albany. The Dutch established a trading post at the most northerly point Hudson had reached, Fort Nassau. Meanwhile, just a few years after the Pilgrim Fathers had sailed to Massachusetts, thirty families left Holland in 1624 to become New York's first **European settlers**.

Most sailed up to Fort Nassau, but a handful – eight families in all – stayed behind on what is now Governors Island, which they called Nut Island because of the many walnut trees there. Slowly the community grew as more settlers arrived, and the little island became crowded; the decision was made to move to the limitless spaces across the water, and the settlement of **Manhattan**, taken from the Algonquin Indian word Manna-Hata, meaning "Island of the Hills," began.

The Dutch gave their new outpost the name **Nieuw Amsterdam**, though following British conquest of the island in 1664 the settlement took its new name from its owner, the Duke of York – **New York**.

Revolution

By the 1750s the city had reached a population of 16,000, spread roughly as far north as today's Chambers Street. As the new community grew more confident, it realized that it could exist independently of the government in Britain. In a way, New York's role during the **War of Independence** was not critical, for all the battles fought in and around the city were generally won by the British, who ultimately lost the war. **George Washington**, who had held the American army together by sheer willpower, celebrated in New York riding in triumphal procession down Canal Street and saying farewell to his officers at **Fraunces Tavern**, a reconstruction of which stands on its original site in the Financial District. On April 30, 1789, Washington took the oath of president at the site of the **Federal Hall National Memorial** on Wall Street. The federal government was transferred to the District of Columbia one year later.

Immigration and the Civil War

The completion of the **Erie Canal** in 1825 allowed New York to expand massively as a port. The Great Lakes were suddenly opened to New York, and with them the rest of the country; goods manufactured in the city could be sent easily and cheaply to the American heartland. It was because of this transportation network, and the mass of cheap labor that flooded in throughout the nineteenth and early twentieth centuries, that New York – and to an extent the nation – became wealthy. The first waves of **immigrants**, mainly **Irish and German**, began to arrive in the mid-nineteenth century, the former forced out of their native country by the potato famine of 1846, the latter by the failed revolutions of 1848–49. The city could not handle people arriving in such great numbers and epidemics of yellow fever and cholera were common, exacerbated by poor water supplies, unsanitary conditions, and the poverty of most of the newcomers. Despite this, in the

1880s large-scale **Italian** immigration began, while at the same time refugees from **Eastern Europe** started to arrive – many of them Jewish. The two communities shared a home on the **Lower East Side**, which became one of the worst slum areas of its day. On the eve of the Civil War (1861–65) the majority of New York's 750,000 population were immigrants; in 1890 one in four of the city's inhabitants was Irish.

When the **Civil War** broke out, caused by growing differences between the Northern and Southern states, notably on the issues of slavery and trade, New York sided with the Union (North) against the Confederates (South). However, none of the actual hand-to-hand fighting that ravaged the rest of the country took place near the city itself – though New York did form a focus for much of the radical thinking behind the war, particularly with **Abraham Lincoln**'s influential "Might makes Right" speech from the Cooper Union Building in 1860. In 1863 a **conscription law** was passed that allowed the rich to buy themselves out of military service. Not surprisingly this was very unpopular, and New Yorkers rioted, burning buildings and looting shops. More than a thousand people were killed in these **Draft Riots**, mostly African-Americans whose increase (if abolition succeeded) was perceived as a threat.

The late nineteenth century

The end of the Civil War saw much of the country devastated but New York intact, and it was fairly predictable that the city would soon become the wealthiest and most influential in the nation. New York was also the greatest business, commercial, and manufacturing center in the country. **Cornelius Vanderbilt** controlled a vast shipping and railroad empire, and **J.P. Morgan**, the banking and investment wizard, was instrumental in organizing financial mergers that led to the formation of the prototypical corporate business.

The latter part of the nineteenth century was in many ways the city's golden age: **elevated railways** sprung up to transport people quickly and cheaply around the city; **Thomas Edison** lit the streets with his new electric light bulb, powered by the first electricity plant on Pearl Street; and in 1883, to the wonderment of New Yorkers, the **Brooklyn Bridge** was completed, linking Brooklyn and Manhattan – at the time it was opened, and for twenty years after, it was the largest and longest bridge in the world. Brooklyn, Staten Island, Queens, and the part of Westchester known as the Bronx, along with Manhattan, were officially incorporated into New York City in 1898. All this commercial expansion stimulated the city's cultural growth; **Walt Whitman** memorialized the city in his poetry, while **Henry James** recorded its manners and mores in such novels as *Washington Square*.

The turn of the century

At the same time, the emigration of Europe's – and China's (beginning in 1884) – impoverished peoples continued unabated. The **Statue of Liberty**, holding a symbolic torch to guide the huddled masses to their new home, was unveiled in 1886. By 1898 New York's population had surpassed three million, making it the largest city in the world. **Ellis Island**, the offshore depot that processed arrivals, was handling two thousand people a day, leading to a total of ten million by 1929, when laws were passed to curtail immigration. During the first two decades of the twentieth century, one-third of all the Jews in Eastern Europe arrived in America, and upwards of 1.5 million of them settled in the city, primarily in the Lower East Side.

The war years and the Depression: 1914–1945

With America's entry into World War I in 1917, New York benefited from wartime trade and commerce. Perhaps surprisingly, there was little conflict between the various European communities crammed into the city. Although Germans comprised roughly one-fifth of the city's population, there were few of the attacks on their lives or property that occurred elsewhere in the country.

The postwar years saw one law and one character dominating the New York scene: the law was **Prohibition**, passed in 1920 (and not repealed until 1933) in an attempt to sober up the nation; the character was **Jimmy Walker**, elected mayor in 1925. Walker led a far from sober lifestyle: "No civilized man," he said, "goes to bed the same day he wakes up," and it was during his flamboyant career that the **Jazz Age** came to the city. In speakeasies all over town the bootleg liquor flowed and writers as diverse as Damon Runyon, F. Scott Fitzgerald, and Ernest Hemingway portrayed the excitement of the times, while musicians such as George Gershwin and Benny Goodman packed nightclubs with their new sounds.

With the **Wall Street** crash of 1929 the party came to an abrupt end. Yet during the **Great Depression** three of New York's most opulent – and beautiful – skyscrapers were built: the **Chrysler Building** in 1930, the **Empire State Building** in 1931, and Rockefeller Center's **GE Building** in 1933. All three typify the Art Deco architectural style, with their stepped pinnacles, metallic ornamentation, and sweeping curves.

The country's entry into World War II in 1941 had little direct impact on New York City, though lights were blacked out at night in case of bomb attacks, two hundred Japanese were interned on Ellis Island, and guards were placed at the entrances to bridges and tunnels. New York's major contribution to the war, rather, was the **Manhattan Project**, which took place behind the scenes at Columbia University and succeeded in splitting the uranium atom, thereby creating the first atomic weapon.

The postwar years

Following racial tensions in the 1950s there was a general exodus of the white middle class out of New York (and indeed out of many major American cities) and into the suburbs – the **Great White Flight**, as the media labeled it. Between 1950 and 1970 more than a million families left the city. Things went from bad to worse during the 1960s with **race riots** in Harlem and in Brooklyn's Bedford-Stuyvesant neighborhood. The **World's Fair** of 1964, held in Queens, boosted New York's international profile, but on the streets the calls for civil liberties for blacks and the protests against US involvement in Vietnam (1964–75) were as loud as those in any US city.

The Twin Towers of the **World Trade Center** opened in 1973, a testament to at least one builder's faith in New York as an international business hub. Nonetheless, the city reached a crisis point in 1975, after spending more than it was receiving in taxes – billions of dollars more. Essential services, long shaky due to underfunding, were ready to collapse as bankruptcy loomed. Fortunately, tourism, spurred by cheap transatlantic airfares, and a new go-get-'em mayor, **Edward I. Koch**, helped save the city. Meanwhile the anything-goes attitudes of the 1970s were taking hold in New York's nightclubs: singles bars sprang up all over the city, gay bars proliferated in the Village, and Disco was King. **Studio 54** was an internationally known hot-spot, and drugs and illicit sex were the main events off the dance floor.

In the 1980s, the real estate and stock markets boomed, and another era of Big Money was ushered in; fortunes were made and lost overnight, and several **Wall Street** bigwigs, most notably Michael Milken, were thrown in jail for insider trading. In Midtown, Philip Johnson designed the controversial AT&T Headquarters with a Chippendale-inspired pediment in 1984, and master builder Donald Trump provided glitzy housing for the super-wealthy.

The **stock market crash** of 1987 ended that high-flying era and led in part to Koch's losing the Democratic nomination for mayor (rare for an incumbent) to the more even-tempered **David Dinkins**, who, after besting the brash young district attorney **Rudolph Giuliani** in the general election, would go on to become the first African-American mayor of New York.

However, by the time Dinkins took office the city had already slipped hard and fast into a **massive recession**: in 1989 New York's budget deficit topped $500 million, and one in four residents was officially classed as poor – a proportion unequaled since the Depression. In the 1993 mayoral elections, Dinkins narrowly lost to his erstwhile adversary Giuliani: New York, traditionally a firmly Democratic city, wanted a change and with Rudy – the city's first Republican mayor in 28 years – it got it.

The Giuliani years

Though it may have been coincidental, **Giuliani's first term** helped usher in a dramatic upswing in New York's prosperity. The city's reputation flourished, with a remarkable drop in crime and a revitalized economy. Such successes helped the mayor withstand a bitter fight over rent control as well as continued concern over serious overcrowding in the public school system and cutbacks in health and welfare programs. Giuliani won re-election in 1997 in a landslide.

The early years of his **second term** were characterized by the continued growth of the city's economy and more civic improvements, such as the cleaning up of previously crime-ridden neighborhoods like Times Square, the renovation of Grand Central Terminal and Bryant Park, and the building of new hotels and office buildings. All these developments greatly boosted tourism (and thus the city's coffers), but they also raised protests that the mayor would do anything to attract national chains to the city, often at the expense of local business and local workers. Several shocking incidents of police brutality, such as the torture of Haitian immigrant Abner Louima while in NYPD custody, led to charges of disregard for minority rights as well. With reports on racial profiling reinforcing the claim, Giuliani's approval ratings, once amazingly high, tanked – though they were soon to be resuscitated in a big, albeit tragic, way.

CONTEXTS | History

9/11 and beyond

Nothing could have prepared New York – or indeed the world – for the events of **September 11, 2001**, when terrorists hijacked four airplanes, crashing two of them into the Twin Towers of the World Trade Center and a third into the Pentagon in Washington DC; the fourth was brought down by a passenger revolt in a field south of Pittsburgh, Pennsylvania. New York was hit hardest by far: within hours, both towers had collapsed, and the fallout and debris destroyed a number of nearby buildings. In all, 2750 people, including 343 firefighters, were killed in New York in the catastrophe.

Over the next nine months, workers carted off 1.5 million tons of steel and debris, and by March 2002 the site was clear, well ahead of schedule. (Some would later ask if the job was perhaps done too quickly: several thousand Ground Zero workers continue to have chronic breathing problems from toxic dust at the site.) So assured was his guidance throughout the ordeal that if Rudolph Giuliani had been able to run again, he most certainly would have won in a landslide. The law, however, precluded him from running for a third term – he set his sights on the presidency instead – and so on January 1, 2002, billionaire businessman **Michael Bloomberg** replaced him as mayor.

Though he had no prior political experience, Bloomberg, who switched his affiliation from Democrat to Republican before announcing his candidacy, proved himself an able leader, using his corporate know-how to shore up the city's shaky finances – the city ended the 2006 fiscal year with a record $6.1 billion budget surplus – and reorganize the school system. One of the mayor's most controversial acts was to follow California's lead and ban smoking in bars, clubs, and all restaurants in 2003. Bar owners, naturally, fought the move, but it turned out to be good for business: patrons seem to drink more and stay longer in a smoke-free environment, and smokers have gotten used to lighting up outside (to the chagrin of the neighbors). In 2004 Bloomberg handily won re-election to a second term, during which he passed a law banning "trans fats" in New York restaurants, introduced a plan to replace the city's taxicabs with hybrid vehicles, and proposed a congestion pricing scheme to reduce traffic in Manhattan similar to the one in London.

By 2007 New York had never seemed so prosperous or so popular: unemployment was down, the stock market up, and real-estate prices continued to defy logic and gravity, with luxury condominiums snapped up as quickly as developers could build them. (Indeed, the construction crane is now a seemingly permanent part of the streetscape.) For tourists and culture vultures, completion of major renovations at the Metropolitan Museum of Art and the Morgan Library came as good news, and none other than David Bowie oversaw the first annual High Line Festival, named after a much-ballyhooed new park that's opening on an abandoned train trestle in West Chelsea in 2008.

By then, the presidential campaign season will be in full swing, and one or more New Yorkers may be in the thick of it. In the build-up to the primaries in 2007, there was much speculation – particularly when Bloomberg switched his affiliation again, from Republican to Independent – that the mayor was considering going head-to-head with his predecessor, Rudy Giuliani, for the race to the White House. Meanwhile, the state's junior senator, **Hillary Rodham Clinton**, was trying to secure her place at the top of the Democratic ticket. The winner, if among this group, would be the first New Yorker in the Oval Office since Franklin Delano Roosevelt.

Books

S ince the number of **books** about or set in New York is so vast, what follows is necessarily selective – use it as a launchpad for further sleuthing. Publishers are given in the order British/American if they are different for each country; where a book is published only in one country, it is designated UK or US; o/p indicates a book is out of print; and UP indicates university press.

Essays, poetry, and impressions

Joyce Johnson *Minor Characters: A Beat Memoir* (Penguin, US). Women were never a prominent feature of the Beat Generation; its literature examined a male world through strictly male eyes. This book, written by the woman who lived for a short time with Jack Kerouac, redresses the balance superbly; there's no better novel on the Beats in New York.

Phillip Lopate (ed) *Writing New York* (Pocket Books, US). A massive literary anthology taking in both fiction and nonfiction writings on the city, and with selections from everyone from Washington Irving to Tom Wolfe.

Federico García Lorca *Poet in New York* (Penguin/Farrar, Strauss & Giroux). The Andalusian poet and dramatist spent nine months in the city around the time of the Wall Street Crash. This collection of over thirty poems reveals his feelings on brutality, loneliness, greed, corruption, racism, and mistreatment of the poor.

Joseph Mitchell *Up in the Old Hotel* (Vintage, US). Mitchell's collected essays (he calls them stories), all of which appeared in *The New Yorker*, are works of a sober if manipulative genius. Mitchell depicts characters and situations with a reporter's precision and near-perfect style – he is the definitive chronicler of NYC street life.

Jan Morris *Manhattan '45* (Penguin/Johns Hopkins UP). Morris's best piece of writing on the city, reconstructing New York as it greeted soldiers returning from WWII in 1945. Effortlessly written, fascinatingly anecdotal, and marvelously warm about the city.

History, politics, and society

Herbert Asbury *The Gangs of New York* (Arrow/Thunder's Mouth Press). First published in 1928, this fascinating account of the seamier side of New York is essential reading; it was also the inspiration for the film of the same name. Full of historical detail, anecdotes, and character sketches of crooks, the book describes New York mischief in all its incarnations and locales. **Edwin G. Burrows and Mike Wallace** *Gotham: A History of New York City to 1898* (Oxford UP). Enormous and encyclopedic in its detail, this is a serious history of the development of New York, with chapters on everything from its role in the American Revolution to reform movements to its racial make-up in the 1820s. **Robert A. Caro** *The Power Broker: Robert Moses and the Fall of New York* (Random House, US). Despite its imposing length, this brilliant and searing critique of New York City's most powerful twentieth-century figure is one of the most important books ever written about the city and its environs. Caro's book brings to light the megalomania and manipulation responsible for the creation of the nation's largest urban infrastructure. **Kenneth T. Jackson** (ed) *The Enyclopedia of New York City* (Yale UP). Massive, engrossing, and utterly comprehensive guide to just about everything in the city. Much dry detail, but packed with incidental wonders as well. **John B. Manbeck** (ed) *The Neighborhoods of Brooklyn* (Yale UP). Wonderfully thorough account of the diversity of Brooklyn's neighborhoods, filled with firsthand accounts, photographs, maps, and local lore celebrating the borough in all its complexity.

Luc Sante *Low Life: Lures and Snares of Old New York* (Farrar, Straus & Giroux, US). This chronicle of New York's underbelly between 1840 and 1919 is a pioneering work. Full of outrageous details usually left out of conventional history, it reconstructs the day-to-day life of the urban poor, criminals, and prostitutes with a shocking clarity. Sante's prose is poetic and nuanced, and his evocations of the seedier neighborhoods, their dives and pleasure-palaces, quite vivid.

Russell Shorto *Island at the Center of the World: The Story of Dutch Manhattan and the Forgotten Colony That Shaped America* (Vintage/Knopf). An intriguing account of how important the Dutch really were to the founding of New York City, and how this colonial nation's sense of adventure kept Manhattan from falling to the English and becoming just another quaint port town. Vividly written and thoroughly researched, Shorto brings his reader back to a pre-skyscraper, pre-asphalt Big Apple.

Art, architecture, and photography

Alain Bergala, Ellen Handy, Miles Barth, and Weegee *Weegee's World* (Bulfinch). The hard-bitten tabloid photographer Weegee (born Arthur Fellig) captures New York City's seamy side – from murder sites to society balls – in black, white, and all shades of gray. A definitive work.

H. Klotz (ed) *New York Architecture 1970–1990* (Prestel/Rizzoli; o/p). Extremely well-illustrated account of the shift from modernism to postmodernism and beyond.

Jacob Riis *How the Other Half Lives* (Dover/Hill & Wang). Republished photo journalism reporting on life in the Lower East Side at the end of the nineteenth century. Its original publication awakened many to the plight of New York's poor.

N. White and E. Willensky
(eds) *AIA Guide to New York*
(Macmillan/Crown). Perhaps
even more than the above,
the definitive contemporary
guide to the city's architecture, far more interesting than
it sounds, and useful as an onsite reference.

Gerard R. Wolfe *New York:
A Guide to the Metropolis*
(McGraw-Hill, US). Set up
as a walking tour, this is a
little more academic – and
less opinionated – than others, but it does include some
good stuff on the outer
boroughs. Also informed historical background.

Fiction

Martin Amis *Money* (Vin-
tage/Penguin). Following
the wayward movements of
degenerate film director John
Self between London and
New York, a weirdly scato-
logical novel that's a striking
evocation of 1980s excess.

🏃 **Paul Auster** *The New
York Trilogy* (Vintage/
Penguin). Brooklyn native
Auster has churned out books
for more than two decades,
but this remains his mas-
terwork – three obsessively
compelling novels with inter-
locking stories and characters,
replete with postmodern
flourishes.

James Baldwin *Another
Country* (Vintage/Penguin).
Baldwin's best-known novel,
tracking the feverish search

for meaningful relationships
among a group of 1960s
New York bohemians. The
so-called liberated era in the
city has never been more
vividly documented – nor
has its knee-jerk racism.

Truman Capote *Breakfast at
Tiffany's* (Penguin/Random
House). Far sadder and raci-
er than the movie, this novel
is a rhapsody to New York
in the early 1940s, tracking the dissolute, youthful
residents of an Uptown
apartment building and their
movements about town.

Don DeLillo *Underworld*
(Picador/Scribner). Bronx
native DeLillo's dazzling
epic of postwar America
starts with a tour-de-force
scene set at the final game

of the 1951 Giants–Dodgers pennant race and careers through the decades to the Nevada desert in the 1990s, then on into cyberspace. His luminous, rhythmic prose is spellbinding even when the story feels faintly ridiculous.

Chester Himes *The Crazy Kill* (Canongate/Knopf). Himes wrote violent, fast-moving, and funny thrillers set in Harlem; this and *Cotton Comes to Harlem* are among the best.

Henry James *Washington Square* (Penguin/Modern Library). Skillful and engrossing examination of the mores and strict social expectations of New York genteel society in the late nineteenth century.

Jonathan Lethem *Motherless Brooklyn* and *Fortress of Solitude* (Faber & Faber/Knopf). Lethem's *Motherless Brooklyn* is a noir-ish modern classic set in the 1970s, starring "The Human Freakshow," a local private investigator with Tourette's syndrome. *Fortress of Solitude*, meanwhile, tells the tale of two Brooklyn boys, white Dylan and black Mingus. Spanning over thirty years in the lives

of these best friends, it's an epic work, and comes highly recommended.

Jay McInerney *Bright Lights, Big City* (Flamingo/Knopf). A trendy, "voice of a generation" book when it came out in the 1980s, *Bright Lights* follows a struggling New York writer in his job as a fact-checker at a literary magazine, and from one cocaine-sozzled nightclub to another. Amusing now, as it vividly captures the times.

Henry Miller *Crazy Cock* (HarperCollins/Grove Atlantic). Semiautobiographical work of love, sex, and angst in Greenwich Village in the 1920s. The trilogy of *Sexus*, *Plexus*, and *Nexus* (HarperCollins/Grove) and the famous *Tropics* duo (*...of Cancer*, *...of Capricorn*) contain generous slices of 1920s Manhattan sandwiched between the bohemian life in 1930s Paris.

Dorothy Parker *Complete Stories* (Penguin). Parker's stories are, at times, surprisingly moving. She depicts New York in all its glories, excesses, and pretensions with perfect, searing wit. "The Lovely Leave" and

"The Game," which focus, as many of the stories do, on the lives of women, are especially worthwhile.

Damon Runyon *First to Last* and *On Broadway* (Penguin, US); also *Guys and Dolls* (River City, US). Collections of short stories drawn from the chatter of Lindy's Bar on Broadway and since made into the classic musical *Guys and Dolls*.

J.D. Salinger *The Catcher in the Rye* (Penguin/Bantam). Salinger's classic, gripping novel of adolescence, following Holden Caulfield's sardonic journey of discovery through the streets of New York.

Hubert Selby Jr. *Last Exit to Brooklyn* (Bloomsbury/Grove Atlantic). When first published in Britain in 1966 the author of this novel was tried on charges of obscenity – and even now it's a disturbing read, evoking the sex, immorality, drugs, and violence of downtown Brooklyn in the 1960s with fearsome clarity. An important book, but to use the words of David Shepherd at the obscenity trial, you will not be unscathed.

Betty Smith *A Tree Grows in Brooklyn* (Arrow/HarperCollins). Something of a classic, and rightly so, in which a courageous Irish girl learns about family, life, and sex against a vivid prewar Brooklyn backdrop. Totally absorbing.

Edith Wharton *Old New York* (Pocket). A collection of short novels on the manners and mores of New York in the mid-nineteenth century, written with clarity and precision.

New York in film

With its dashing skyline and rugged facades, its mean streets and swanky avenues, New York is probably the most filmed city on Earth – or at least the one most instantly recognizable from the movies. It would be fruitless to enumerate them all; we've just given a small sampling below of films that best capture the city's atmosphere, its pulse and style, and, if nothing else, give you a pretty good idea of what you're going to get before you get here.

Twelve great New York movies

Annie Hall (Woody Allen, 1977). Oscar-winning autobiographical comic romance, which flits from reminiscences of Alvy Singer's childhood living beneath the Coney Island rollercoaster to life and love in uptown Manhattan, is a valentine both to then-lover and co-star Diane Keaton if not to the city. Simultaneously clever, bourgeois, and very winning. All of Allen's movies are New York–centric; don't miss **Manhattan** (1979), which, with its Gershwin soundtrack and stunning black-and-white photography, is probably the greatest memorial to the city ever made.

Breakfast at Tiffany's (Blake Edwards, 1961). This most charming and cherished of New York movie romances stars Audrey Hepburn as party girl Holly Golightly amid the glittering playground of the Upper East Side. Hepburn and George Peppard run up and down each other's fire escapes and skip down Fifth Avenue, taking in the New York Public Library and that certain famous jewelry store. **Do the Right Thing** (Spike Lee, 1989). Set over 24 hours on the hottest day of the year in Brooklyn's Bedford-Stuyvesant section – a day on which the melting pot is reaching boiling point

– Spike Lee's colorful, stylish film moves from comedy to tragedy to compose an epic tale of New York.

The French Connection (William Friedkin, 1971). Plenty of heady Brooklyn atmosphere in this sensational Oscar-winning cop thriller starring Gene Hackman, whose classic car-and-subway chase takes place under the Bensonhurst Elevated Railroad.

The Godfather Part II (Francis Ford Coppola, 1974). Flashing back to the early life of Vito Corleone, Coppola's great sequel re-created the Italian immigrant experience at the turn of the century, portraying Corleone quarantined at Ellis Island and growing up tough on the meticulously re-created streets of Little Italy.

Midnight Cowboy (John Schlesinger, 1969). The odd love story between Jon Voight's bumpkin hustler and Dustin Hoffman's touching urban creep Ratso Rizzo plays out against both the seediest and swankiest of New York locations.

On the Town (Gene Kelly and Stanley Donen, 1949). Three sailors get 24 hours' shore leave in NYC and fight over whether to do the sights or chase the girls. This exhilarating, landmark musical with Gene Kelly, Frank Sinatra, and Ann Miller flashing her gams in the American Museum of Natural History was the first to take the musical out of the studios and onto the streets.

On the Waterfront (Elia Kazan, 1954). Few images of New York in this unforgettable story of long-suffering longshoremen and union racketeering are as indelible as Marlon Brando's rooftop pigeon coop at dawn and those misty views of New York Harbor (actually shot just over the river in Hoboken).

Rosemary's Baby (Roman Polanski, 1968). Mia Farrow and John Cassavetes move into their dream New York apartment in the Dakota and think their problems stop with nosy neighbors and thin walls until Farrow gets pregnant and hell, literally, breaks loose. Arguably the most terrifying film ever set in the city. Compare to **Panic Room**, a thrilling game of a film starring Jodie Foster (David Fincher, 2002) and also set in the Upper West Side.

The Sweet Smell of Success (Alexander Mackendrick, 1957). Broadway as a nest of vipers. Gossip columnist Burt Lancaster and sleazy press agent Tony Curtis eat each other's tails in this jazzy, cynical study of showbiz corruption. Shot on location, and mostly at night, in steely black and white, Times Square and the Great White Way never looked so alluring.

Taxi Driver (Martin Scorsese, 1976). A long night's journey into day by the great chronicler of the dark side of the city – and New York's greatest filmmaker. Scorsese's New York is hallucinatorily seductive and thoroughly repellent in this superbly unsettling study of obsessive outsider Travis Bickle (Robert De Niro).

West Side Story (Robert Wise and Jerome Robbins, 1961). Sex, singing, and Shakespeare – it's based on *Romeo and Juliet* – in a hyper-cinematic Oscar-winning musical (via Broadway) about rival street gangs. Lincoln Center now stands where the Sharks and the Jets once rumbled.

Travel
Store

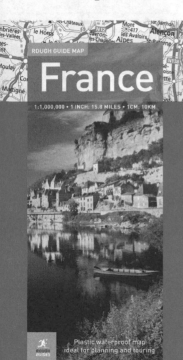

WHEREVER YOU ARE,

WHEREVER YOU'RE GOING,

WE'VE GOT YOU COVERED!

Rough Guides Travel Insurance

Visit our website at www.roughguides.com/insurance or call:

- ☎ UK: 0800 083 9507
- ☎ Spain: 900 997 149
- ☎ Australia: 1300 669 999
- ☎ New Zealand: 0800 55 99 11
- ☎ Worldwide: +44 870 890 2843
- ☎ USA, call toll free on: 1 800 749 4922

Please quote our ref: *Rough Guides books*

Cover for over 46 different nationalities and available in 4 different languages.

NOTES

NOTES

NOTES

NOTES

NOTES

NOTES

NOTES

Small print &
Index

A Rough Guide to Rough Guides

Published in 1982, the first Rough Guide – to Greece – was a student scheme that became a publishing phenomenon. Mark Ellingham, a recent graduate in English from Bristol University, had been travelling in Greece the previous summer and couldn't find the right guidebook. With a small group of friends he wrote his own guide, combining a highly contemporary, journalistic style with a thoroughly practical approach to travellers' needs.

The immediate success of the book spawned a series that rapidly covered dozens of destinations. And, in addition to impecunious backpackers, Rough Guides soon acquired a much broader and older readership that relished the guides' wit and inquisitiveness as much as their enthusiastic, critical approach and value-for-money ethos.

These days, Rough Guides include recommendations from shoestring to luxury and cover more than 200 destinations around the globe, including almost every country in the Americas and Europe, more than half of Africa and most of Asia and Australasia. Our ever-growing team of authors and photographers is spread all over the world, particularly in Europe, the USA and Australia.

In the early 1990s, Rough Guides branched out of travel, with the publication of Rough Guides to World Music, Classical Music and the Internet. All three have become benchmark titles in their fields, spearheading the publication of a wide range of books under the Rough Guide name.

Including the travel series, Rough Guides now number more than 350 titles, covering: phrasebooks, waterproof maps, music guides from Opera to Heavy Metal, reference works as diverse as Conspiracy Theories and Shakespeare, and popular culture books from iPods to Poker. Rough Guides also produce a series of more than 120 World Music CDs in partnership with World Music Network.

Visit www.roughguides.com to see our latest publications.

Rough Guide travel images are available for commercial licensing at www.roughguidespictures.com

Publishing information

This third edition published
February 2008 by
Rough Guides Ltd, 80 Strand,
London WC2R 0RL.
345 Hudson St, 4th Floor, New
York, NY 10014, USA.
Distributed by the Penguin Group
Penguin Books Ltd, 80 Strand,
London WC2R 0RL
Penguin Group (USA), 375
Hudson Street, NY 10014, USA
14 Local Shopping Centre,
Panchsheel Park, New Delhi
110017, India
Penguin Group (Australia), 250
Camberwell Road, Camberwell,
Victoria 3124, Australia
Penguin Group (Canada), 10
Alcorn Avenue, Toronto, ON M4V
1E4, Canada
Penguin Group (New Zealand),
Cnr Rosedale and Airborne
Roads, Albany, Auckland, New
Zealand
Typeset in Bembo and Helvetica
to an original design by Henry Iles.

Printed and bound in Italy by
LegoPrint S.p.A.
Cover concept by Peter Dyer.
© Martin Dunford and Rough
Guides 2008
No part of this book may be
reproduced in any form without
permission from the publisher
except for the quotation of brief
passages in reviews.
368pp includes index
A catalogue record for this book is
available from the British Library
ISBN 978-1-85828-619-8
The publishers and authors
have done their best to ensure
the accuracy and currency of
all the information in The Mini
Rough Guide to New York City,
however, they can accept no
responsibility for any loss, injury,
or inconvenience sustained by any
traveler as a result of information
or advice contained in the guide.
1 3 5 7 9 8 6 4 2

Help us update

We've gone to a lot of effort to
ensure that the third edition of **The
Mini Rough Guide to New York
City** is accurate and up-to-date.
However, things change – places
get "discovered", opening hours
are notoriously fickle, restaurants
and rooms raise prices or lower
standards. If you feel we've got
it wrong or left something out,
we'd like to know, and if you can
remember the address, the price,
the phone number, so much the
better.

Please send your comments
with the subject line **"The Mini
Rough Guide to New York City
Update"** to ©mail@roughguides.
com.
We'll credit all contributions and
send a copy of the next edition
(or any other Rough Guide if you
prefer) for the very best emails.
Have your questions answered
and tell others about your trip at
Ⓦcommunity.roughguides.com

Rough Guides credits

Text editors: Patricia Cunningham, Amy Hegarty
Layout: Dan May
Cartography: Maxine Repath
Picture editor: Nicole Newman

Production: Rebecca Short
Proofreader: Diane Margolis
Cover design: Chloë Roberts
Photographer: Nelson Hancock, Angus Oborn

Acknowledgments

Martin Dunford: Thanks to Patricia Cunningham, Amy Hegarty, and all who worked on the guide. I'd like to dedicate the book to my friend Jon Crowley, who would have made the best New York company.

Shea Dean: Thanks to my cheerful and talented editors: Patricia Cunningham, for her astute comments, and Amy Hegarty, for patiently seeing the

guide through to production. Thanks also to Andrew Rosenberg and Steven Horak for their continued support.

Zora O'Neill: Thanks to the residents of NYC's outer boroughs for building such fascinating neighborhoods and cooking such tasty food, as well as Amy Hegarty and Patricia Cunningham for editing all this goodness into manageable bites.

SMALL PRINT

Index

Map entries are in color.

C

D

E

F

INDEX

NOTES

WHEREVER YOU ARE,

WHEREVER YOU'RE GOING,

WE'VE GOT YOU COVERED!

Rough Guides Travel Insurance

Visit our website at www.roughguides.com/insurance or call:

☎ UK: 0800 083 9507

☎ Spain: 900 997 149

☎ Australia: 1300 669 999

☎ New Zealand: 0800 55 99 11

☎ Worldwide: +44 870 890 2843

☎ USA, call toll free on: 1 800 749 4922

Please quote our ref: *Rough Guides books*

COLUMBUS
Travel Insurance

ROUGH
GUIDES

Cover for over 46 different nationalities and available in 4 different languages.

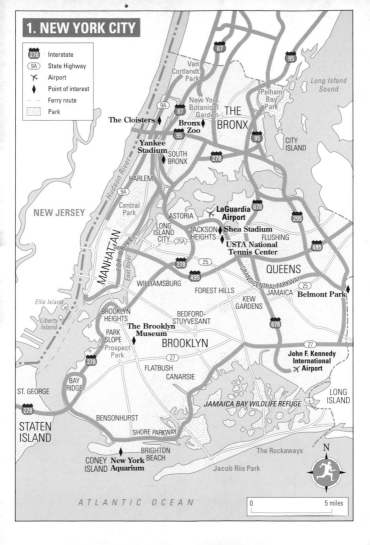

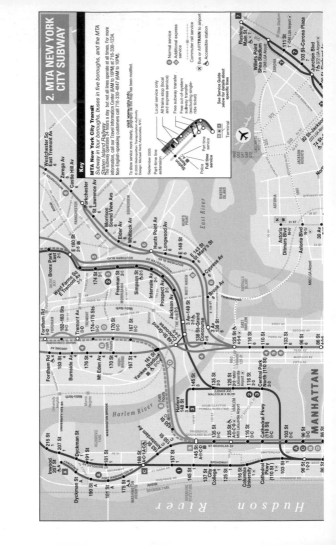

2. MTA NEW YORK CITY SUBWAY

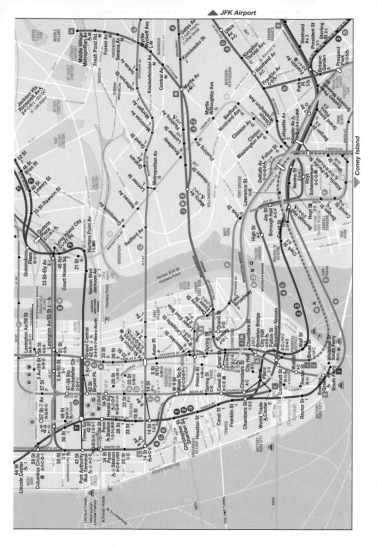

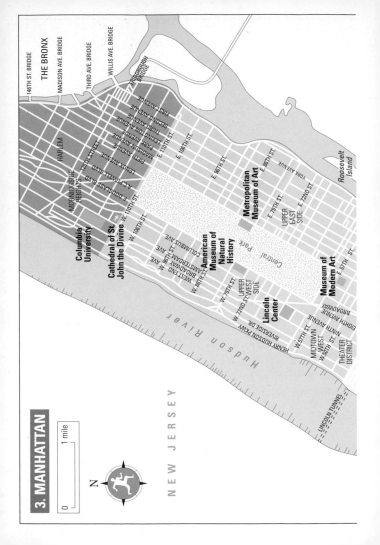

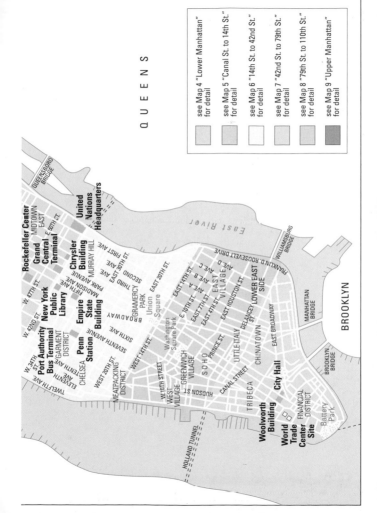

QUEENS

see Map 4 "Lower Manhattan" for detail

see Map 5 "Canal St. to 14th St." for detail

see Map 6 "14th St. to 42nd St." for detail

see Map 7 "42nd St. to 79th St." for detail

see Map 8 "79th St. to 110th St." for detail

see Map 9 "Upper Manhattan" for detail

East River

BROOKLYN

QUEENSBORO BRIDGE

Rockefeller Center

MIDTOWN EAST

W. 47TH ST.

Grand Central Terminal

E. 42ND ST.

United Nations Headquarters

Chrysler Building

MURRAY HILL

New York Public Library

Empire State Building

PARK AVENUE

MADISON AVE.

EAST 34TH ST.

FIFTH AVE.

THIRD AVE.

SECOND AVE.

FIRST AVE.

W. 42ND ST.

W. 34TH ST.

Port Authority Bus Terminal

GARMENT DISTRICT

Penn Station

CHELSEA

GRAMERCY PARK

EAST 20TH ST.

SIXTH AVE.

SEVENTH AVE.

BROADWAY

WEST 14TH ST.

Union Square

1ST AVE.

AVE. A

AVE. B

AVE. C

AVE. D

EAST 14TH ST.

EAST 9TH ST.

EAST 4TH ST.

EAST 1ST ST.

W. 10TH STREET

Washington Square Park

EAST VILLAGE

EAST HOUSTON ST.

TWELFTH AVE.

ELEVENTH AVE.

TENTH AVE.

WEST 20TH ST.

MEATPACKING DISTRICT

WEST VILLAGE

GREENWICH VILLAGE

SOHO

PRINCE ST.

LITTLE ITALY

DELANCEY ST.

LOWER EAST SIDE

HUDSON ST.

TRIBECA

CANAL STREET

CHINATOWN

EAST BROADWAY

FRANKLIN D. ROOSEVELT DRIVE

WILLIAMSBURG BRIDGE

MANHATTAN BRIDGE

HOLLAND TUNNEL

Woolworth Building

World Trade Center Site

Battery Park

City Hall

FINANCIAL DISTRICT

BROOKLYN BRIDGE

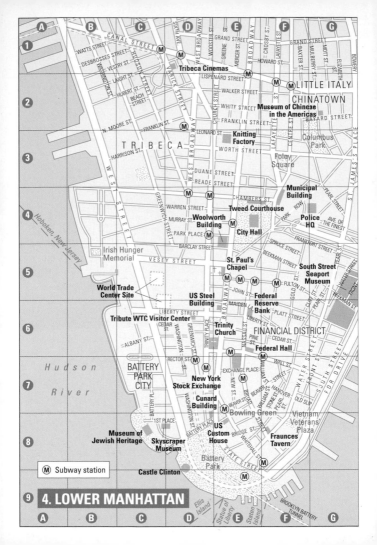

4. LOWER MANHATTAN

A   **B**   **C**   **D**   **E**   **F**   **G**

1
CANAL STREET
WATTS STREET
DESBROSSES STREET
VESTRY ST.
LAIGHT ST.
HUBERT ST.
BEACH STREET
GRAND STREET
Greene
Mercer ST.
HOWARD ST.
Tribeca Cinemas
WEST BROADWAY
WOOSTER ST.
SIXTH AVE.
BROADWAY
CROSBY ST.
LAFAYETTE ST.
GRAND STREET
BAXTER ST.
MULBERRY ST.
MOTT ST.
ELIZABETH ST.
BOWERY

2
N. MOORE ST.
FRANKLIN ST.
LISPENARD STREET
WALKER STREET
WHITE STREET
FRANKLIN STREET
HUDSON STREET
VARICK STREET
CHURCH STREET
LITTLE ITALY
CHINATOWN
Museum of Chinese in the Americas
BAYARD STREET
CENTRE ST.
JAMES PLACE
Columbus Park

3
TRIBECA
HARRISON ST.
LEONARD ST.
DUANE STREET
READE STREET
WORTH STREET
WEST BROADWAY
Knitting Factory
Foley Square

4
Hoboken, New Jersey
WARREN STREET
MURRAY ST.
PARK PLACE
BARCLAY STREET
GREENWICH STREET
CHAMBERS ST.
Tweed Courthouse
Woolworth Building
City Hall
PARK ROW
SPRUCE STREET
Municipal Building
Police HQ
AVE. OF THE FINEST
FRANKFORT STREET
PEARL STREET

5
Irish Hunger Memorial
VESEY STREET
World Trade Center Site
US Steel Building
St. Paul's Chapel
BEEKMAN STREET
JOHN ST.
FULTON ST.
GOLD ST.
South Street Seaport Museum
WATER STREET

6
Tribute WTC Visitor Center
LIBERTY STREET
CEDAR ST.
World Financial Center
GREENWICH STREET
WASHINGTON
Federal Reserve Bank
MAIDEN LANE
PLATT STREET
CEDAR ST.
Trinity Church
FINANCIAL DISTRICT
Federal Hall
FRONT ST.
CLIFF ST.

7
Hudson River
BATTERY PARK CITY
ALBANY ST.
RECTOR ST.
TRINITY PLACE
New York Stock Exchange
EXCHANGE PLACE
WALL ST.
PINE ST.
BEAVER ST.
WILLIAM ST.
HANOVER ST.
STONE ST.
PEARL ST.
OLD SLIP
WATER ST.
FRONT ST.
SOUTH ST.
FDR DRIVE

8
Museum of Jewish Heritage
1ST PLACE
Skyscraper Museum
BATTERY PLACE
Cunard Building
US Custom House
Bowling Green
Fraunces Tavern
BRIDGE ST.
WHITEHALL ST.
STATE STREET
Vietnam Veterans Plaza

9
Castle Clinton
Battery Park
BROOKLYN BATTERY TUNNEL
Ellis Island
Statue of Liberty
Staten Island

Ⓜ Subway station

A   **B**   **C**   **D**   **E**   **F**   **G**

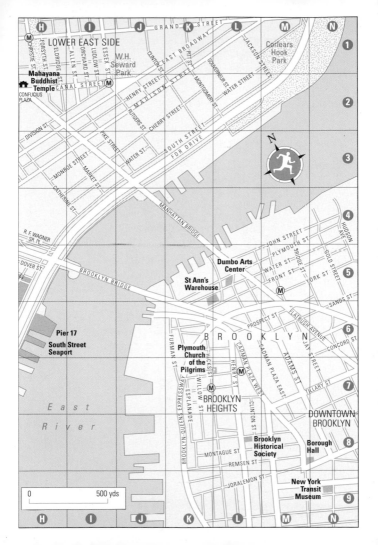

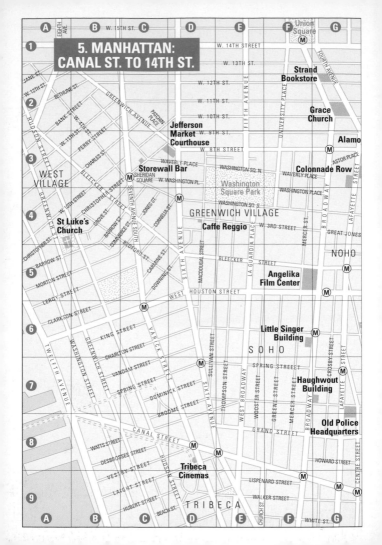

M   E. 14TH STREET   0   600 yds

E. 13TH ST.

EAST
VILLAGE

E. 12TH ST.

E. 11TH ST.

St. Mark's-in-
the-Bowery
Church

E. 10TH ST.

Russian
& Turkish
Baths

E. 9TH ST.

Tompkins
Square
Park

E. 8TH ST.

M Cooper
Union

ST. MARK'S PLACE

E. 7TH ST.

COOPER
SQUARE

McSorley's Old Ale House

E. 6TH ST.

Public Theater

ALPHABET CITY

E. 4TH ST.

E. 3RD ST.

ST.

E. 2ND ST.

BOND ST.

E. 1ST ST.

EAST HOUSTON STREET

Hamilton
Fish Park

M

Katz's Deli

STANTON STREET

NOLITA

St. Patrick's
Old Cathedral

LOWER
EAST SIDE

RIVINGTON ST.

PRINCE STREET

Lower East Side
Tenement
Museum

M

DELANCEY STREET

KENMARE STREET

M

BROOME ST.

i

GRAND STREET

M

GRAND STREET

LITTLE
ITALY

W.H.
Seward
Park

HESTER STREET

HESTER STREET

CANAL STREET

EAST BROADWAY

☆ Eldridge Street
Synagogue

M

EAST BROADWAY

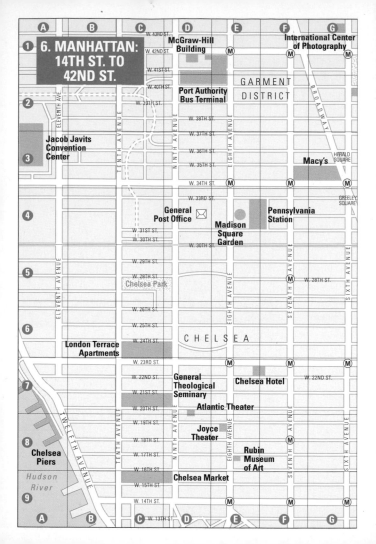

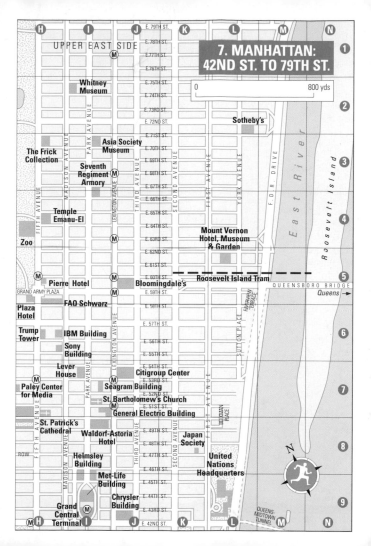

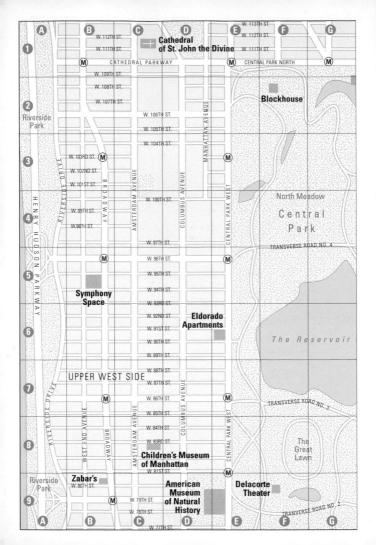

A   **B**   **C**   **D**   **E**   **F**   **G**

1

W. 112TH ST.

W. 111TH ST.

W. 113TH ST.

W. 112TH ST.

W. 111TH ST.

✚ **Cathedral of St. John the Divine**

Ⓜ CATHEDRAL PARKWAY   Ⓜ CENTRAL PARK NORTH   Ⓜ

W. 109TH ST.

W. 108TH ST.

W. 107TH ST.

2

Riverside Park

Blockhouse

W. 106TH ST.

W. 105TH ST.

W. 104TH ST.

3

W. 103RD ST. Ⓜ

W. 102ND ST.

W. 101ST ST.

Ⓜ

North Meadow

W. 100TH ST.

W. 99TH ST.

C e n t r a l

W. 98TH ST.

4

P a r k

W. 97TH ST.

TRANSVERSE ROAD NO. 4

Ⓜ   Ⓜ

W. 96TH ST.

W. 95TH ST.

5

Symphony Space

W. 94TH ST.

W. 93RD ST.

W. 92ND ST.

Eldorado Apartments

6

W. 91ST ST.

W. 90TH ST.

T h e   R e s e r v o i r

W. 89TH ST.

W. 88TH ST.

UPPER WEST SIDE

W. 87TH ST.

7

Ⓜ

W. 86TH ST.

TRANSVERSE ROAD NO. 3

W. 85TH ST.

Ⓜ

W. 84TH ST.

W. 83RD ST.

8

Children's Museum of Manhattan

The Great Lawn

W. 81ST ST.

Ⓜ

Zabar's

American Museum of Natural History

Delacorte Theater

Riverside Park

W. 80TH ST.

9

Ⓜ W. 79TH ST.

W. 78TH ST.

TRANSVERSE ROAD NO. 2

W. 77TH ST.

A   **B**   **C**   **D**   **E**   **F**   **G**

HENRY HUDSON PARKWAY

RIVERSIDE DRIVE

BROADWAY

AMSTERDAM AVENUE

COLUMBUS AVENUE

MANHATTAN AVENUE

CENTRAL PARK WEST

WEST END AVENUE

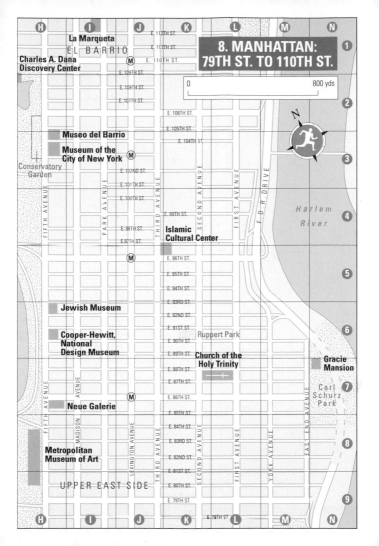

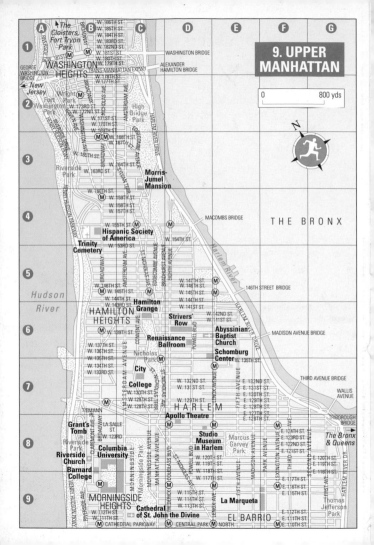